Operations Management Strategy

Operations Management Strategy

Mike Harrison

Head of the Division of Operations and Information Management
The Business School, Staffordshire University

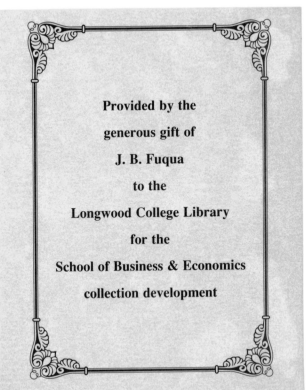

PITMAN
PUBLISHING

Pitman Publishing
128 Long Acre, London WC2E 9AN

A Division of Longman Group UK Limited

First published in 1993

Reprinted 1993

© Mike Harrison 1993

British Library Cataloguing in Publication Data
A CIP catalogue record for this book can be obtained from
the British Library.

ISBN 0 273 60119 9

Printed and bound by Bell and Bain Ltd., Glasgow

CONTENTS

LIST OF FIGURES

PREFACE

Many texts have recently been produced on operations management, some with a general orientation and others emphasizing the particular needs of specific sectors such as service industries. Most texts address strategic problems to a limited extent at least, but few concentrate their attention on strategic issues in operations and there the main concern is often only with manufacturing strategy.

This book addresses issues in operations strategy with three main purposes in mind. The first is to attempt to bridge the gap between business strategy and operations management, partly through a 'top-down' approach showing how operations may contribute positively to strategic planning but also through a 'bottom-up' approach describing how the best operations management practice is forward-looking and integrative in pursuing organizational objectives.

The second purpose of the book is to deal with manufacturing, service and office operations at the same time. The simple reason for this is that most organizations are involved in all three. A 'manufacturing firm' not only converts materials but also provides a service to customers while needing to process large amounts of information effectively. The operational effectiveness of a supermarket equally depends on a mixture of activities, with the added complication that the customer provides much of the labour in material handling. Even the most service-oriented organizations, such as those in the National Health Service, may find manufacturing models and analogies of value in scheduling key activities through scarce resources, and this should in no way detract from their primary mission in caring for individuals on a personal basis.

The third purpose in writing this book is to complement the checklist – dominated practitioner manuals with an essentially educational text which takes time to discuss some of the basic issues in this area and to critically examine underlying models.

The book is specifically intended for individuals taking higher-level management courses such as the MBA, whether by full-time or part-time attendance or through using distance-learning materials. It is assumed that the reader has previously studied general management and has a reasonable knowledge of other functional areas. Though no specific detailed knowledge of operations management is required, it is likely that the reader has either taken a general course in this area or has worked in operations. If this is not the case, then reference may be required to one of the texts mentioned in Chapter 1 in order to fill in some background knowledge of basic operations terminology and methods.

It is also advantageous if the reader is currently studying other areas of management at a strategic level and therefore has the opportunity of relating ideas in operations strategy to corporate strategy and to other functional strategies. Though these are the subject of Chapter 3 in this text, a more comprehensive examination through complementary studies will enrich the reader's view of this challenging area of work.

However, no specific experience of operations management is necessary in using this text and final-year undergraduates as well as full-time students will, with a little imagination, be able to relate to the ideas presented. In particular, when introducing new concepts, examples have been chosen which are easy to visualize and relate to everyday experiences. Indeed one of the advantages of studying operations, particularly service operations, is that the situations being depicted are not remote from everyday life. Unfortunately this does not mean that solutions to operational problems are always easy to find.

This book also has a number of sub-themes which regularly recur. For instance, the use of technology in operations is widespread and likely to increase dramatically in the future. However, no prior technical knowledge of information or manufacturing technology is assumed. Similarly, the appropriate use of human resources is an underlying preoccupation of the operations strategist. A short discussion of ethics in operations is included in Chapter 9.

The book contains a number of short case-type episodes and a few longer cases, all based originally on real organizational situations though now adapted to illustrate particular points. These may usefully be complemented by other texts which concentrate on case presentations, as described in the Introduction.

At several points in the text, examples are given based on spreadsheet models. Further details of these are available if you write to me at the address shown below.

A great number of personal acknowledgements should have been made at this point to colleagues and students who have supported this writing venture, often unwittingly, as well as to staff at Pitmans and my family, who have been all too aware that manuscript production has been in progress. However, as I work in a large Business School and have been teaching managers for over 20 years, attempts to give credit where it is due would no doubt only offend far greater numbers through omission. Nevertheless, I am acutely aware of, and grateful for, the range of inputs that have been available.

Mike Harrison
Staffordshire University Business School
Stoke-on-Trent, Staffs.
January 1993

LIST OF ABBREVIATIONS

ACME	Application of Computers in Manufacturing Engineering
AGV	Automated Guided Vehicle
AMT	Advanced Manufacturing Technology
APICS	American Production and Inventory Control Society
APS	Anthropocentric Production Systems
ATE	Automated Testing Equipment
BCG	Boston Consulting Group
BOM	Bill of Materials
BPICS	British Production and Inventory Control Society
CADCAM	Computer Aided Design, Computer Aided Manufacture
CAPM	Computer Aided Production Management
CATWOE	Mnemonic in SSM
CIB	Computer Integrated Business
CHIM	Computer and Human Integrated Manufacturing
CIM	Computer Integrated Manufacturing
CMS	Cost Management System
CNC	Computer Numerically Controlled
CumNPV	Cumulative Net Present Value
DCF	Discounted Cash Flow
DP	Data Processing
FMS	Flexible Manufacturing System
JIT	Just in Time
MIS	Management Information System
MPS	Master Production Schedule
MRP	Materials Requirements Planning
MRPII	Manufacturing Resources Planning
NPV	Net Present Value
OPT	Optimised Production Technology
PDCA	Plan, Do, Check, Act cycle
QFD	Quality Function Deployment
ROI	Return on Investment
SFP	Single Factor Productivity
SIS	Strategic Information System
SMED	Single Minute Exchange Die
SPACE	Strategic Position and Action Evaluation
SSC	Scientific Stock Control
SSM	Soft Systems Methodology
TFP	Total Factor Productivity
TQC	Total Quality Control
TQM	Total Quality Management

INTRODUCTION

This book provides an exploration of the general area of operations management strategy along with critical analysis of a number of key issues. It is assumed that the reader has a good general knowledge of management and more specifically has studied financial aspects of business, human resource management and marketing to an introductory level at least. Some background theory in corporate strategy is provided here with an obvious emphasis on operations issues. It is assumed that this will be complemented by more comprehensive studies in corporate policy making either concurrently or at a later date.

It is likely that the reader will have some background and experience covering the techniques and day-to-day practices of operations management. Though not essential, it is hoped that the reader will, through the above, have some feel for operational issues. Some of the arguments in this book may appear a little abstract if taken out of context and this would be unfortunate in an area which is firmly rooted in experience and real practicality.

The following are typical textbooks to which the reader might wish to refer to complement our discussion in terms of details of actual techniques and examples of their application:

Dilworth, J.B. (1992) *Operations Management*, McGraw Hill, New York
Hill, T. (1991) *Production/Operations Management: Text and Cases* (2ed), Prentice Hall, New York
Schroeder, R.G. (1989) *Operations Management* (3ed), McGraw Hill, New York
Vonderembse, M.A. and White, G.P. (1991) *Operations Management* (2ed), West Publishing, St Paul

Summary of chapter contents

Chapter 1 includes an extended discussion of the systems terminology and methodologies which underpin our models of operations strategy. Of particular importance here is the basic model of operations as a transformational system, differences between manufacturing, service and office operations and the concept of systems models as necessary simplifications of reality which, nevertheless, must be adequate in representing the key features of the situation being modelled. Chapter 1 ends with a brief discussion of the environment, introducing themes which continually recur in later chapters.

One feature of this book which may be noted at this point is the necessary mixture of details and discussion of broad issues. One of the challenges which faces any strategist is the need for a broad and integrated vision of a situation combined with detailed knowledge relating to key parts of the situation and in particular to implementational issues. Grand plans can fail because of small, ignored details. Strategy is not merely vague waffle about environments and missions. Similarly it is not endless elaborate detail about technology and scheduling. It must encompass the essential features of both the large and small pictures. The best practitioners of strategy have always been able to master this art of simultaneous holistic and reductionist thinking.

In Chapter 2 we introduce some quite technical issues in systems management. We explore the world of productivity measurement, finding here a need for cooperation between accountants and operational staff which has often been lacking in the past. We examine the learning curve, considering also why this argument in favour of mass production and service must also relate to more general learning in the context of rapid product innovation. We reflect on some of the difficulties inherent in that crucial word 'flexibility' and finally we argue that forecasts are inevitable and that forecasting should be approached in a systematic manner. These four issues are, of course, tightly interwoven and underlie much later discussion.

Chapter 3 allows us to take a small step outside the narrow confines of operations and to consider corporate strategy as a whole. Corporate policy making, whilst integrative in purpose, makes detailed reference to strategy formulation in the major functional areas of marketing, human resource management, finance and operations. Thus as well as providing a corporate framework for operations strategy it also provides a mechanism for functional integration.

We follow this general approach with a brief examination of the problems of strategy formulation in a declining industry. Then three sections deal with financial matters, in particular costing systems, the financial modelling of working capital and finally the appraisal of major investments. Each of these is of particular concern to operations managers, though one may not have thought so from previous literature. As a major generator of revenue and incurrer of cost, operations must have clear systems for the measurement of cash flows and sensible procedures for ustifying capital expenditure.

In Chapter 4 we now return to mainstream operational matters. We concentrate first of all on classifying the key policy areas in operations strategy. Then the general principles underlying two major areas of decision making, that is process choice and capacity management, are analysed in depth. This is followed by three illustrative case exercises. Though this book is not based on case studies, it is strongly recommended that the reader makes use of the ones included, preferably as the basis for group discussion. The cases in this book, though drawn from general experience of organizational practice, are constructed to allow easy access to issues of operations strategy rather than tell the story of individual companies (with the one exception as noted in the text). As we discuss below, many sources include other cases which can then be used as further practice in relating strategic ideas to the real world.

Chapter 5 continues this theme but in the separate contexts of manufacturing and service operations management. It also includes a brief section on the particular problems facing small manufacturing companies.

The remaining four chapters are each devoted to a particular area of concern in operations strategy.

Chapter 6 deals with the highly fashionable and important area of quality management, including total quality management though this is rapidly becoming a general management philosophy rather than an extension of the traditional quality control function. This is followed in Chapter 7 by a consideration of the management of material flow, an opportunity to examine the reality behind such acronyms as MRP, JIT, OPT and so forth. In particular the human and implementational problems behind computer aided production management are discussed in some depth.

If Chapter 7 is orientated towards the management uses of technology, Chapter 8 is devoted entirely to it. Of particular note here, and continued in Chapter 9, is an analysis of computer integration in manufacturing (CIM), a very important technology, thought by some to be the destiny of all major manufacturers. The organizational implications of massive data integration are causing concern to many writers and we consider these issues at some length.

The final chapter relates to human resource issues in operational strategy. This in itself deserves a book and in practice much of this book relates to it in some form or another. This chapter therefore summarizes some issues and introduces others such as ethics in operations management.

In total all areas of operational policy making and all sectors are not considered in the above chapters in the same degree of detail. The emphasis is on areas where there has been considerable research in the past and in which awkward problems are known to arise. Manufacturing industry in general receives a more comprehensive coverage due partly to the vast amount written in this area but also to the breadth of disparate organizations covered under the 'service' banner. However, service operations (which may take place within manufacturing industry) and office operations (which are widespread) are regularly referred to and the latter may well be the major area for future consideration as the design office and the service back room play a more important part in adding value for the customer.

Case studies in operations management

In contrast to some texts on operations strategy (for example Garvin (1992) and Samson (1991)), this book contains only a few case exercises. If a text is to contain meaningful, and therefore extensive, real cases in strategy then most of its content must be devoted to them, and the intention in this book is to concentrate on the analysis of issues and problem areas.

However, a number of excellent sources of appropriate cases are available. The following is a selection of accessible and comparatively short cases from Johnston et al (1993), listed with reference to the chapter in this book which explores associated issues:

Case 3 – Aylesbury Pressings
Relates to JIT implementation and therefore to Chapters 7 and 9.

Case 4 – Warwick Castle
Service strategy and quality are explored, see Chapters 4 and 6.

Case 5 – Executive Holloware
Quality in a manufacturing context, see Chapter 6.

Case 7 – Problems in total quality implementation at Company A
See Chapters 6 and 9.

Case 14 – Beaver Engineering Group
Relates to computer aided production management and to advanced manufacturing technology; see Chapters 7 and 8.

Case 15 – Massey Ferguson JIT Purchasing and Supply
Discussion particularly relates to Chapter 7 but also has implications for manufacturing strategy.

At the end of Chapter 5 we give a further list of cases from this source. These have particular reference to Chapters 4 and 5. Furthermore a number of texts include comprehensive cases relating to business strategy. These will often lend themselves to analysis from an operational point of view. The reader is referred to books mentioned in Chapter 3 in particular.

CHAPTER 1

Operations management, systems and the environment

OPERATIONS MANAGEMENT – DEFINITIONS AND KEY CONCEPTS

A number of authors have produced definitions relating to operations management which, though differing in detail and emphasis, present a consistent picture of this key organizational function. To use one text as an example, Vonderembse and White (1991) define operations as transformational processes in an implicit systems' framework:

> Operations are the processes by which people, capital and materials (inputs) are combined to produce the services and goods consumed by the public (outputs).

They also describe what is seen as a key feature of operations:

> Consumers are willing to pay more for an organization's services and goods than the total cost of the inputs. In essence, operations add value to the final product over and above the product's cost.

The idea that operations add value, or in conjunction with the customer create value, is crucial to a consideration of quality, productivity and cost effectiveness. A good characterization of operations might also indicate how effectiveness might be pursued. Vonderembse and White divide operations management into three sets of activities essential for building a competitive advantage:

- Designing the system
- Planning the system
- Managing and controlling the system

An interesting point to consider is whether these sets of activities are intended to be carried out in the above order and by whom. It is quite easy to map them onto a hierarchic and functional organizational structure but this is by no means the only way to proceed. In particular the idea of continuous improvement entails the systems design processes being in some way never ending, that is design space is left free for future change rather than rigid procedures instituted from the start.

A different form of definition is given by other writers who concentrate on the human resources required for operations or on its managerial requirements:

> The operations function is performed by that group of persons in a business who are responsible for producing the goods or providing the services that the business offers to the public ... one of the three primary functions within a business, the other two being finance and marketing. (Dilworth 1992)

> Operations managers are responsible for producing the supply of goods or services on organizations. Operations managers make decisions regarding the operations function and the transformation system used. Operations management is the study of decision making in the operations function. (Schroeder 1989)

> Operations management is that function of an organization which is concerned with the design, planning and control of resources for the production of goods and the provision of services. (Bennett et al 1988)

These definitions therefore assume that a body of individuals, or at least a set of functional roles, have been identified to carry out the tasks associated with operations management. Two points should be considered in this context. The first is that this organizational model seems more appropriate for the larger organization. In small companies operations decisions are commonplace and pervasive. Operations is everyone's business. The second point is that a functional model of operations might be seen to imply that operational ideas are of importance to only one group of employees. This is totally contrary to concepts of total quality management, to give one example. It may well be that in traditionally concentrating on factory issues and more recently on direct service provision, many writers on operations have either missed issues in office based operations or wrongly assumed that they are covered by factory-style concepts.

Thus to summarize, operations may be defined as a transformational process which adds value, while operations management is the decision making and control function associated with it. As Krajewski and Ritzman (1990) point out, there are three possible views of operations management. It may be seen as a function in the context of an organizational structure. It may be characterized by a particular set of decisions. Finally it may be seen as an emerging profession.

It is not entirely clear whether the 'professionalization' of operations management is desirable. Operations is not a narrow and peripheral discipline but is central to the working lives of very many people. Operations, along with human resource management and some simple financial ideas, constitutes general management for much of the working population. However, many of the concepts and techniques of 'operations management' as a discipline are not widely known and many employees would find them difficult to apply. Whilst there is a core set of techniques (often associated with TQM or with Japanese-style problem solving) which are intended to be widely applied, many of the more strategic ideas are quite subtle and complex.

Yet, as we point out below, one key to success in strategic planning is the development of a set of consistent functional strategies and thus it may be argued that the competent operational strategist is in effect a good business strategist with a deep appreciation of operational issues. On balance it appears that the effective operational manager is a good manager with extensive knowledge and experience of operations. Certainly this personal 'added value' should be recognized both within organizations and through academic qualifications, but if removed from the context of general management such specialization seems counterproductive.

Though certainly not the intention of most modern writers on operations, it is all too easy to view operations management in a tactical way by narrowly concentrating on day-to-day decision making. Though the trouble-shooting role is important, the definitions given above also emphasize the more structural role of operations management in designing systems and implementing systems' change. We also note that operational activities must be at least consistent with other functions and contribute to meeting organizational objectives.

This leads us to a consideration of operations strategy. Most general texts on operations insist that their approach is 'strategic' but their actual content is mainly tactical with an appreciation of the long-term ramifications of operational decision making. A recent line of argument counters this as follows:

> The strategic approach to operations differs from the traditional approach on almost every count. Operating decisions are made on the basis of their strategic impact and their contribution to long-run competitive advantage, not on narrow financial criteria ... operating decisions become part of an overall strategy, to be assessed in combination, rather than as discrete, independent events. (Garvin 1992)

Garvin's approach is top-down in the sense of basing operational decisions on corporate plans, and therefore implicitly assumes that the organization in question has a well developed strategic planning process and that operational managers have sufficient status to be able to contribute effectively in this planning process. This latter point has been explored by Hill (1985) who deplores the often low status of manufacturing managers in particular.

Another point made by Garvin is the rejection of 'narrow financial criteria'. Much attention is currently being paid to the potentially counterproductive effects of traditional financial systems of investment appraisal and management accounting if unimaginatively used in the context of modern automated systems. Thus the idea that the fundamental decisions underlying operations management should be based on a strategic planning process is most welcome.

It should, however, be noted that Garvin's approach, though referred to as 'operations strategy' is, in effect, like several other influential texts, related to 'manufacturing strategy'. Therefore we must be careful in relating such ideas to operational decisions in non-manufacturing areas as work. Though the word 'operations' may be substituted for the word manufacturing' in many texts concentrating on the latter, this may lead us to the idea that the agenda of issues for manufacturing management and strategy is identical to that for non-manufacturing operations. Though in fact many issues (for example facilities layout, quality management ...) are common to all forms of operations, the differing characteristics of manufacturing, service and office management may lead to quite different recommended approaches in each case.

In order to pursue the implications of strategic thinking in this context, it is important that we view the process of strategic planning in some detail. This is the subject of a later chapter though at this stage it is useful to sketch out some of the key concepts.

As corporate strategy, by definition, addresses issues concerning an organization as a whole there is a potential problem of complexity in this area which is best addressed by concentrating on simple and explicit models and techniques. Typically a standard text (Johnson and Scholes (1989)) approaches this in a clear way by dividing strategic decision making into the following categories:

- *Strategic analysis*
  - Environment
  - Resources
  - Expectations, objectives and power
- *Strategic choice*
  - Generation of options
  - Evaluation of options
  - Selection of strategy
- *Strategic implementation*
  - Resource planning
  - Organizational structure
  - People and systems

Whilst it is recognized that a simple linear progression through these activities is unlikely, such a list forms a useful reminder of what needs to be done. Johnson and Scholes also make a number of comments on the character of strategic decisions as summarized below with some additions relating to operational issues:

- Strategic decisions are concerned with the scope of an organization's activities, that is they define what the organization will and will not do.
- Strategic decisions match the activities of an organization to the environment as far as this can be forecasted, an important point as organizations seek to operate in increasingly global and turbulent markets.
- Strategic decisions match the activities of an organization to its resource capability as exists at the present and as far as can be forecasted into the future. The emphasis here must be on resource capability, that is what can actually be achieved with resources – a crucial challenge for operations management.
- Strategic decisions have major resource, and hence financial, implications.
- Strategic decisions affect operational decisions and the way in which operational decisions are made, which relates to the decision making infrastructure (with a particular emphasis on information flows).
- Organizational strategy is affected by the values and expectations of those who have power in the organization. Thus the status of operations as a function is very important if operations is to be proactive.
- Strategic decisions affect the long-term direction of an organization. In particular many operational decisions regarding equipment, skills and systems may affect resource capability for many years into the future.
- Strategic decisions are often complex in nature, due to the high degree of uncertainty, the need for an integrated approach and the need to manage major change.

In one of the most influential books on manufacturing strategy, Hayes and Wheelwright (1984) go to some lengths to explore in detail how corporate and operational strategies are linked. Following their line of argument:

> We define a company philosophy as the set of guiding principles, driving forces and ingrained attitudes that help communicate goals, plans and policies to all employees and that are reinforced through conscious and subconscious behaviour at all levels of the organization.

In similar fashion to comments made above, strategy is characterized by Hayes and Wheelwright as follows:

- It deals with an extended time horizon
- Its impact is significant
- It requires a concentration of effort
- The resulting pattern of decisions must be consistent
- It is pervasive through all levels of a company

They define three levels of strategy (though note that this characterization seems most appropriate to a large, multi-divisional organization):

- *Highest level*
  Corporate strategy specifies all areas of overall interest to the organization: the definition of the businesses in which the corporation will
  participate ... and the acquisition and allocation of key corporate
  resources to each of those businesses.
- *Second level*
  A business strategy specifies (1) the scope (product/market/service
  subsegments) of that business in a way that links the strategy of the
  business to that of the corporation as a whole, and (2) the basis on
  which that business unit will achieve and maintain a competitive
  advantage.
- *Third level – functional strategies*
  A manufacturing strategy consists of a sequence of decisions that,
  over time, enables a business unit to achieve a desired manufacturing
  structure, infrastructure and set of specific capabilities.

Two points must be noted here. First of all the discussion is concentrated on
manufacturing, though the sense is basically retained if 'operations' is insert-
ed in place of 'manufacturing'. Secondly the automatic insistence on the need
to achieve a competitive advantage might require modification if the operational characteristics of a public sector organization are being analysed.

For Hayes and Wheelwright the key characteristics for evaluating a
(manufacturing) strategy are its consistency with corporate, business and
other functional strategies and its contribution to competitive advantage.
This latter point is elaborated in an oft-quoted characterization of manufacturing's role in a company. Hayes and Wheelwright identify four stages in
the evolution of manufacturing's strategic role:

- *Stage 1 – internally neutral*
  The modest objective here is to 'minimize manufacturing's negative
  potential', essentially a damage limitation exercise.
- *Stage 2 – externally neutral*
  Here the objective is to 'achieve parity with competitors', a goal
  which traditionally one feels is as far as many companies would be
  willing or able to go.
- *Stage 3 – internally supportive*
  If one takes on board the fundamental ideas of operations strategy
  then to 'provide credible support to the business strategy' becomes a
  minimum objective.
- *Stage 4 – externally supportive*
  The ideal situation is seen to be to 'pursue manufacturing based competitive advantage', that is operations is positive and proactive in the
  contribution which it makes.

Though once again the discussion, based on past literature, is manufacturing based it requires little imagination to see in principle at least how

these ideas may be reflected in a modified form in a wider range of organizations and to a wider set of activities.

A further valuable contribution to the debate is made in Hill (1985) which presents a framework for linking corporate and manufacturing decision making. This is briefly outlined in the following five-stage model:

1 Define corporate objectives
2 Determine marketing strategies to meet these objectives
3 Determine how products win orders in the market place
4 Choose the most appropriate process
5 Provide the manufacturing infrastructure to support production.

Of note here is the importance given to the formal expression of marketing strategies (step 2) and the determination of qualifying and order winning criteria (step 3). These are used very directly as support for steps 4 and 5 and thus clearly show the interrelationship between corporate and functional strategies. This material is explored in later chapters.

A word of warning is appropriate here on the use of the word 'operations' in some general and strategic texts. For example Porter (1985), whilst making operations a key ingredient in his value chain approach (see Chapter 3) unfortunately appears to identify operations with manufacturing processes. In fact many of his 'primary activities' relate to operational issues in the sense in which we use the term in this book.

The final point to be made here relates to the nature of strategic operational decisions. Having defined operations, its management and the need for a strategic approach it remains to consider the actual strategic decisions likely to be of concern to the operations strategist. The basic list, whose ramifications are explored in much of the remainder of this book, is given in Figure 1.1. The first four items refer to the choice of basic operational processes while the latter six items are concerned with key infrastructural issues.

> Scope and span of process
> Process choice, focus and flexibility
> Facilities, location and layout
> Process technology
> Work design and human resource development
> Capacity
> Quality management
> Material flow control
> Information management
> New products and services

Figure 1.1
Policy issues in operations strategy

Thus to summarize this section, we have seen in the above how operations, its management and its strategy can be defined and we have briefly explored some of the issues in the development of a coherent operations strategy. We return later to a more detailed analysis of a systems view of operations management strategy.

SYSTEMS MODELS IN OPERATIONS MANAGEMENT

Definitions and properties of systems

The word 'system' is widely used in management writings as well as in computing, engineering, the natural sciences and everyday language. Indeed it is in danger of losing all meaning through its application to almost every phenomena. In this book we use the word in a very definite way and in this section we explore the fundamental ideas underlying 'systems models' and show a number of illustrations of systems language applied to operational management.

In very general terms a system is a description of the world in terms of a number of elements which relate to each other in some meaningful way. A boundary can be identified which defines membership of the system, that it separates elements which are in the system from those which are not. A system also has a relationship with outside elements which is defined in terms of its inputs and outputs. The environment of a system is those outside elements which are relevant to its operation.

Two points should be noted about the use of the word 'environment'. First of all, management literature often refers, confusingly, to the internal environment of a system and to its external environment. We invariably use the word to mean the latter. Secondly the word has taken on a special meaning in terms of conservation. Though this meaning may be used if relevant (for example operations managers have a major role to play in conserving energy and reducing waste) we use environment to refer to anything outside the system that we must consider in order to understand the system and its operation.

It should be emphasized that whenever we speak of systems we are referring to descriptions of the real world, that is to models. It is assumed that the world in itself is endlessly complex and that implicit in any model is a set of choices about which elements should be included, their relationship and so forth. One of the main intentions of systems modelling is to be as clear as possible about the assumptions underlying a model and the reasons why it was constructed in a particular way. Thus when the word 'system' is used it should be understood that a systems model is being referred to. One interesting question that should always be asked is 'who built the model and why?'.

All the systems we will consider are processes, that is they do work by transforming inputs into outputs. This in turn entails the concept of feedback whereby information on the work done by systems elements is in some way shared in order to control the transformation process. Feedback may be implicit in our models of a system or we may explicitly show it as an external control mechanism whereby information on outputs is fed back to the management of inputs in some defined way. We do however note the importance of information and communication in all systems models. There is a danger in considering 'information systems' as a separate form of modelling with its own specialists and arcane terminology. Information flows should be considered in all systems models and conversely the meanings and uses of information must be carefully weighed up even when the primary concern is data handling.

It is possible for us to draw our systems boundaries in such a way that we may consider a system as 'closed', that is the environment is so stable that only the action of the system itself is of importance. Strictly a system is closed if it has no inputs and outputs, but this is hardly a useful model of any management situation. We may, however, wish to describe a situation as if the inputs and outputs were totally predictable and unchanging. Our concentration is then on the internal mechanisms of the system and we refer to this as a closed system. However, much of our argument in this book is against such descriptions of the world and in favour of models which characterize situations of interest as 'open systems'. Such systems should be able to continue their transformational processes in the context of a changing environment, a feature technically called homeostasis or more generally referred to as adaptability. In a somewhat curious and pedantic use of terminology, a system is considered to be 'purposive' if capable of carrying out a transformation to meet a purpose, goal or objective and said to be 'purposeful' if the purpose is self generated. This distinction is explored more fully in Ackoff and Emery (1972).

Another feature of systems models is their inherent focus. Do we model a company, a department, a process or even a set of activities (as in work and methods study, for example). A useful way of looking at systems is as a hierarchy whereby full systems at one level of the hierarchy are considered as elements of another system at a different hierarchic level. This is an approach which is also used extensively by engineers and computer specialists (often confusingly called 'systems analysts'!). One danger is that this can lead to a mechanistic and over-ambitious attempt to characterize what is essentially a social system. Referred to as 'hard systems analysis', Checkland (1981) contrasts this to the soft systems methodology (SSM) described below.

Systems models which adopt a very tight focus or a narrow view of their constituent elements are sometimes referred to as reductionist. This is contrasted with holistic views of the world. However, this debate misses the simple point that all levels of model have their use. In this book we use a very varied set of models depending on the subject matter under discussion. Each has their place in enriching our understanding of the world and providing useful tools for the practising operations manager.

A very important idea in this context is the notion of the emergent properties of a system. A simple physical example might be that though our bodies can be analysed as consisting of quantities of a range of chemicals, our behaviour cannot be entirely predicted on the basis of the science of chemistry. To use a well known phrase, the whole is more than the sum of the parts. As a system we exhibit 'synergy' in that our constituent elements, their relationships, internal control mechanisms and relationship with the environment give us a distinct identity as a species and individuality depending on our genetic inheritance and experiences since birth. Organizations and other human groupings similarly exhibit general and individual characteristics which are the emergent properties of interest to the management scientist and practitioner.

Three obvious levels of systems hierarchy are frequently used in studies of management. These are the organization as a whole, functions (finance, operations and so forth) and work units (typically individuals or small groups). Some attention should also be given to intermediate systems which might be important. Corporate strategy uses notions such as business units, product groups and so forth. Implicit in, for example, product life-cycle models and experience curves is the idea of a product as having a separate identity and emergent characteristics. Of course in practice even individual products change over time in terms of the characteristics evident to the consumer and the processes required to make them. However, the product over its life cycle is a useful unifying concept.

Examples of systems models in operations

Many areas of operations management may be better understood through a consideration of their implicit view of systems focus. Thus in Chapter 7 we consider material flow control. Traditional methods of scientific stock control use a very tight focus, based mainly on individual items of stock. This has utility in terms of attempting to minimize costs in this narrow context but severe drawbacks through ignoring the integrated flow of materials and human aspects of materials management. Material requirements planning takes a more integrated view through central control of a wide range of stocks and flows (a wider systems perspective) though is fairly mechanistic in its treatment of human and organizational aspects. The classic Just-in-Time approach is essentially integrated with great attention given to human and quality aspects. However it requires a stable environment for its effective operation.

Another area where changes in practice may be analysed in terms of differing views on systems focus is quality control. In its traditional form, quality control consisted of an independent check on the output of a production process, a form of external control system that may have fed rejected items back into the process as inputs for rework. A similar check is often carried out on raw materials and components received from a supplier. This became more sophisticated as statistical product control, one of whose outputs is an occasional instruction to stop the process and reset its working parameters. Such methodologies may be refined further as vendor rating systems.

An alternative approach is statistical process control (SPC) where the control system addresses problems of process capability and continuing performance. This is an example of an internal control system and is an important feature of the more general methodology of total quality management (TQM). In TQM a very wide range of organizational transactions are considered suitable candidates for systematic control. Such transactions are subjected to an analysis of client needs and producer (or service provider) capability before operating parameters are set up and the operation monitored. The whole transactional process should also be continually reviewed with a view to incremental improvement. Thus emphasis is placed on changing client needs and the providing system is expected to be adaptive to those needs and to take advantage of new technologies. This form of control may be in place at an individual operation or for a business unit as a whole. It should also, like many modern ideas on quality management, be sensitive to human needs and behaviour. The quality gurus, such as Deming, place great emphasis on human aspects of quality management, in sharp contrast to more traditional mechanistic approaches. Thus TQM is adaptive, can be applied at varying levels in an organization, and TQM itself as management practice can be seen as an integrative system whose output is general improvements in quality awareness and performance.

In their excellent summary of recent systems thinking, Flood and Jackson (1991) include a discussion of TQM which clearly shows how it draws on a range of systems methodologies in order to achieve its aims. We expand on these methodologies in a later section.

Each of these examples involves a range of choices in arriving at appropriate intermediate systems structures. Indeed many current operational management concerns come down to a choice of the most suitable scope of system which should be considered. In operations strategy we have a natural tendency to broaden the scope and see relationships with corporate systems. However, this should in no way detract from the contribution made by operational management and associated professions (such as work study practitioners) where a greater degree of systems focus is appropriate and desirable. Both approaches should be complementary and in total support organizational objectives.

Measures of systems performance

For a variety of reasons, including control and communication as well as reporting to outside agencies, the measurement of systems performance is an important issue. By choosing an appropriate focus, performance measurement always comes down to a consideration of the key characteristics of input and output (that is internal control can be examined by narrowing the system focus so that a producing sub-system is seen as separate from a controlling sub-system).

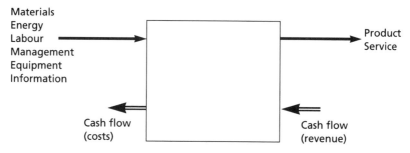

Figure 1.2
Input-output systems

As we see in Figure 1.2, two types of input/output are usually present in commercial systems. One is concerned with the primary transformation intended by the system. Thus a production system takes in raw materials, energy, labour, management, equipment and information and produces a product. A personal service system takes in the above as possible inputs as well as the client and produces a 'changed client' as output. Measurements may be taken relating to any of these features. A dual economic system may also be characterized whereby payment is received from the client, often some time later than the product or service is received, and cash paid for the resources used, hopefully leaving a surplus or profit to be distributed in some appropriate way or reinvested in the structure of the system (which may be interpreted as providing further input resources). The mechanics of this economic process is of course handled by the accounting function and can usefully be analysed in a systemic fashion.

A great deal of time and effort has been spent in the past in setting up the rules by which this dual system operates for a trading enterprise which must produce an annual report. However, it must be understood that a wide range of conventions and standard practices are involved in producing a set of accounts, for example relating to asset valuation, depreciation and so forth. These affect the reliability of the resulting performance measures which may be subject to considerable manipulation by the creative accountant. Further difficulties may be experienced in setting up this dual system for parts of an organization. This may involve transfer prices being agreed along with all the complexities of fixed cost apportionment, subjects which require the attentions of specialist cost and management accountants.

The measurement of systems performance therefore depends on a mixture of financial and non-financial information and is affected by data availability and timeliness as well as secrecy due to commercial sensitiveness and the propensity of individual managers to hide and distort unfavourable information.

Dubious performance measures abound, for example:

- Measures related entirely to input quantities ('I've worked hard this week ...')
- Measures related entirely to financial inputs ('The NHS has spent £999M this year on ...')
- Measures related entirely to output quantities ('We produced 26 cars this week ...')
- Measures related entirely to revenue ('Sales are up 25 percent this month ...')
- Measures relating output volume to a single input ('We produced three cars/worker/year but, in Japan ...')
- Capacity-related measures, relating to the utilization of a single input ('Our restaurant was full for three evenings this week ...' or 'We've been working flat out all year ...')

However in defence we should say that the above may summarize all the information which is readily available. It should also be remembered that the working lives of many people centre on inputs, for example time spent or work done, and real final outputs may seem remote. Several years ago when questioning a group of production middle managers from a major electronics factory I discovered they neither knew nor cared where the output of their work was going. More recently in that same factory anyone working on the lines will know exactly who is the final customer for a given batch ('This is for Acme, it's part of a £300,000 order, they need it next Wednesday, it has three modifications from the standard and I have 3.2 hours of machine time to make it in.'). Such is the effect of a determined application of TQM.

Some further difficulties must be understood. All measures, in particular financial ones, may be totals or averages relating to a long period and may hide important fluctuations in performance. The remedy here may be more effective electronic methods of data capture but this in turn can lead to information overload if care has not been taken in advance to specify what control data is really important, what information must be sent to whom and by when. A further point is that all performance measures must be seen in the context of expectations, performance standards, targets and budgets. In particular the classic difference between efficiency (relating inputs to outputs) and effectiveness (relating inputs, outputs and agreed intentions) is crucial.

The concept of return on investment in financial reporting may unfortunately reinforce the idea that all performance characteristics can and should be reduced to a single performance measure. A far more valuable approach in operational terms is the use of a range of performance indicators to represent performance over time on a variety of fronts. Such an approach is employed by Berry and Carter (1992), jointly with the police and other agencies, in monitoring the performance of a series of crime prevention initiatives. Thus in the examination of a campaign to reduce car-related crime in a major city, 50 indicators were identified as being of relevance with a final short list of around a dozen being used intensively over a period of time to show different aspects of a complex control situation.

Most public sector organizations (including educational ones) should be able to identify a range of performance indicators which together not only relate to client satisfaction but also to resource usage and the development of future capability. Similarly, though profit making organizations may emphasize return on assets, or even share price, it is often difficult for individual employees to relate their actions to such global statistics. It is also unlikely that such organizations really are judged in so narrow a way in the long term by all stakeholders (see Chapter 3). The use of a range of performance indicators may be helpful in both these contexts. Prompted by problems in operations management, Goldratt (1986) proposes a quite different approach to performance measurement based on the concept of throughput and with an emphasis on relating individual operational actions to global measures. This whole area has been the subject of much recent research.

The theme of performance measurement is taken further in Chapter 2 by a specific consideration of the details of productivity measurement in manufacturing and service operations. Some related issues in cost management accounting are explored in Chapter 3.

General classifications of systems methodologies

A number of very specific contributions to systems theory have been made in the past few years through the development of a range of methodologies, each aimed at uncovering important aspects of systemic behaviour. Flood and Jackson (1991) provide a very clear introduction to this difficult area. They identify five prominent systems 'metaphors' as follows:

- The machine or closed system view which is mainly useful in modelling repetitive tasks carried out in a stable environment. It is often associated with Taylor's original view of scientific management and with mechanistic views of bureaucracies.

- The organic or open systems view, borrowing from concepts in biology, which emphasizes adaptive response to environmental change. Though very influential in the last 30 years, it may be criticized as assuming too high a level of agreement between organizational members on the purposes of an organization and for being reactive to environmental change rather than proactive.

- The neurocybernetic or viable systems view. Based very much on the work of Stafford Beer (in a management context), see Beer (1981, 1985), it centres on the concept of requisite variety in a control system (cf the central nervous system of the body) and the need for active learning and proactive adaptation. Its organizational prescriptions are dramatic and often problematic in the sense of implementation in the context of real power (see Beer's attempts to influence the government of Chile prior to Allende's assassination). It also, like the previous two metaphors, assumes an objective rather than a socially constructed view of organizational life.

- The culture metaphor which relates to organizational culture, that is how things are actually done in a given context with particular emphasis on values, beliefs and norms of behaviour. Studies of Japanese operations, for example, have led to considerable speculation on their transferability to other cultures and to research on the performance of 'transplants' in the UK. It may lead senior management to the view that culture manipulation is a good way to run a firm but is somewhat short of prescriptions. This may not be a bad thing.

- The political metaphor which explicitly addresses issues of power, influence and competition within an organization. This view dominates much current general management writing, both journalistic and based on thorough research. There is a temptation in operations management to recognize that issues of power are important but then to relegate them to common sense rather than careful analysis, except perhaps in the sphere of industrial relations.

The first three metaphors have an obvious resonance in traditional operations management thinking and practice, in particular to the extent that production management, say, has in the past borrowed from an engineering culture. Such ways of looking at an organization are of great practical value and may also lead to prescriptions for systems design that transfer from one organization to another. More recent ideas, such as TQM and JIT, are more subtle in their views of how people behave but one wonders if they are being applied in many contexts as mechanistic techniques. If Deming is seen merely as SPC plus a few aphorisms about people then little progress has been made. Perhaps the challenges of international operations and the increased attention being given to operations management in personal service contexts will help reinforce an awareness of the subtleties of human behaviour and the need for well prepared employees to provide 'requisite variety' in adapting to such a complex environment.

An alternative diet of metaphors is provided by Morgan (1986) whose *Images of Organization* includes the five given above plus such offerings as the organization as a psychic prison or an instrument of domination. The approach of most writers in this area is that there is no one correct metaphor but that all may be useful and that one should cultivate the difficult art of seeing the same organization is a variety of ways.

Flood and Jackson go further and suggest a way of comparing systems methodologies based on a simple, two-way classification structure. The first dimension in this structure is systems complexity. Remembering that the discussion refers to systems models, we differentiate between:

- Simple systems where a fairly small number of elements interact in a regular way.
- Complex systems where a larger number of elements exhibit probabilistic and evolutionary behaviour in a purposeful manner.

The other dimension relates to people and contrasts three possibilities:

- Unitary relationships where participants tend to agree on values, interests, objectives and all contribute to decision making.
- Pluralistic relationships where interests and objectives are compatible, all participate in decision making but compromises may have to be reached on issues of value and means to achieve ends.
- Coercive relationships where agreement does not exist on interests, values, objectives or methods and some subgroupings coerce others to accept decisions.

The juxtaposition of these two dimensions gives six groupings of systems methodologies which are explored at length in Flood and Jackson (1991). We will draw attention to only three which seem currently to form the basis of thinking in operations management. This is not to say, of course, that future approaches may not strongly develop the other possibilities.

If a simple and unitary approach is pursued as the basis for analysing operations, then we are in the area of classic, mathematically orientated operational research (OR), systems analysis and the simulation approach often referred to as systems dynamics (for the latter see Wolstenholme (1990)). It should be said immediately that current OR practitioners have developed more varied approaches (see for example Rosenhead (1989)). However, the basic 'hard systems' approach is aimed at problem solving and optimization and perhaps should only be used when other approaches have identified the key issues and concrete prescriptions are now required.

A complex and unitary approach may lead one in the direction of viable systems or the older socio-technical systems approach. If one is convinced that unity of purpose and agreement on fundamental values really exists then these methods can be highly illuminating though quite difficult to apply, which is inevitable if real complexity must be faced up to.

Noteworthy is the category of complex and pluralist systems methodologies which includes the very well known soft systems methodology (SSM). Though underpinned by deep theoretical considerations, the basic approach is straightforward and surprisingly intuitive and seems capable of immediate use. A recent description is found in Checkland and Scholes (1990) and it should be emphasized that cases of its practical use are of particular value to the novice.

Soft systems methodology emphasizes the subjective nature of systems models. It is in itself an 'enquiring process' aimed at continual improvement in our views of real-world problem situations. It centres on purposeful activity systems which are seen as transformational processes and described through root definitions. In any situation a variety of root definitions are possible, thus reflecting a plurality of views in a cooperative climate of enquiry. A mnemonic, CATWOE, is usually employed to help with the construction of root definitions. This includes:

C Customers - the beneficiaries of the transformation
A Actors - those who perform the transformation
T Transformation - the conversion of input to output
W Weltanschauung - or world-view which provides a meaningful context for the transformation
O Owners - those who could stop the transformation
E Environment - other relevant elements outside the system

The real challenge in using this method comes from seeing the variety of response from a range of individuals attempting to describe the same transformational system. This has often been found in practice to lead to an enrichment of one's view about a process (particularly in service or office contexts). Wilson (1984) shows how this can be taken further in terms of systems design and application though a range of analysis and design techniques (e.g. in information systems) now seem to have taken SSM on board, if only as a brainstorming technique in the preliminary stages of systems investigation.

Thus to summarize, we would like to be able to finally represent most operational management situations as simple and unitary, either by design or by training. That is, we would like to be able to train operations staff in procedures which are basically simple though effective. However, the real world is endlessly complex and great care must be taken in such design activity.

In a tightly controlled factory context, individual transformations may be modelled as simple and unitary. A sub-system becomes seen as a collection of agreed tasks. Such a view may not be appropriate, for example when a poorly designed piecework system of wage payment is in use and the relationship between management and workers is far from unitary. Much general management literature shows the dangers of such a view applied in a broader factory context. Indeed it would be a most inappropriate starting point for operational analysis and design where complexity and potential conflict should be addressed before simple procedures are designed.

However, in modelling some operational contexts it is doubtful whether it is ever desirable to aim for a simple and unitary view of the world. When in direct contact with a client one must always ask whether both parties really have the same interests and objectives. Though many routine services assume agreement on the package on offer, in terms of specification and price, the whole issue of service quality addresses the perceptions of both parties of the actual value of a specific transformation. At best this seems to be an inherently pluralist situation and total quality management (TQM), by emphasizing the need for continuing communication and negotiation between provider and client, appears to recognize this and imply a simple-pluralist view of individual transformations. If TQM is seen as permeating all management situations then this fundamental assumption on how we see the world goes with it.

Some professional services, for example in health and education, may to a large extent work with agreed objectives between client and provider. Here, though, great skill may be required in actual delivery, for example medical diagnosis and operations. A complex-unitary view may be appropriate, which then places different demands on operations management, in particular training and retention of professional providers. In a cynical mood one might note that some selling situations pose as complex-unitary where in actuality they are simple-pluralist. The insurance salesman may wish to appear to be applying great skill in choosing a product which is best for everyone while in actuality is making simple choices, based on sophisticated materials, with the objective of maximising commission.

To carry this further, some operational situations seem inherently complex and pluralistic. For instance commercial negotiation over long-term material supplies contracts may be multi-faceted and competitive. In this context one may view with some interest current ideas on the value of cooperative sole-supplier agreements. Are they, in actuality, unitary or coercive? Though soft systems methodology may be recommended for complex-pluralist situations it is hard to see it applied in situations where openness in stating one's position may not be a wise move.

One further role for the operational strategist, much explored in this book, is to relate corporate needs and plans to operational reality. A general rule for the operational strategist is that though complexity and plurality must again be faced in the real world of markets and finance, we need models which are as simple and robust as possible while providing the basis for effective actions. Much work in corporate strategy is aimed at precisely this requirement and examples, such as the Porter models, are briefly described in Chapter 3. Their use, however, requires care and judgement. To take an example, Discounted Cash Flow models of the financial implications of capital investment decisions are simple and unitary in form but may be highly misleading if not embedded in a view of the world which addresses complexity and competition.

Perhaps this is a good place to make the observation that 'simple', in this classification of systems, is not the same as 'easy'. Many simple models, with few variables and a single objective, are quite difficult to learn and may exhibit unusual features. If well chosen and carefully explored one hopes that simple models will become easy to use and to relate to richer views of the world.

A further point to note here is that engineering and computing systems methodologies are often good at providing ways of modelling complexity in an essentially unitary framework. The common sense views of experienced managers often reflect a subtle understanding of human nature and competition whilst inevitably simplifying the detail workings of a system. These two approaches taken together seem complementary except that their respective practitioners often lack the training and experience to integrate them. Methodologies such as SSM and corporate modelling may therefore be useful in providing a basis for such integration.

Finally we must never divorce the above issues from our need, at an individual and corporate level, to continuously learn and improve. Our modelling must never be static but must include mechanisms for change, hence the emphasis in TQM and JIT for continual monitoring, reflection and adaptation. Viewed in this way, many traditional operational approaches seem simple, unitary and static – a fatal combination.

Modern systems thinking therefore provides a rich and varied range of approaches. Unfortunately this might seem more confusing than helpful. The following simple framework may therefore be of value. We differentiate between four levels of systems:

- *Level 1*
  General definitions of systems (including such language as boundary, feedback and so forth) which are common to all systems approaches, plus classification schemes (such as Flood and Jackson's two dimensions).

- *Level 2*
  Specific systems methodologies, such as SSM, systems dynamics, viable systems methods which have been developed to be of value in a range of contexts but have implicit assumptions that place them in

particular parts of the Flood and Jackson scheme.
● *Level 3*
Derived approaches in operations management which are aimed at particular, frequently occurring problem contexts. Examples are TQM, manufacturing systems audit models and so forth. On careful analysis they can be seen to have implicit assumptions also.
● *Level 4*
Actual systems models and descriptions relating to real operational contexts, these may be seen as Level 2 or 3 approaches with actual data added.

Of course the end point of the work of the operational manager is the implementation of Level 4, that is changing things to improve performance. This section has outlined some of the tools which may be of value in at least describing the context which is to be changed.

A SYSTEMS VIEW OF OPERATIONS MANAGEMENT

In the previous section we developed an extended view of systems terminology as applied to operations. The basic building block in our systems approach is an input-output system as shown in Figure 1.2. The action of the system is a process we refer to as a transformation. Though in systems theory such a process may cover a wide range of possibilities, in the context of this book we mainly concentrate on the following:

● Manufacturing systems where a range of material and human inputs are transformed into product outputs.
● Service systems where the external customer is both an input and an output. Other inputs will of course be necessary to effect a transformation.
● Office systems where information flows are key inputs and outputs.

The use of these ideas requires a little imagination. For example a product design system may be seen in terms of information flows, that is information inputs reflecting customer needs and technological possibilities are transformed into outputs specifying suitable products.

It should be noted in all cases that one system output which is almost always present though frequently neglected is information which reflects the actual performance of the system and which may be valuable in promoting learning. Indeed, associated with all operational transformational systems are managerial control systems which show how operational decision making is effected. These are discussed in Chapter 2 in the context of evaluation, learning and continual improvement.

An example of a manufacturing system is given in Figure 1.3. Another associated system for each operational transformation is one reflecting cash flows and other financial matters. A typical example is shown in Figure1.4. It should be noted that the relative timing of material and cash flows is often an important issue and therefore a time dimension should be added to our systems representations as illustrated in Figure 1.5.

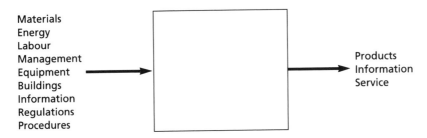

Figure 1.3
A manufacturing system

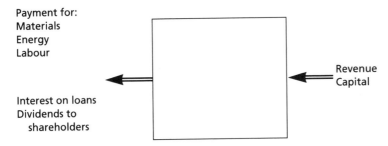

Figure 1.4
Cash flows in a manufacturing system

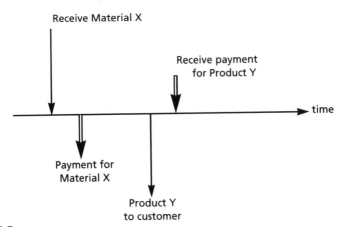

Figure 1.5
Cash flow timing

Using only this basic set of systems ideas, we may now move on to a classification of operations systems. This further explains our three-fold division of systems as introduced above.

A classification of operations systems

There are a number of taxonomies of operations management, the simplest of which is the division of operations into 'manufacturing' and 'service'. As operations management has grown out of the discipline of production management there is a continuing tendency for production concepts to explicitly and implicitly underpin operational thinking. To counter this, operations management academics and practitioners (for example through the annual conferences and publications of the Operations Management Association (UK)) have made a determined effort to promote service orientated thinking and to show how cross-fertilization between manufacturing and service research may be of value.

Two examples may help to illustrate this process in mainstream operations management. The concept of just-in time manufacturing may be seen as echoing the basic service situation where 'stocks of service' are not possible and therefore production has to match consumption. The total quality management ideology places an emphasis on continuing customer-supplier relationships, very important in service situations but sadly neglected in much of the classic manufacturing 'quality control' literature with its emphasis on the mechanistic policing of quality standards. However, many texts on operations management still include service issues as adjuncts to well developed manufacturing themes or discuss service situations using manufacturing concepts and metaphors. If the latter is meant as a helpful teaching approach then it fails with the increasingly large body of students whose whole work experience is in service and public sector organizations.

However, it must be said that many manufacturing orientated techniques are well developed and thoroughly tested and a re-invention of the wheel is hardly appropriate. Also the application of techniques in a manufacturing context is often simpler than in a service context where the customer is present, though this is often spoilt by the over-elaboration of such techniques in manufacturing in search of elusive optimization.

An example of the tendency to over-elaborate is the development of network analysis techniques such as CPA, PERT and so forth from the 1950s onwards. As shown in Lockyer(1984) it is possible to endlessly pursue the logic of network analysis and resource allocation in ways which are interesting and analytically satisfying but which hardly reflect the turbulent conflict of real project situations. One may cynically reflect whether such tools as GERT (see Meredith and Mantel (1989), a text which otherwise emphasizes organizational issues) are of most value as therapy for the technically brilliant but organizationally naive project leader requiring a means of demonstrating professional ability in situations beyond his control. It is noticeable that more recent literature explores the social context of project management, organizational design for project management and the competencies required of the project manager (see for example Boddy and Buchanan (1992)). Yet even here a word of caution is in order. It is quite foreseeable that recent developments in project management software, which not surprisingly emphasize networking and user-friendly interfaces, allied to expert systems will enable highly complex algorithms to support the project management decision making while the technical details remain invisible. Whether this will produce better managed portfolios of projects or confusion remains to be seen.

Another example of the care which must be taken when transferring techniques from one context to another is seen in the area of queuing theory. Most elementary operations textbooks contain some of the basic formulae for the calculation of queue lengths and queuing times, though these do scant justice to the complexity and real mathematical difficulty of this subject. In addition some discussion of the use of simulation to model queuing situations is likely to be included. Now both analytical and simulation-based approaches are of great value in the engineering analysis of manufacturing situations and throw some light on situations where human beings rather than materials are queuing, for example in supermarkets, on roads, at hospitals and so forth. However, the management of 'human queues' has a number of added dimensions of complexity. People are quite adept at queue avoidance, that is modifying their behaviour when faced with the possibility of having to queue by adopting such strategies as taking their custom elsewhere. This helps queue management but may not be in line with the objectives of the organization which is being avoided. An interesting alternative approach to queue management is given by Maister (see Lovelock (1988)) in an article on 'The psychology of Waiting Lines'. Here we are not given probabilistic formulae on queuing times but a series of propositions on how it feels to be a member of a queue and strategies which may be adopted to ease the annoyance of having to queue.

Thus we note the care with which manufacturing and service concepts should be developed. Two further points must also be made which dramatically affect our analysis. The first, which we develop in later chapters, is that operations management in small organizations is not merely a scaled down version of large organizational practice. Managers in the smaller firm have a different agenda of issues and are constrained in different ways from those in large organizations or even in small offshoots of large organizations. In particular financial, organizational and strategic issues cannot be separated from operational issues in the convenient manner assumed in much standard theory.

The second point was brought home to me by working with a number of mature general management students whose experience is in neither manufacturing nor service, if the latter is narrowly defined as personal service to an outside customer. They work in offices! Their work may be mundane or highly professional and it may be done in the general context of manufacturing, service or public sector organizations but the issues of operations management relevant to their context appears to be little explored beyond traditional operations management allied to the extensive use of computer technology.

Now this may seem an unfair point to make as service operations specialists have often used the 'front office' and 'back room' dichotomy. Yet it appears that so much of the innovative thinking reflects the handling of front office situations (where the customer is present). We might also note that much of the activity in manufacturing companies takes place away from the actual factory. It is just as useful to discuss the strategy of office operations as that of a factory. Value is added, or subtracted, in offices as much as in other parts of organizations and TQM concepts are of particular relevance here.

In view of the points made above we will adopt a simple systems approach in this book as follows:

All operational systems are concerned with transformations of inputs to outputs which add value.

We differentiate between three major transformational situations:

- The **FACTORY** where the primary transformation involves materials
- The **SHOP** where the primary transformation involves external customers
- The **OFFICE** where the primary transformation involves information

We refer above to 'primary transformations' because, for example, in the factory information gathering may take place, customers may be consulted and so forth. However, we assume that in a factory the conversion and movement of materials is the main activity. Mixed situations also exist such as a **FACTORY-SHOP** where the customer is fully involved in material transformation. A supermarket is such a situation where the customer also supplies the labour necessary in moving goods from shelves to the checkout point. Indeed customer involvement in service provision may be seen as a movement from a shop to a factory-shop environment. Such situations provide a particular challenge for operations management.

In the factory, the transformation of materials may take a variety of forms, of which the most obvious are:

- Direct alteration of the material through cutting, bending, assembling, packing and so forth.
- Movement of materials.
- Examination of materials (e.g. quality inspection) and recording of relevant information.

In the shop there is a wide variety of ways in which people may be 'transformed' (indeed the use of the word 'Shop' is a compromise between a host of different terms). Some examples are:

- Ownership, that is customers are sold a standard product.
- Personal transformation, such as a haircut or a medical operation.
- Receive information and advice.
- Be entertained.

Naturally many service situations are a mixture of these. A customer walks into a travel agent to receive brochures (a standard, free product giving information), to discuss possible holiday destinations, to buy a package holiday and subsequently to complain when things go wrong. Each of these may require different forms of service and backup to be effective. In particular one notes the extent to which service delivery and selling (and therefore operations management and marketing) are interrelated in the shop.

In the office, data and information from a variety of sources is handled to provide a range of outputs for internal and external customers. Such data may refer to physical quantities, financial amounts and times. Recording may be manual or electronic and may take the form of text, numbers, pictures or audio/visual media. Much attention is likely to be given to issues of communication, security and the transferring of information from one media to another (e.g. voice on a tape to electronic database to letter to external customer).

THE OPERATIONS ENVIRONMENT

The management of operations is inseparable from the environment in which operational activity takes place. As trade becomes more global, so must operations. If labour shortages exist then operational activity must be modified to take this into account. Whether we are referring to manufacturing, service or office operations the environment has an obvious and considerable effect.

We are here using the word 'environment' in its general systems meaning to refer to anything outside the business system which is relevant to its operation. The word has also recently taken on connotations of social responsibility regarding the management of the earth as a whole, the so called 'Green' movement. Though not the principal concern of this book, this approach may be seen as a long-term view of the preservation of the operational environment. Many of the messages of the Green movement regarding waste avoidance, efficient uses of energy and so forth translate directly into cost-effective operations.

The growth of the service sector as a major employer and provider has been charted in a number of places (see Lovelock (1992) for a summary).

This has been partly due to rises in the standard of living in the West, thus leading to the massive global travel and recreational industries, for instance. More generally consumers are seeing services as adding value to purchased products. In the computer industry, for example, the material and direct manufacturing processing costs may represent only a fraction of the price paid by the consumer while most of the remaining cost is the result of design and service operations.

Thus discussion centred on manufacturing industry is not exclusively about manufacturing operations. Indeed manufacturing companies represent an opportunity to discuss all types of operational problems and strategies. An excellent example of this is the extended analysis of the global car industry in Womack et al (1990). Whilst covering engineering and production, this study makes extensive reference to the relationship with suppliers, to issues in the management of design, to marketing and selling, indeed to a wide range of operational activities which are shown to relate to one another in a number of ways.

The relationship between the environment and competitive strategy in manufacturing industries is effectively explored in a study undertaken by PA consultants on behalf of the DTI (DTI (1989)). This classifies environmental influences under five headings, showing potential opportunities and threats under each:

- Economic factors – opportunities in Europe and the Pacific Rim may be contrasted with the current recession.
- Demography and lifestyles – on the one hand an ageing and affluent population presents market opportunities, though labour and skill shortages may provide problems.
- Green issues – market opportunities for environmentally safe products contrast with resource depletion and pollution.
- Market factors – demand for niche products and short life cycles are balanced by global competition.
- Technology – obvious advances are accompanied by greater sophistication and need for training.

It might also be noted that the summary of environmental influences in this study, though fairly recent, takes little account of changes in Eastern Europe or the currency problems of the European Community for example. Future projections of the environment will always be at the mercy of political change.

Of the factors listed above, particular note should be taken of demographic changes. The market effects of an ageing population are quite marked in terms of demand for a number of categories of product and service ranging from recreational products to medical treatment. As operations is a major employer, changes in the labour market in terms of numbers and skills are of primary importance.

Manufacturing industry is adapting continually to changing environmental conditions and also as learning takes place on a world-wide basis regarding the major strategies for a modern manufacturing enterprise. A series of global manufacturing projections were undertaken in the 1980s, mainly to contrast differing responses in Japan, USA and Europe. Ferdows et al (1989) showed that concern for standards of quality in manufacturing was the highest concern for companies in all three regions for most of the early part of the decade, followed by control of overhead costs and new product introduction. Japanese companies were, however, more interested in developing flexible manufacturing systems for the future than their overseas counterparts.

In a recent updating of this work relating to 1990 (comments based on a presentation at the 1992 Operations Management Association (UK) conference) conformance quality still appears to be a prime issue in the USA and Europe while the Japanese have moved on. All regions showed a concern for delivery as a key competitive weapon. Somewhat interestingly, and contrary to arguments later in this book, companies in the West have found robotics, activity based costing and even bench-marking to be 'low pay off activities'!

A key point to make here is that there are few eternal truths in operational strategy formulation; no straight path to guaranteed success. Each organization must find a strategy which fits its objectives in the current environment and provides the basis for long-term competitiveness. The problem is that resources have often to be committed, in terms of location, technology and people, far in advance of the point in time when actual operations occur. There is little wonder that faced with the current global environment, many managers will insist that any chosen strategy carries the prefix 'flexible'.

CHAPTER 2

Productivity, learning, flexibility and forecasting

INTRODUCTION

In this chapter we are concerned with four key aspects of systems management. These may be summarized in the form of a series of simple questions which may be asked for any operational system.

Productivity

How much input is needed to achieve the required output?
How effective is the system in transforming input into output?

Learning

How is the input-output relationship changing as the system gains operating experience?

Flexibility

Can the system adapt to changing needs?

Forecasting

What are future needs likely to be?
How will the system behave in the future?

Unfortunately it is unrealistic to always expect simple answers to simple questions. Each of the above areas has a substantial body of theory relating to it and theory in this instance is not merely academic elaboration of the obvious. There are major difficulties in arriving at sensible and reliable answers to these questions.

In the following sections we explore these areas in the context of operational decision making and lay the foundation for a number of issues to be addressed in later chapters.

PRODUCTIVITY MEASUREMENT

The concept of productivity seeks to explore the quantitative relationship between the inputs and outputs of a system. Productivity measurement attempts to answer the basic and apparently simple question of how much input is required to achieve a particular output. This question may be posed for a single machine, service encounter, manufacturing cell, factory or an entire economy. Thus productivity measurement is of interest to the engineer, the business manager and the economist. It is of particular interest to the operations manager as productivity measurements and forecasts are a crucial part of operational planning and control systems. Similarly the operational strategist is concerned with facilitating operations management and also with understanding the dynamic relationship between productivity and profitability and how this relationship may be improved over time.

One point should be mentioned at this early stage. Productivity assessments may be based on simple crude statistics which are readily comprehensible to a wide range of employees and there are distinct benefits in using such measures if one expects understanding and motivation to follow. Unfortunately it can be readily shown that simple measures are frequently misleading. A typical example is the 'number of cars produced per employee' measure that has often been used to show the relative success of motor manufacturing plants. Such a statistic ignores the degree of vertical integration of a manufacturing unit and the extent to which automation has been adopted. However, a more complete analysis requires large amounts of data and leads to a highly complex picture of the relationship between a range of inputs and outputs. Productivity measurement is an area where careful choices must be made regarding the complexity of analysis which is required, this in turn being dependent on the decisions and controls being informed by the productivity measures. The operations strategist may well need a highly complex form of analysis which is subsequently simplified for tactical operational decision making.

There are two ways of quantifying productivity. The first uses the physical properties of inputs and outputs as follows. Suppose we are concerned with the manufacture of a product which we refer to as Model A. Past data shows that typically in order to make 100 units of Model A we use 40 kg of a substance we will refer to as Material 1. We may express this relationship in either of the following simple ways:

- as a technology coefficient, that is Model A requires 0.4 kg of Material 1 to make a unit of Model A;
- as a 'single factor productivity' measure, that is 1 kg of Material 1 produces 2.5 units of Model A.

Thus though both measures relate quantities of input and output, technology coefficients compute input divided by output while single factor productivity (SFP) statistics show output divided by input. This may cause confusion and therefore it is important always to state the units of measurement used, for example the SFP in this case is 2.5 units/kg.

Some words of caution are necessary even at this early stage. First we should be clear whether the measurement given expresses a historical fact, a forecast or a standard. That is we should be clear which of the following applies:

- last Thursday we used 40 kg to actually make 100 units;
- we usually need 40 kg if we are making 100 units and expect this to continue in the future;
- if the production unit is properly set up we should only need 40 kg to make 100 units.

We refer to the first of these as a measure of actual performance and the last of these as a productivity standard. Productivity is often intimately related to expectations of performance and quality, particularly in service situations, and hence such standards are very important in communicating management expectations.

The second point to note is the implicit assumption of linearity in forming a ratio of inputs and outputs. Suppose the situation is that Model A is made in batches, the first 2 kg of Material 1 being used to test the quality of a batch, and the amount of Material 1 consumed depends on the machine used in manufacture. However, suppose that we still use a simple aggregate productivity measure without recording the machines used or the batch sizes. This simple ratio may still record average performance or expectations but is of less value in prompting managerial action (e.g. on which machine to use or whether to change the testing method). Indeed such measures may lend credence to past bad practice. Once again we make the point that the form of measurement used must relate to the decision making situation. While it is tempting to try to design the productivity measure which expresses the ultimate truth about a given situation it is more realistic to design measures which are useful in highlighting inefficiencies and guiding future action.

It should not be thought that productivity is only a manufacturing concern. Service productivity is also a central issue in all organizations. However, productivity measurement in this instance is complicated by a number of factors as explored in Hill (1991), Lovelock (1992) and Mill (1989). In particular we note that in a service situation:

- It may be difficult to relate service output and customer goals directly to the activity of particular worker (for example, in a hospital it might be possible to measure the productivity of a surgical team but harder to characterize the productivity of nursing staff providing continuing care).
- It may be hard to measure output, particularly as output quality is linked in complex ways to the inputs provided (in this case consider, as an example, a personal advice consultancy).
- Inputs and outputs may be dramatically separate in time (a salesperson's production of quotations for proposed work may bear partial fruit some considerable time later).

Thus our concentration on manufacturing in this section is a reflection of the comparative simplicity afforded by a concrete example. We return to some specific issues in service operations management later and in Chapter 5.

Though single factor productivity measures based on physical properties are an important building block in our productivity measurement systems they are limited in two important ways. First of all they do not reflect the actuality of transformational systems where a set of inputs produces a set of outputs. Secondly they do not directly relate to the financial objectives of an organization. In addressing both of these issues we are led to the use of costs and prices in our measurement systems.

Most current texts recommend the use of total factor productivity (TFP) measures where inputs are somehow aggregated. This is not easy as the physical measurements of inputs are likely to be quite different (e.g. hours of labour, kg of material and so forth). We illustrate the use of TFP measures through a development of our previous example.

In Figure 2.1 we show data relating to the manufacture of Model A in two different time periods. In Year 1 we made 10,000 units of this product and this required 5,500 hours of labour, 3,800 kg of Material 1 and so forth. Thus the SFP for labour is calculated as 10,000/5,500, i.e. 1.818 units of Model A per labour hour. SFPs are similarly calculated for the other resources for Year 1 and for Year 2 and the percentage change is then found

	Ouput: Model A	Inputs: labour	Material 1	Material 2	Machine X	Total
	Units	Hours	Kg	Kg	Hours	
Physical analysis:						
Year 1:						
Amount	10,000	5,500	3,800	26,000	24,000	
SFP		1.818	2.632	0.385	0.417	
Year 2:						
Amount	12,000	7,200	5,040	28,800	30,600	
SFP		1.667	2.381	0.417	0.392	
SFP change		−8.33%	−9.52%	8.33%	−5.88%	
Financial analysis:						
Prices (£)	£25.00	£9.80	£8.10	£1.90	£3.20	
Total revenue and costs:						
Year 1	£250,000	£53,900	£30,780	£49,400	£76,800	£210,880
Year 2	£300,000	£70,560	£40,824	£54,720	£97,920	£264,024
Financial ratios:						
Year 1		4.638	8.122	5.061	3.255	1.186
Year 2		4.252	7.349	5.482	3.064	1.136
Change		−8.33%	−9.52%	8.33%	−5.88%	−4.15%

Figure 2.1
Productivity measurement

for each separate resource. Thus we see that labour productivity has declined by 8.33 percent. Only Material 2 has apparently improved in terms of effective usage between Years 1 and 2.

This simple form of analysis is useful and easy to comprehend but limited in conveying an impression of productivity as a whole. We therefore continue by finding TFP measures and immediately encounter a basic problem. We cannot sensibly aggregate physical quantities of labour, materials and so forth. One approach might be to find average SFPs for each period but this assumes that each resource is of equal importance in making Model A. We can for example imagine a readily available input resource costing only small amounts of money which happens to have dramatic changes in SFP and thus distorts the total picture. The approach normally taken here is to use financial weights of some kind to reflect the comparative importance of the inputs. Typically these will be costs and prices but the weights must be kept constant for differing time periods otherwise the resulting SFP and TFP changes will reflect price as well as productivity fluctuations. In our example the Year 2 price of Model A and unit costs of the resources have been used as weights. Alternatively some form of standard costs could have been used. The important judgement here is that the weights chosen reflect the relative importance of the inputs.

To continue our calculations, the price weights have been multiplied by the input and output quantities to give data for total revenue and cost for each of the two years. For Year 2 these will be actual revenues and variable costs as the appropriate financial data has been used. However, our need to use constant weights has led us to multiply Year 2 prices by year 1 quantities, a move which may seem strange but is typical of this form of index number calculation. We can now find total 'costs' for both periods and the financial equivalents of SFPs. The latter is calculated by dividing total 'revenue' by the total 'cost' of each resource. Thus for example we now find that each £1 spent on labour in Year 2 produced £4.252 of Model A. In particular it is now possible to find TFPs for each year, i.e. each £1 spent on resources produced £1.186 of output in Year 1 and £1.136 of output in Year 2, a productivity reduction of 4.15 per cent. We note in passing that though the financial SFPs differ from the physical ones, the percentage changes must be identical in each case as constant weights have been used.

Total factor productivity measures were used by Hayes and Clark (1986) as an essential variable in the study of factory productivities and their relationship with other key variables such as age of equipment, inventory levels and work force policies. The result is not only a convenient tool for statistical analysis but one which is meaningful to employees. Thus one can readily see why this device is becoming accepted as a standard productivity measure (see also Hill 1991).

Hayes, Wheelwright and Clark (1988) develop a limited framework for profitability analysis based on TFPs and this clearly shows the value of modelling the financial effects of productivity improvement policies. However, a more extensive development of this theme is found in Kaplan and Atkinson (1989), leading to an approach we illustrate in a further extension to our productivity example. Their approach is based on the 'nine box' model of cost analysis. In Figure 2.2 we show the obvious derivation of profit changes from those of cost and revenue. In carrying out productivity analysis it is convenient to base our analysis of profit changes on a different set of variances as shown in Figure 2.3. In essence we split profit changes into effects caused by changes in productivity, in sales activity (volume and mix) and in price recovery. By 'profit changes' we may be referring to variances from budgets and standards, to inter-period changes or to alternative scenarios as we attempt to model the effects of managerial action. In each case it is convenient to use the same basic framework with small appropriate adjustments.

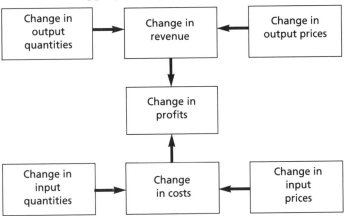

Figure 2.2
Profit, cost and revenue

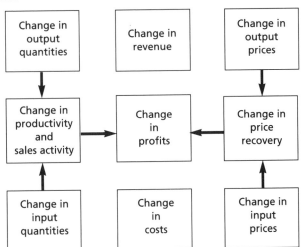

Figure 2.3
Nine box model

In Figures 2.4 to 2.7 we show an extensive worked example based on three types of output and two periods of trading. The details of the calculations closely follow Kaplan and Atkinson (1989). Our calculations show productivity changes between Years 1 and 2 for three products which each require four input resources.

In Figure 2.4 we show data and analysis for Year 1. This includes the following features:

1 A technology specification showing how much of each resource we expected to use in the manufacture of a unit of each product.
2 Details of technology performance, that is how much resource was actually used on average in manufacturing a unit of each product.
3 The actual input quantities and unit costs, from which total variable and fixed costs can be calculated.
4 The actual output quantities and prices, from which total revenue can be found.
5 An income statement summarizing revenue, costs and profit.

			Model A	*Model B*	*Model C*
Technology specification					
Direct labour (hr/unit)			0.50	1.50	3.00
Material 1 (kg/unit)			0.40	0.40	0.50
Material 2 (kg/unit)			2.60	2.90	4.30
Machine X (hr /unit)			2.60	2.00	3.10
Technology performance:			*Model A*	*Model B*	*Model C*
Direct labour (hr/unit)			0.55	1.60	3.20
Material 1 (kg/unit)			0.38	0.37	0.47
Material 2 (kg/unit)			2.60	3.10	4.30
Machine X (hr/unit)			2.40	1.70	3.00
Input:	*Quantity*	*Unit cost*			
Direct labour	21,500 hours	£10.00			
Material 1	7,230 kg	£8.00			
Material 2	55,100 kg	£2.00			
Machine X	40,600 hours	£3.00			
Overhead	1	£105,000			
Output:	*Quantity*	*Price*			
Model A	10,000 units	£24.00			
Model B	8,000 units	£39.00			
Model C	1,000 units	£80.00			
Income statement					
Sales		£632,000			
Direct labour	£215,000				
Material 1	£57,840				
Material 2	£110,200				
Machine X	£121,800				
Variable costs		£504,840			
Overhead		£105,000			
Profit		£22,160			

Figure 2.4
Example – Year 1 data

We then move to Figure.2.5 which shows similar data for Year 2. In this case:

1 The technology specification has been adjusted slightly in line with the experience gained in Year 1.
2 Technology performance shows some improvements and also some problems when compared with Year 1.
3 Input quantities have changed and so have unit costs, some showing inflation and some showing reductions due to changed working practices.
4 Output quantities have changed, Model A being more successful in volume terms while Models B and C have reduced sales. The latter may be due to price rises which were kept to a minimum for Model A.
5 The income statement for Year 2 shows extra profit but we are unsure from where this improvement actually came.

Technology specification		Model A	Model B	Model C
Direct labour (hr/unit)		0.53	1.50	3.10
Material 1 (kg/unit)		0.40	0.40	0.50
Material 2 (kg/unit)		2.50	3.00	4.30
Machine X (hr /unit)		2.50	1.80	3.00
Technology performance:		Model A	Model B	Model C
Direct labour (hr/unit)		0.60	1.55	3.05
Material 1 (kg/unit)		0.42	0.43	0.55
Material 2 (kg/unit)		2.40	2.80	4.40
Machine X (hr/unit)		2.55	2.05	3.20
Input:	Quantity	Unit cost		
Direct labour	21,420 hours	£9.80		
Material 1	8,748 kg	£8.10		
Material 2	53,600 kg	£1.90		
Machine X	48,740 hours	£3.20		
Overhead	1	£126,000		
Output:	Quantity	Price		
Model A	12,000 units	£25.00		
Model B	7600 units	£43.00		
Model C	800 units	£89.00		
Income statement				
Sales		£698,000		
Direct labour	£209,916			
Material 1	£70,859			
Material 2	£101,840			
Machine X	£155,968			
Variable costs		£538,583		
Overhead		£126,000		
Profit		£33,417		

Figure 2.5
Example – Year 2 data

We attempt to analyse these many changes through variance analysis. Two forms of variance analysis are of interest here. The first, a traditional form of income statement variance analysis shown in Figure 2.6, shows the favourable profit variance (i.e. profits went up by 51 per cent) but a confusing pattern of sales and resource changes based on actual quantities and prices.

		Year 2	Year 1	Variance	Percentage
Sales		£698,000	£632,000	£66,000 (F)	10.44%
	Direct labour	£209,916	£215,000	(£5,084) (F)	−2.36%
	Material 1	£70,859	£57,840	£13,019 (U)	22.51%
	Material 2	£101,840	£110,200	(£8,360) (F)	−7.59%
	Machine X	£155,968	£121,800	£34,168 (U)	28.05%
Variable costs		£538,583	£504,840	£33,743 (U)	6.68%
Overhead		£126,000	£105,000	£21,000 (U)	20.00%
Profit		£33,417	£22,160	£11,257 (F)	50.80%

Figure 2.6
Example – income statement variance analysis

The second analysis, the results of which are shown in Figure 2.7, splits the profit change in a different way. The details of this set of calculations are not shown but follow the format used in Kaplan and Atkinson (1989). Our main interest is in the results of such an analysis.

Sales-volume variance	£9,439	(F)	42.59%	
Sales-mix variance	(£13,059)	(U)	−58.93%	
Sales-activity variance		(£3,620) (U)		−16.34%
Sales-price variance	£49,600	(F)	223.83%	
Input-cost variance	£21,979	(U)	99.18%	
Price-recovery variance		£27,621 (F)		124.64%
Productivity-variance Yr 1	£940	(U)	4.24%	
Productivity-variance Yr 2	£18,564	(U)	83.77%	
Usage-standards variance	(£4,880)	(F)	−22.02%	
Productivity variance		(£12,744) (U)		−57.51%
Total profit variance		£11,257 (F)		50.80%

Figure 2.7
Example – productivity variance analysis

Thus we see that changes in profit resulted from:

Sales-volume variance

Increases in sales volume considered in isolation increased profits by £9,439. (The percentages given relate these changes to the profit made in Year 1.)

Sales-mix variance

Unfortunately sales volume changes included a move away from Models B and C to the less profitable Model A which had the effect of reducing profits by £13,059.

Sales-activity variance

The net effect of these two changes in sales policy was a profit reduction of £3,620.

Sales-price variance

Increases in the prices charged for the three models improved profits by the considerable amount of £49,600.

Input-cost variance

Increases in unit costs, however, reduced profits by £21,979.

Price-recovery variance

The net effect of these two changes was a profit increase of £27,979.

Productivity variance Year 1

Relative to Year 1 standards, as shown in the technology specification, Year 1 actual performance showed an unfavourable variance of £940.

Productivity variance Year 2

Relative to Year 2 standards, Year 2 actual performance was very poor. The unfavourable variance was £18,564.

Usage-standards variance

However, the standards have been changed and this in itself 'caused' a favourable variance of £4,880.

Productivity variance

The net effect of the three productivity related variances is a profit reduction of £12,744. This is calculated as £18,564 − £940 − £4,880, which may seem strange if one is not accustomed to accounting variance analysis, but does reflect the changes made.

The above may once again be aggregated to give a total profit variance of £11,257.

	Ouput: all models	Inputs: labour	Material 1	Material 2	Machine X	Total
Total revenues and costs:						
Year 1	£632,000	£215,000	£57,840	£110,200	£121,800	£504,840
Year 2	£698,000	£209,916	£70,859	£101,840	£155,968	£538,583
Variance	£66,000	(£5,084)	£13,019	(£8,360)	£34,168	£33,743
	10.44%	−2.36%	22.51%	−7.59%	28.05%	6.68%
Productivity ratios:						
Year 1		2.940	10.927	5.735	5.189	1.252
Year 2		3.325	9.851	6.854	4.475	1.296
Change		13.12%	−9.85%	19.51%	−13.75%	3.52%

Figure 2.8
Example – total factor productivity analysis

Thus using an analysis of this form, productivity changes can be separated from other variables. We may also present this data in the form of a total factor productivity analysis, see Figure 2.8 which is similar in format to Figure 2.1. Each form of analysis throws light on a different aspect of a situation while maintaining consistency. Such analysis may in theory be carried out at any level of system focus, though the lack of reliable disaggregated financial data may be an impediment in many instances.

LEARNING AND EXPERIENCE CURVES

Introduction

One of the most important empirical findings in the analysis of manufacturing productivity is that resource usage, and therefore unit cost, tends to decrease as more product is manufactured. There appears to be a learning effect whereby efficiency is improved as experience is accumulated.

Though this finding is consistent with current ideas of 'continual improvement', the effect and its associated quantification have been known for some time. It has now taken a central place in manufacturing strategy and underpins certain aspects of the Boston Consulting Group (BCG) approach to corporate strategy. Common sense suggests that such ideas will also relate to office and personal service situations.

In the context of the BCG approach we might note that it is quite natural to link the quantification of the learning curve with a 'learning curve strategy' whereby increasing cost advantage is used as the key competitive weapon. While this is certainly a valid approach it should be remembered that learning is a feature of a range of operational systems and the learning curve thus has far wider application. As continuous learning becomes more and more a central part of operational thinking then the learning curve should be seen as a general tool for exploring and representing such learning as appropriate. Although writers on corporate and human resource policies recognize the value of learning, most texts in these areas lack details on appropriate models, such as the learning curve approach. One of the significant features of operations management, as a discipline, is that such detail is pursued to levels where its operational application is possible.

One of the key papers in describing this concept is Abernathy and Wayne (1974) which dates the wider appreciation of the learning curve concept to the mid 1950s. These authors differentiate between the following:

● The learning curve which models the reduction of manufacturing costs for a standard product as a function of cumulative production.

● The experience curve which models reductions in total costs (or possibly price or added value, see later discussion) for a product over an extended period of time.

Thus the learning curve is essentially a tool for the engineer and the operations manager examining the details of cost changes in an otherwise stable situation. The experience curve is more appropriate either for a corporate strategist or an external analyst looking at more general price movements and in particular the structural advantages of high volumes of production.

The experience curve may be thought of as a form of dynamic economy of scale, though, as the detailed formulation shows, it is somewhat different from the conventional ideas of a scale economy (see Porter (1985)). Substantial expositions of the experience curve concept are to be found in Hayes and Wheelwright (1984) and in McNamee (1985). The former relates experience curves in detail to manufacturing strategy while the later is concerned largely with product portfolio approaches to corporate strategy. This is an area where careful study is repaid with real insights into one of the main sources of strategic advantage and the above references, along with the Abernathy and Wayne paper are to be recommended as initial reading. The latter in particular contains a most interesting historical digression into the long-term prices and costs of the Model T Ford. As we know, this car had a long period of success before being challenged and superseded by rival offerings. The data given here complements more recent studies (in particular Womack et al (1990) on the complex strategies of the motor trade.

Service-related applications of learning curves

Whilst the learning curve concept has been extensively developed in the context of manufacturing, its application in the controlled environment of office work is fairly clear. This is particularly true as data capture relating to the productivity of electronic work (for example speed and accuracy of text entry in word processing) becomes routinely possible and productivity improvements can be monitored and controlled. However, the application to personal service delivery is more complex and it is appropriate at this stage to explore some of these complexities in order to isolate the particular contribution of the learning curve approach.

Obviously learning by individuals is a key aspect of their service delivery. It is obviously present in routine activities as observation of varying speed of operation of supermarket checkout staff shows all too well (though precisely how this is related to experience may not be evident to the customer). Similarly experience may be allied to enhancements in knowledge and judgement, as one hopes will occur with professional workers, for example general medical practitioners. In the latter case, however, it is not unknown for experience to be translated into increased speed of patient throughput.

Thus experience may be translated into conventional productivity or into service improvements. An experienced provider may take longer to deliver a far better service. If the price of the service is unchanged then cost-based productivity measures may remain static or even show unfavourable variations, that is input costs remain the same and output revenues decrease though far more intangible output quality has been provided.

A detailed example may help us to explore this further. Imagine a guide conducting parties of tourists round a stately home. With experience the following changes may occur:

- Basic skill enhancements (knows way around the site, ability to handle minor problems).
- Knowledge enhancements (has far more to communicate on the history of the site, the families who owned it and so forth).
- Inter-personal skills (is better at dealing with an audience, gaining attention, eliciting questions).

This set of changes has a complex set of results in terms of:

- Durations of tours
- Quality of tours
- Number of customers in a touring group.

Thus the experienced guide may be able to give short, high quality tours with a large number in the group, therefore scoring positively on all performance criteria. Alternatively longer tours may result, or even lower quality if improvements in knowledge are lost due to poor presentation skills to a large group. A similar complicated set of outcomes may occur in teaching, consultancy and other professions where formal presentations are an important form of communication.

It appears then that learning curve models, which usually track changes in resource inputs and output volumes assuming constant output quality, may be most easily applied in service situations where a culture of productivity control is appropriate and the customer expects a standardized service (fast food outlets, supermarkets). Such situations are most like factories and offices.

In other situations the advantages of learning may be more subtle. For example a restaurant may operate with mainly fixed labour costs in the short term. Here experience may result in either of the following depending on the situation at a particular time:

- A better quality of meal and table service.
- Faster turn-round of customers, for the benefit of the customer or to increase the capacity of the restaurant.

That is, experience may be managed to give a range of outcomes depending on circumstances. Experience translates into capability. This is actually also true in a wide range of office and factory situations but if it is assumed that standard outputs are required then increased capability will most obviously be channelled into increased productivity. Yet if the order winning criteria for a particular product include, say, tailoring the product to a customer's needs then it might be more appropriate if capability be translated into flexibility or into quality enhancing activities. In this way manufacturing takes on a 'service' culture, assuming that the organizational infrastructure supports such a change.

A further point which must be noted here, particularly in a service context, is that we have spoken of experience, learning and capability as features of individuals. Yet much of the manufacturing literature refers to organizational learning, in particular the changes in procedures and the organization of work which improve productivity. In service provision also such changes may be of primary importance and be seen through:

- Changes in facilities and layout design.
- Improved training and motivation.
- Improved information and back-up for the actual service deliverer.
- Operational decision making and control systems which quickly adapt to changing situations.

Thus learning should not be left entirely up to the individual, even in a context where the actual service encounter is of prime importance. The organizational context must support the service provider in a variety of ways and must therefore be continually improved. This should be aimed at the improvement of a range of performance measures of which productivity is likely to be one.

The learning curve model

Our particular interest, having briefly summarized general findings in this area, is to show how the detailed application of such models can aid operational management decision making in both tactical and strategic ways. This requires an exposition of the details of learning curve models (though without the mathematical proofs). The qualitative concept that costs decline with cumulative volume produced is usually operationalized through an explicit quantitative model as shown below. The same model is used for both learning and experience curves and it should be emphasized at the outset that this represents, as do all models, an approximation to reality. Although a number of different mathematical formulations are possible, the one given below is almost invariably used.

We define the following variables (given here with an extended discussion of their meaning which may be ignored on first reading but should subsequently be returned to):

i = cumulative production count (that is we simply label the first item produced as '$i=1$' and continue upwards)

It should be noted from the outset that this is a slightly unusual idea and not without problems in its application to real world situations. For instance do we start our count with the first prototype or the first unit of normal production (if that can be defined)? Do we include rejected items in our count? Do we restart the count if a substantial change takes place in the specification or manufacturing method used?

These are real problems which strike at the basis of our use of this model. A change may on the one hand temporarily increase costs and seem to justify restarting the count but it should be remembered that the physical mechanism of the learning curve is continual change – if one continually restarts the count one loses the effect being modelled! Certainly experience curve applications are intended to reflect long-term experience including a number of tactical changes. The learning effect does not, of course, happen by chance. It is the result of the management of change. Improvement is not guaranteed but only imperfectly reflected by this mathematical device.

$y(i)$ = resource used for producing the ith unit

The learning curve model may be applied to a single resource (traditionally labour though this is hardly appropriate in a highly automated system) or a more aggregated form of productivity measure may be used. The measure may reflect physical units of resource or the cost of resources, though in the latter case care must be taken to remove the effects of inflation to give measures of 'real cost'. When the model is used by an outside analyst, the only data available may be general cost trends and prices which must be treated with care due not only because of inflation effects but also due to distortions introduced by the allocation mechanisms for fixed costs.

R = learning rate parameter, usually expressed as a percentage

A learning rate of $R = 80$ per cent, for example, means that a doubling of cumulative volume (the i variable) produces a reduction of resources used (the $y(i)$ variable) to 80 per cent of its previous value, that is a 20 per cent reduction. For mathematical convenience this process is assumed to occur steadily, that is each unit produced is slightly cheaper than the last. The learning rate will depend on the situation, that is the actual product and process characteristics as well as managerial effectiveness in reducing costs. Though assumed to be constant in this model it may well fluctuate and be quite hard to measure in practice.

B = reduction rate parameter

This variable is introduced only to give a neater exposition of the model. It is a function of the learning rate parameter as given by the relationship:

$B = -\log(R)/\log(2)$

Any base of logarithm may be used. The result is shown in Figure 2.9 for standard values of R.

Learning rate	Reduction parameter
(R)	(B)
100%	0.0000
95%	0.0740
90%	0.1520
85%	0.2345
80%	0.3219
75%	0.4150
70%	0.5146
65%	0.6215
60%	0.7370
55%	0.8625

Figure 2.9
Learning rate parameters

Having defined our variables we express the learning curve effect as:

$y(i) = y(1)\ i^{\wedge}(-B)$

That is, the resource used to produce the ith unit is equal to that needed for the first unit multiplied by a reduction factor which depends on how much has been produced before and on the rate of learning which is being achieved by management.

Some further formulae are of value in using this concept. If we consider any two items labelled i and j (with $j>i$) then:

$y(j) = y(i)\ (j/i)^{\wedge}(-B)$

Thus our use of this model is not dependent on our measurement of the costs of producing the first item (which is fortunate as this may reflect particular non-recurring problems) but is dependent on the accuracy of the count. It can readily be seen that if $j = 2i$, costs will have reduced by the amount required by our specification of a learning rate. It may also be shown that if we define the following (resource usage may reflect physical performance or cost):

$T(i)$ = cumulative resource usage up to and including the ith item

$T(i,j)$ = cumulative resource usage from the $(i+1)$th to the jth item $(j>i)$

$A(i)$ = average resource usage up to and including the ith item

$A(i,j)$ = average resource usage from the $(i+1)$th to the jth item $(j>i)$

Then the following can be derived (though an approximation is involved which gives some inaccuracies for low values of i. The enthusiastic reader is encouraged to experiment with a spreadsheet to explore the extent of such inaccuracies in a given situation):

$T(i) = (y(1)/(1-B))\ i\wedge(1-B)$

$T(i,j) = (y(1)/(1-B))\ (j\wedge(1-B) - i\wedge(1-B))$

$A(i) = (y(1)/(1-B))\ i\wedge(-B) = y(i)/(1-B)$

$A(i,j) = (y(1)/(1-B))\ (j\wedge(1-B) - i\wedge(1-B))/(j-i)$

These formulae may easily be used in a spreadsheet environment to forecast production rates and also may be used as part of more general operational forecasting models. Some examples are given later.

If we plot $y(i)$ and $A(i)$ against i we obtain graphs similar to those shown in Figure 2.10 for illustrative values of the learning rate. If such a graph is

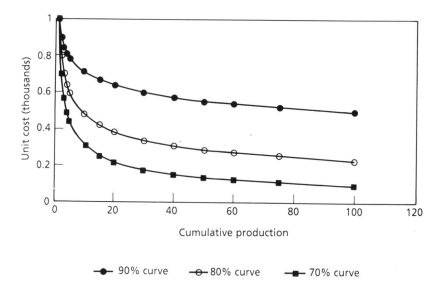

Figure 2.10
Learning curves

plotted on log-log paper then a straight line is the result, a possibility which makes forecasting easy by being visual.

In using this model we may wish to fit a learning curve to past data either to extrapolate forwards in order to forecast future learning for an existing product or to study past learning experiences in order to guide future policy (see below). Such estimation may be carried out by trial and error but a more efficient use of past data is achieved by using linear regression. If we take logs of both sides of the basic equation we obtain:

$$\log(y(i)) = \log(y(1)) - B \log(i)$$

If data can now be obtained on a number of pairs of i and $y(i)$ values then these can be used to estimate $y(1)$ and B as shown in Figure 2.11 and also to check whether learning does appear to follow the given equation. It should be noted that the estimates of $y(1)$ and B will be subject to sampling error. A number of pieces of software exist to facilitate manipulation of the learning curve model.

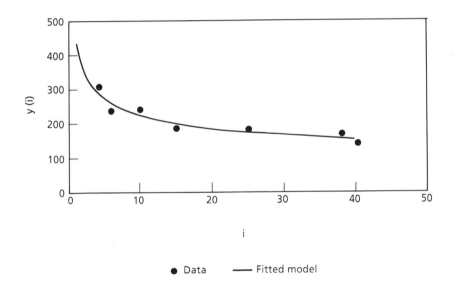

Figure 2.11
Estimation of learning curve parameters

The strategic use of learning and experience curves have been extensively studied (for useful summaries see Hayes and Wheelwright (1984) and McNamee (1985)). We now examine in more detail problems which must be addressed when using this model and policies which facilitate learning.

Key issues in using experience curve models

Unit of analysis

Learning and experience curve models may be applied to individual components, products or groups of products at the level of an individual company or an industry. There is no unique right way to use them. Similarly, judgement must be exercised in deciding what is a 'product' as features change over time. This is a common problem when analysing change over time (for example note the difficulties which occur with the product life cycle model) but in no way invalidates attempts to model such phenomena. As with all modelling and forecasting situations experience must be gained in the use of models in a given setting.

Shared experience

A further problem for the learning curve analyst is that products are built up using a mixture of components. Their production, in turn, is likely to involve differing learning rates and past experience as existing components are used in new products and common components are used for a variety of products.

Starting the count

It will be noted that the cumulative production count is a key variable and yet as we commented when initially defining this variable it is by no means clear how counting is to proceed. Once again this points to the need for attention to detail and a willingness to experiment when using such models.

Cost estimation problems

A number of problems exist in the area of cost estimation. The first concerns which costs should be included in the analysis. The impact of fixed costs, if included, may well be dependent on the allocation mechanisms used but such costs can hardly be ignored entirely in long-term experience curve analysis. There is also some doubt in the literature whether total cost or value added should be used. One view is that value added (which excludes material costs) is the appropriate variable as it concentrates on costs which are under factory management control. A contrasting view is that total cost should be used to reflect policies of vertical integration and supplier choice and price negotiation. The latter seems by far the better argument though such analysis might well include disagreggated modelling to show the impact of each cost factor on learning curve characteristics.

The costs included must be adjusted for inflation, a problem with all long-term cost analysis. However, this presents a real problem in this case as inflation adjustment factors will relate to real time periods rather than the 'count' for a particular product. In addition it is quite likely that all but the most sophisticated costing systems will average costs over periods of time, such as a year, even if appropriate data is collected at all. Though no doubt such problems can be solved by the application of time and effort, there is a strategic decision here on the scope and sophistication of cost data capture systems. Whilst one may imagine a vast cost database which can be endlessly manipulated to provide any information the reality is likely to be less useful.

Such problems are magnified if the data required is from outside our organization, for example competitor and supplier information is necessary for a full strategic analysis in this context. In many cases we will have to use prices as surrogates for cost information though this may distort the result. Similarly, we may be unsure of both the prior experience and the use of shared experience by outsiders, both features which have been shown may systematically distort our results and affect plans.

The above collection of problems should in no way deter the operational strategist from this form of modelling. The exploration of such issues in a given real situation is of great value in itself in enabling one to come to terms with the peculiarities of a particular context. Learning effects may be so great that any analysis which takes them into account is better than ignoring them.

Policies for learning

We now ask the simple question, why does the learning curve effect occur and what can be done to facilitate it?

Labour issues

The main basis for early learning curve studies was the examination of changes in labour productivity. As experience in making things is accumulated individual skills are improved (though it should not be assumed that this will inevitably lead to productivity gains), quality issues are addressed and the organization of work is likely to be adjusted to improve characteristics such as layout and material flow. A variety of policies and actions will be necessary both to encourage improvements in individual performance (for example through training and motivation), to improve the environment in which work takes place, to optimize job design (possibly through specialization or through forms of group working as appropriate) and to be sure that learning is actually fed through into improvements in costs and output.

Production processes

Capital investment in equipment may reduce unit costs through improved machine productivity or through varying the resource mix (substituting machines for labour if such automation is appropriate). Available economies of scale may be fully exploited through increased levels of automation provided necessary flexibility is not lost. Similarly, continuous modifications to equipment may be possible as particular production processes become better understood.

The above may relate to a phenomenon usually referred to as 'technical conservatism' whereby the potential performance of new or unfamiliar equipment is underrated when initially planning its use. One obvious source of early learning is the adjustment of expectations of what performance is feasible.

Product changes

Some standardization or simplification of the product may be possible as consumer needs become better understood, though the dangers of this approach must always be recognized. Similarly value analysis may be used to adjust the product specification, materials to be used or necessary manufacturing processes. It is widely recognized that large amounts of cost may be 'stripped' from many products once the situation of their manufacture is fully understood.

The systematic exploitation of shared experience (through the use of common components for example) is one way of achieving cost reductions though this must be balanced against the use of new designs and new materials to achieve cost breakthroughs. Another potentially fruitful source of cost reduction is the improved management of the material supply interface, an issue which is returned to many times in this book. Suppliers also gain experience and therefore their costs should similarly come down with cumulative production.

This last issue is explored in Hayes and Wheelwright (1984) in the context of vertical integration strategies. It would appear that vertical integration is most valuable where good opportunities for learning and cost improvement are available. Presumably one must back one's own ability to learn as against the ability of material suppliers and to use this to move along the experience curve at a greater rate than one's competitors. This reinforces the argument given earlier that experience curve analysis should be based on total costs rather than value added.

A word of warning is perhaps appropriate here as the culmination of the above learning policies may be the Ford Model T experience discussed by Abernathy and Wayne (1974). Pursuit of the learning curve in the narrow sense of cost reduction may lead to disabling reductions in flexibility. The learning curve should be part of a total policy and only in particular situations should it provide the main strategic thrust to operations.

FLEXIBILITY

The word 'flexibility' is used with great regularity in operations management, as it is in manufacturing engineering. Any set of objectives is likely to include it along with productivity, cost effectiveness and high quality.

Engineers speak of flexible manufacturing systems (FMS), but are they using the word in the same way as business specialists? Indeed a good test of anyone's understanding of this concept is to ask precisely what it means in a given context.

This question has been put to practising managers by researchers, but before looking at their results and at the categorizations of flexibility to be found in the operations literature we will attempt to explore the use of the word in a simple context. Imagine a small factory capable of manufacturing a range or catalogue of standard products. The reader might like to stop for a moment and attempt to frame some questions for the operations manager of this factory to explore how flexible the factory really is.

Some typical questions are the following:

- How many different standard products can you make, that is how many items are in your 'catalogue'?
- How quickly can you change from making one product to making another?
- How soon can you change from making one product to making another?
- How soon could you make a product which is not in your catalogue (if at all)?

The questions above relate to output, that is they represent a customer's view of the factory. The first might be referred to as 'range' rather than 'flexibility'. The second and third are distinct in an important way and their differences should be unravelled further. Though it might be possible to change quickly from one product to another there might be some delay before such a change could be initiated. There might be a long order book for the first product or such a change might be expensive. In particular speed of change and delay are likely to vary with different product combinations and also likely to be affected by the current environment. Thus flexibility is an attribute of a total system as well as relating to an individual resource, machine or department. The fourth question is a rather more stringent test of flexibility which may apply to a company as a whole rather than our factory, that is, it may include design and general business considerations.

In fact it could be argued that the customer is less concerned with flexibility than with delivery promises and reliability. Flexibility is therefore an internal matter. So we may wish to reframe our questions as follows:

- How many different parts can be made on machine X?
- What is the set-up time for machine X?
- What is the batch size for the part currently being made on machine X and what is scheduled for this machine in the future?
- Can we make part Z on this machine?

It may be argued that in terms of systems transformations we are now merely using a tighter focus. We are talking about a machine rather than a factory and the machine still has 'customers', albeit internal ones. Thus rather than delivery we might now talk about manufacturability to a given schedule.

As we examine this idea in more detail it is becoming obvious that 'flexibility' is not only an elusive concept but also an incomplete one. Thus, for example, are we speaking of particular behaviour (replacing product X with product Y) or of general or average behaviour (replacing any product with any other product in our catalogue)? In the latter case should our average be weighted depending on the frequency with which particular changes actually take place?

A further point is that this discussion cannot be isolated from some broader issues, for example:

● What are the economics of the proposed changes? Will the making of a particular change affect the cost-effectiveness of other operations?
● How is our flexibility affected (positively or negatively) by other functions or operational areas?
● Can the discussion be widened to include systems inputs as well as outputs?

Yet the word 'flexibility' is widely used with apparent coherence and therefore we will briefly summarize some empirical work in this area. An excellent reference is Slack (1987) which reports on a study of managers in manufacturing organizations to show the uses they made of the word 'flexibility' and the way this affected their decision making. Slack summarizes this by ten 'observations' which tend to reflect managers' partial and functionally orientated perspectives. These are related in turn to some positive attempts to classify 'flexibility', including the following:

The four main types of flexibility:

● Product flexibility – the ability to modify existing products or introduce new ones.
● Mix flexibility – the ability to change the range of products made within a given period.
● Volume flexibility – the ability to change the aggregate level of output.
● Delivery flexibility – the ability to change delivery dates.

An interesting point to note here is that, in an earlier paper, Slack had put forward the idea of 'quality flexibility' but found no support for it in his empirical work. Managers might wish to improve quality but would not admit to varying it depending on the circumstances. If by quality one simply means conformance to specification (see Chapter 6) then this is a reasonable view, but in a TQM framework the idea of flexibility does seem to have a valid meaning in terms of the speed of a producer or a service provider in adapting to a client's changing and newly articulated quality needs. Even so it must be admitted that the phrase 'quality flexibility' may be misunderstood.

Returning to Slack (1987) it is noted that trade-offs exist between different types of flexibility. It is also noted that the word is habitually used in two quite different ways:

- Range flexibility – the set of capabilities of a system.
- Response flexibility – the ease of change, in terms of cost and time, with in existing capabilities.

Range flexibility might be seen as taking a long-term view of a system while response flexibility has a more short-term flavour and therefore may be seen as being of more pressing concern.

Slack also shows that flexibility, as characterized here, is viewed by many managers as a means to an end, that is as a way of improving productivity and delivery performance. This appears to reflect an internally orientated use of response flexibility which might in turn reflect the pressures on operational middle management. He also shows how views on the desirability of differing forms of flexibility are affected by the variety of operations and by uncertainty in the environment.

A final categorization is that flexibility can be seen at different levels in an organization, the following four being identified:

- Resources (i.e. flexible technology, labour and infrastructure).
- Tasks (the classifications mentioned above).
- Functional performance.
- Organizational performance.

Regarding resource flexibility, most manufacturing managers would be quite happy talking about flexible labour and machining systems but be unsure about 'flexible infrastructure'. Manufacturing planning and control systems (i.e. JIT, OPT and MRP; see Chapter 7) have very different flexibility characteristics. For instance JIT is low on product range flexibility but high on mix responsiveness. OPT, in contrast, scores highly on almost all types of flexibility.

In a later paper, Slack (1991) explores strategic flexibility with a particular emphasis on carrying out a flexibility audit and arriving at priorities for flexibility improvement. A 'flexibility analysis' can provide a rich picture of a manufacturing organization but great care must be taken in such an analysis to define one's terms and be clear about the meaning of 'flexibility' in a given context. This point is reinforced in Hill and Chambers (1991) where the concept of flexibility is related to Hill's manufacturing strategy framework, drawing on case studies of a number of companies.

It will not have escaped the reader's attention that all the above discussion is in terms of manufacturing operations. This reflects the literature which is concerned with the very real problems of flexibility in manufacturing industry. Of course flexibility is a central issue in shop and office operations. The basic conceptual structure shown above is still of value though care must be taken in many service situations to define what is meant, for example, by the product/service range. In the context of professional service delivery this may be potentially very large. Also the issue of quality flexibility recurs as quality issues must always be treated with care in a service context. We return to service flexibility in Chapters 4 and 5 in the context of capacity planning.

FORECASTING

The operations strategist has two reasons for being interested in forecasting. The first is the need for long-term forecasts to support strategic decision making. The second is that operations, on a day-to-day basis, need forecasts and a forecasting system must therefore be set up as part of the operational infrastructure.

Though many management texts tacitly assume that forecasting is sales forecasting, all decisions are about the future and are therefore based on forecasts of environmental features as well as the results of actions. Using our systems framework, decision making for transformational control can be seen to involve a multitude of assumptions about the state of future environments and the results of the future actions of all actors associated with the system, that is employees, stakeholders and competitors.

It is to our advantage if the forecasting approach we adopt has the following characteristics:

- The assumptions underlying forecasts are made explicit. This will facilitate communication, debate and understanding.
- The collection of data which we know we will need as a basis for our forecasting methods is done in a routine and regular way. Thus data is available when required and its collection is cost-effective.
- We routinely learn from the effectiveness or otherwise of our forecasting methods and engage in continuous improvement of forecasting.

However, the production of forecasts is not in itself the final output of most organizations (the exception being those which offer a professional service advising, say, investors on stock market trends). In most situations forecasts are part of a decision making and control context. We must differentiate between the following:

- Predictions of what is thought will happen in the future, which in turn may be categorized as follows:
  - passive predictions of events and trends beyond our control or influence;
  - predictions of the results of our actions, which may be:
    - to do nothing;
    - to continue with current plans;
    - to react to unfavourable prior predictions by taking actions intended to change things;
  - predictions of the results of competitor actions, which may in turn include any of the three sub-categories above.
- Plans, that is statements of goals and objectives and agreed strategies and actions in some form of timetable.
- Budgets which are in essence control mechanisms, hopefully reflecting plans but possibly merely based on previous budgets.
- Targets, motivational devices which may be linked to rewards and the payment structure of an organization.

A simple and unitary view of organizations might lead one to expect that predictions are made and these form the basis of future plans. This is followed by an implementation phase. The detailed control of actions in a planning framework requires budgets, and the required motivation to achieve objectives requires explicit targets.

However, as common sense might suggest, a considerable amount of game playing takes place in this context. Studies of actual budgeting processes have shown that individuals and groups, who may wish to have low and achievable targets and ample budgets, manipulate the forecasting and information flow systems in order to reinforce their claims. Taking this view one always spends last year's budget and, whilst reaching last year's targets, always exaggerates the difficulty this involves. Managers may respond by adopting other methods, initially or in response, such as setting wild targets and minuscule budgets and only changing these under great pressure.

To use the systems framework described in Chapter 1, we may view our organizational system as simple and unitary, in which case the statistical techniques shown in almost all operational management texts will apply, or we see our organization as pathologically complex and coercive in which case the use of any quantitative technique is problematic due to the dubious nature of available information. A view somewhere in between, say complex and pluralist, is more constructive provided it does reflect organizational reality. Thus issues of value and working culture affect forecasting systems.

Assuming the organizational climate is right, operations need a large number of predictions covering different time horizons. These relate to demands, costs, supplier lead-times and reliability, productivity and many other routine features. This in turn entails that a range of forecasting processes are used.

In simple terms, a quantitative forecast is a point estimate for a future variable along with an assessment of likely error in the estimate. A qualitative forecast is a statement, story or scenario of what is thought will happen along with some discussion of alternatives. Each will depend on a set of assumptions about other aspects of the future, that is all forecasts are conditional to some extent.

An effective forecasting process produces forecasts, as above, and also monitors its own performance and engages in learning and continual improvement.

A large number of forecasting techniques exist, some of which track past data with limited prior assumptions of expected pattern (exponential smoothing, regression analysis and so forth). Some methods assume features such as seasonality of demand and others apply in special situations such as the launch of a new product. There are also a range of 'technological forecasting' methods, such as the Delphi technique, which are aimed at providing a consensus of experts on future trends and the timing of expected events. Details of this vast area of work are found in many texts, for example Twiss (1992) and Makridakis and Wheelwright (1989).

One important commonsense approach to operations management is forecasting avoidance! This recognizes the inherent uncertainty of a situation and manages operations in such a way as to cope with a wide range of futures. Thus buffer stocks of materials avoid a precise knowledge of demand, though to be economic require some forecasting of demand parameters. You may not be able to stock a service but you may require people to form a queue. In particular the whole concept of flexibility revolves around managing in situations of imperfect forecasts. Similarly being proactive in a competitive situation and seizing the initiative is a good strategy if one wishes to control events rather than predict and react.

The popular management literature includes such exhortations as 'Thrive on Chaos' (see Peters (1987)). Such ideas gain some support from attempts to adapt the concepts of the mathematical theory of chaos in natural systems to social situations (see Stacy (1991)). However, we cannot avoid making some assessments on the structure of the future. The important thing is to embed these assumptions into a decision making and control context and be aware of the sensitivity of predicted outcomes to uncertainty in other forecasts.

The techniques of forecasting may be applicable in a mechanistic way as part of computer-based planning systems or may be seen as ways of structuring and debating an uncertain future. They may act as therapy for the confused manager or may deceive through their concreteness and air of professional mystery. They cannot be avoided but must be handled with great care.

CHAPTER 3

Corporate, market and financial strategies

INTRODUCTION

In this chapter we review the essential mechanisms of a 'top-down' view of business planning through the process of corporate strategy formulation. Whilst in Chapter 1 we introduced the principal areas of corporate policy making, we now expand this framework by concentrating on:

- The main issues
- Representations and techniques
- Links with operations strategy

It should be emphasized that this chapter is not intended as a mini-text in corporate strategy. Indeed it is assumed that the reader either has some familiarity with this area or is studying it concurrently with operations strategy and therefore most of the ideas in this chapter will be heavily dependent on other writings and will explicitly show these links in order to facilitate study. Texts in corporate strategy and business policy are often gargantuan in size and scope, the bulk being due in part to the extensive use of large case studies. Therefore it is important that we adopt a simple framework in order to structure the ideas we will examine.

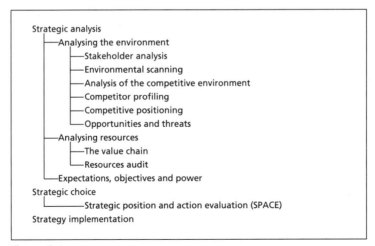

Figure 3.1
Corporate strategy framework

The framework we use is based on Johnson and Scholes (1989), as introduced in Chapter 1, and is illustrated in Figure 3.1. This text provides an accessible introduction to the ideas of corporate strategy and a useful platform for relating these to basic issues in operations strategy. We supplement this with references to the more technique orientated exposition in Rowe, Mason, Dickel and Snyder (1989). This latter text includes details and worksheets for no less than 62 explicit methods of strategic analysis. A number of mentions will be made of Porter's models of competitive strategy and Porter (1985) provides a basic reference for these. Porter's way of analysing competitive business situations has a considerable appeal for operations strategists as the links between corporate and operational issues are clearly shown (though Porter uses a more restricted definition of 'operations'). In particular his value chain model provides a useful way of handling the concept of 'value added' in the context of a supply chain.

It should always be remembered that the study of corporate strategy can easily become the study of everything! Almost anything in the environment may be relevant. Every aspect of running an organization must be taken into account. Thus texts on corporate strategy may be viewed as universal prescriptions for all organizational ills.

One must be particularly careful in the arena of competitive strategy. There is no one guaranteed way to win; no golden road to success; no substitute for creativity, experience, analysis, a willingness to learn from mistakes and a determination to succeed. A parallel may be drawn from the chess books of Fred Reinfeld who wrote *'How to Win with the White Pieces'* and *'How to Win with the Black Pieces'*. Though both are filled with good advice for the novice, what happens when a reader of one plays a reader of the other? Of course chess books give you ideas, methods of analysis, heuristics for good play and the moves played in previous expert games (cf. case studies) with annotations. Chess computers give you an environment in which to practice, similar to the role of business games. None of the above could possibly guarantee success.

Whilst on the topic of games as metaphors for business activity, contract bridge provides an alternative competitive environment where analysis is complemented by partnership with all its problems of communication and conflict. For many people, the main competitors in organizational life are within the organization rather than in the environment. Such analogies are valuable but no substitute for directly addressing business and other organizational problems.

In the next three sections we add some detail to our framework and attempt to show the relevance of certain well established techniques for the operational strategist. Two major areas of concern are then handled in separate sections. The first concerns the relationship of operations to the design function, a critical area of strategic concern as product life cycles become more compressed and product design is considered one of the most important sources of competitive advantage. The second is the relationship between operations and the accounting and finance function. As Hill discusses at length (Hill (1985)), the relationship between accountants and production managers has often been problematic to say the least. We will show in outline some simple ways in which this relationship may be improved.

STRATEGIC ANALYSIS

It is all too easy for the operations manager to assume that strategic analysis should be carried out by staff in some other function. Thus environmental analysis is obviously the work of marketing people, resource analysis frequently comes down to financial issues and issues in the area of power, organizational structure and objectives are the concern of top management. An alternative view is that operations may provide opportunities which are only evident after a careful analysis of appropriate environments. A large amount of organizational resources, particularly people and technology, are under the control of operations staff. Therefore operations strategists should be key players in teams of analysts.

Thus we make no apology for developing the ideas of strategic analysis at some length, though even then hardly doing justice to the richness of the situations under scrutiny or the techniques available.

Analysing the environment

The first part of strategic analysis is an analysis of the environment, that is systems outside the boundaries of the organization which are nevertheless relevant to its operation. Following a slightly extended version of the approach in Johnson and Scholes (1989) we use the following six steps, amplified by references to other texts as appropriate.

Stakeholder analysis

An audit of environmental influences is an important, and often highly illuminating, first stage. Rowe et al suggest a formal stakeholder analysis should be undertaken. This explores individuals and groups in the environment who are in some state of mutual dependency with the organization, and therefore broadens the debate beyond a consideration only of shareholders and customers. It certainly includes suppliers, employees, competitors, banks and government agencies. Depending on circumstances it might also include local pressure groups, educational providers, unions, employer federations, independent research establishments and so forth.

Stakeholders are likely, to a greater or lesser extent to be supportive of your strategic intentions or resistive to them and the extent of likely reactions needs to be estimated. Staff in manufacturing and office operations may only be in regular contact with a limited range of stakeholders but this in no way diminishes the potential impact of the others. Service staff are likely to have a wider view due to client contact and may indeed come to identify more strongly with stakeholder objectives than with those of the organization. This may be seen, for example, where personal delivery staff become identified with the needs of clients and other interest groups rather than the financial objectives of their own organization.

Such analysis is also implicit in the use of a soft systems approach (see Chapter 1) but this raises an issue of importance in much of corporate modelling. Texts such as Rowe et al use a large number of techniques which may, unintentionally, give the impression that corporate analysis is a totally objective and quantifiable discipline. In fact all the texts emphasize the need for judgement and experience in using these techniques. They are, in practice, structured methods for exploring and presenting our decisions in selecting what is important. They are invaluable tools for facilitating debate. The soft systems methodology is particularly strong in putting forward this fundamental point and therefore has considerable value used in conjunction with other methods.

Environmental scanning

Some form of environmental scanning and forecasting is now desirable and it is a fairly standard procedure to divide the organizational environment into the following:

- Economic environment: mainly macro-economic dealing with factors such as inflation, demand, saving, employment, investment, interest rates and with an emphasis on international comparisons.
- Political environment: at the local, national and international levels this includes a concern with power, interest groups and political stability.
- Social environment: including demographic factors, income distribution and spending patterns, mobility, education and social values and culture in general.
- Technological environment: relating to raw materials, product and process opportunities and information technology.

In addition to the above general features which are likely to be relevant to almost all organizations, other categories may be used to reflect the needs of particular situations, for example:

- Competitive environment
- Material supply factors
- Geographical location and infrastructure
- Ecological factors and pressure groups

The links between these groups of environmental factors and operational activities are so obvious and numerous for their study to need no further motivation. However, the sheer extent of environmental interactions with operations brings its own problems of managing complexity, a major theme implicit in much of this book.

Rowe et al emphasize the need for a careful analysis of international environments if intended as markets or as locations for operations (particularly in partnership with indigenous companies). A formal application of some type of political risk assessment analysis is essential along with careful consideration of differing cultural settings. They use Japan as an example in this context and the need to consider very carefully current ways of doing business and the likely future effects of changes in the major trading nations such as Japan, USA, Europe (West and East) should be obvious. In this context reference to up-to-the-minute explorations of the situation in other countries (both academic and journalistic) are of great value in shaking up our preconceptions that other countries are similar to ourselves and unchanging (see for example Reading (1992), provocatively titled *Japan, The Coming Collapse*).

This is not the place to go further into details of how long-term forecasting and scenario writing may be carried out. Specialist references such as Amara and Lipinski (1983) and Mercer (1992) cover this complex ground in detail.

The first stage listed above represents a formidable undertaking which should nevertheless be complemented with a rather more subtle second stage which is an assessment of the complexity, uncertainty and dynamism of the environment.

Complexity may arise from the large range of environmental influences which must be considered or from their interconnectedness. Even if a large range of factors were fully understood, predicting their effects on an organization is likely to be a formidable task.

Uncertainty relates to our knowledge of current and future features of the environment. Such uncertainty always exists but its extent is likely to be highly variable between differing factors and situations.

Dynamism relates to the speed of change of environmental features. Problems of uncertainty and complexity are likely to be increased if the environment is also unstable.

There is a considerable literature in this area though much of it seems speculative and esoteric. One of the more approachable and prescriptive texts is Ansoff and McDonnell (1990). At the base of their approach is a classification of management styles, which is expanded into an operational context below:

● Management through monitoring current performance and control against agreed goals and standards. The basic control loop of classic operations management which in effect pursues efficiency in a slowly changing environment.

● Management by extrapolation where change occurs and adaptation is necessary through forecasting based on data trends. The future is quantitatively different but qualitatively sufficiently similar for existing systems and styles of management to cope.

● Management by anticipation where discontinuous change occurs but planned response is possible and manageable within a traditional managerial framework. Change of this type is likely to be handled through some form of project management.

● Management through flexible and rapid response where many significant challenges develop too rapidly for anticipation. Information flows and flexible delivery systems are essential in such contexts.

Many production managers will feel that the last of these categories has been in existence for many years at the level of operations. However, this may often have been due to organizational inefficiencies. The situation is somewhat different if the environment is inherently unpredictable much of the time and in many dimensions.

This model is further expanded in Ansoff and McDonnell (1990) to cover five levels of turbulence and a set of prescriptions for managerial style. These are summarized in Figure 3.2. Their prescriptive models cover the relationship between turbulence and uncertainty in the environment and the required urgency of response. This raises an important point relating to operations where revolutionary and evolutionary changes represent contrasting styles of management. The need for an urgent response may necessitate immediate and revolutionary action even when environmental turbulence and uncertainty are high. This is only safe in an information-rich organization whose structure facilitates quick response. A further point worthy of note is that one way to operate in an uncertain and turbulent situation is to take the initiative and create the future yourself. Such proactive responses may be based on Hayes and Wheelwright's 'Stage 4 Externally Supportive' operations (see Chapter 1).

Level of environmental turbulence	Managerial style
Repetitive	Custodial (suppresses change)
Expanding	Production (adapts to change)
Changing	Marketing (seeks familiar change)
Discontinuous	Strategic (seeks new change)
Surprising	Flexible (seeks novel change)

Figure 3.2
Turbulence and managerial style

A final point on the subject of environmental turbulence is that such radical uncertainty might provide a limit to what aspects of the future one may forecast. The fashionable area of Chaos theory has given us explicit models of systems which are highly sensitive to initial conditions. In such situations very short-term forecasts may be possible as may long-term forecasts based on the average behaviour of the system, but medium-term forecasts are very difficult to obtain. The much quoted but still useful example is the weather. We are able, based on extensive computer modelling, to forecast the weather for the next few days and also we have a good understanding of general seasonal trends in terms of average temperature, precipitation and other major features. We have some difficulty, unfortunately, in predicting the weather two weeks hence or the path of a hurricane. Though one must exercise great care in transferring models of natural phenomena to the social world, this is at least a useful analogy for doing business.

Analysis of the competitive environment

The third stage in our model of environmental analysis is to carry out a structural analysis of the competitive environment. However, it is necessary here to note that the word 'competitive' may seem inappropriate for many organizations which are either sole providers of a service (for example a voluntary body or a public sector organization) or are non-profit-making. For instance the NSPCC has an obvious mission, in collaboration with other agencies, in promoting the well-being of children but must compete for donations with other charities. Indeed its fund-raising activities may be seen as a distinctive set of operational activities which need financing and managing in a business-like way.

One of the most widely used models of the structure of an industry in terms of competitiveness is that popularized by Porter and usually referred to as the five forces model (see Figure 3.3). Porter argues that before one can assess the competitive position of a company or prescribe appropriate future strategies an analysis of the company (or business unit's) industry must be undertaken. The point is that some industries are inherently more profitable than others and the road to success will vary depending on the industry structure and the competitive stance of its constituent firms.

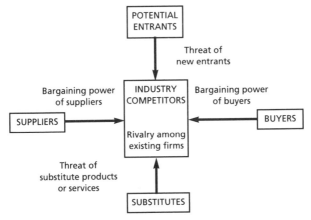

Figure 3.3
Porter's five forces model

The five forces in this model are as follows:

- The threat of entry: this refers to the ease with which a new competitor may enter the arena. Typical barriers to entry include the cost of entry, the need for scale economies (static and dynamic), access to distribution channels and the reputation built up by existing companies in the industry.
- The threat of substitutes: rather than enter a market with a similar product or service, a competitor may seek to capture a market with an alternative offering which acts as a substitute, or possibly a similar product based on different materials or technology. In the entertainment industry, for example, quite different products may attract revenue away from existing ones (an obvious example being the relationship between the cinema and television, now complicated by the availability of films on video). In a more general sense, charities may find themselves in competition with one another for the limited total amount that the general public is willing to donate.
- The power of buyers: the power of customers and clients is likely to differ between industries. Commercial buyers, in particular, may be few in number and able to buy in such volumes that they control an industry, particularly if supply exceeds demand. The key determinants of buyer power are therefore bargaining leverage and also price sensitivity.
- The power of suppliers: in contrast the converse situation applies where a concentration of suppliers may give them a considerable advantage, particularly if the costs of switching from one supplier to another is high. These two forces are particularly evident to operations managers. Buyer power may disrupt schedules, change specifications and necessitate tight cost control. Supplier power may have exactly the same effects for different reasons.
- The intensity of rivalry within the industry: this is the most obvious form of competition and is likely to depend on:
  - the relative sizes of the competitors,
  - the extent to which they are backed up by major organizations,
  - the ease with which capacity changes may be made,
  - the cost structure (i.e. the extent to which fixed cost investments are necessary),
  - productive effectiveness and learning,
  - growth rates in demand,
  - the ease with which product or service differentiation is possible, and
  - the height of the exit barriers.

It is possible to go further in this analysis, depending on circumstances, and include such factors as the links with complementary products and services, the complexity of technology used by particular companies, the rate of innovation which can be sustained and in general management capability.

Competitor profiling

The fourth stage in environmental analysis is the identification and profiling of competitors. Having listed competitors and identified likely future competitors, careful investigation into published sources, augmented by empirical work, is necessary to draw up a comprehensive picture of how such organizations work, what they offer and how effective and profitable they are.

The first stage is the identification of key characteristics. This will include market and financial features but operations staff should be able to contribute a clear picture of how operations are managed in other similar companies with reference to such features as technology employed, process quality, material flow control and the management of the workforce.

As case study writers and financial analysts have long known, a great deal of information is available about most organizations if one knows where to look and if one has developed judgement on the validity of varying sources. An obvious source is company annual reports, whose collection and analysis has recently been made far easier by the existence of computerized databases of company information. The press is another rich source of detail, provided one has the time and determination to search through a large amount of information. Trade associations and the reports of specialist consultants, added to the above, should enable a rich picture of competitors to be formed.

In many organizations such detective work is largely left to marketing staff but it should be obvious that investigations by other specialists will bring alternative perspectives and judgements to this task. Such activity, which might be grouped under the general heading of benchmarking, reflects an outward looking attitude of mind not always found in operations managers but one which should be cultivated.

Competitive positioning

Having ascertained who competitors are, the fifth stage is the identification of an organization's competitive position and comparing this with the positions of other organizations. It should be remembered that an organization competes not only for customers but also for resources, the latter also being true for public sector and non-profit organizations as we explained above.

Thus a set of key characteristics of organizations should be drawn up in an attempt to show both how the organizations compete at present and how the basis of competition may change with movements in environmental factors. There are a number of techniques which may be used to facilitate this form of analysis. An example is product positioning where a conceptual map is drawn up, based on detailed consumer research, of the alternative ways in which competing organizations attempt to meet consumer needs on a variety of key dimensions.

This is an appropriate place to introduce another of Porter's models, in this case a very simple classification of 'generic' competitive strategies. Having described industry structure, Porter (1985) asks how a company can create a sustainable competitive advantage. His reply centres on the alternative general strategies of cost advantage and differentiation. Each of these may in turn may be applied to a broad set of market segments or to a narrowly targeted group of customers. The latter is termed a focus strategy and may in turn involve cost-focus or differentiation-focus.

To achieve cost leadership, an organization must first of all offer products and services which are fully acceptable to the consumer. Indeed such offerings may be considered 'high quality' in the sense of conformance to specification. This may involve the organization in some hard choices to be sure that its products and services exactly match consumer needs with no extra, costly features. With a focused cost leadership strategy this will involve careful market research and some imagination in defining the needs of a distinctive market segment. The cost leader must now provide output at a price which will give an economic (and usually substantial) market share and this in turn entails provision at the minimum possible cost, building a low cost (but not a low quality) culture into every aspect of organizational work. The cost profiles of competitors must be continually monitored (hence the importance of competitive benchmarking, see Chapter 6) and effective programmes of continual improvement must be in place. Thus it can easily be seen that operations has a central and crucial role in the implementation of a cost leadership strategy.

A differentiation strategy also begins with the customer and looks for product and service features which are particularly valued by the customer (in broad or narrow market segments) and which will therefore attract a premium price. The resulting uniqueness must be communicable to the consumer and must be capable of being protected through patents, unique features of the organization or simply by continually improving the product/service mix to remain always ahead of the competition. Being unique is likely to involve some extra costs but once again these must be carefully controlled or the price advantage will not translate into the expected profit margin. Operations once again may provide key sources of advantage in following such a strategic path.

Several points will be evident from this description. The first is that these strategies are not dissimilar (see Bowman (1990)) and it may be argued that they merely represent extreme formulations of the basic notions of employing good market research, choice of appropriate market segment, good product and service design, cost effective delivery and continual improvement. The second point is that Porter appears to go further and argue that being 'stuck-in-the-middle' and not firmly following one of the stated four policies will lead to inferior performance. Yet common sense suggests that a very progressive company may be able, through technological innovation, to provide an enhanced product at low cost. Objection may also be taken to the notion that differentiation must involve uniqueness or one must be the lowest cost provider. Though possibly true in some industries this seems an unnecessarily harsh view of others where a number of roughly similar offerings seem to coexist. These lines of argument are quite beside the point which is that a competitive position must be carefully chosen to match consumer needs and organizational capability and to offer a real route to long-term profitability. Finally it should be obvious that there is room in most industries for a range of different strategies to be applied, to the benefit of all concerned. This profusion may be limited more by lack of imagination and the unwillingness to take risks in trying something new than any iron law of market behaviour.

Another central idea in the analysis of competitive position is likely to be the notion of product and market life cycles. This approach sees products as going through a cycle of change from introduction to growth, maturity and decline. Whilst it should be emphasized that the real world is often far more complex than this, the product life cycle is a useful unifying concept in that a number of ideas may be linked to it, in particular competitive actions at differing points in time. Thus, in the field of manufacturing strategy, Hill (1985) emphasizes how order winning criteria change at different points in the life cycle and therefore fundamental aspects of manufacturing must also adapt (see Chapters 4 and 5).

A further point to make is that the Boston Consulting Group (BCG) approach is related to life-cycle ideas and in turn relates to the concept of experience curves (see Chapter 2). Indeed there is a grouping of similar strategic analysis models (including also the PIMS approach) which can be most useful in exploring the comparative competitive positions of organizations in an industry and also give some guidance in forecasting future movements in competitive position. This area is covered at great length in the texts already mentioned and many others.

Opportunities and threats

The sixth and final stage in our environmental analysis is to attempt to use information gathered in earlier stages to identify opportunities and threats to the organization. This may be seen as half of a SWOT analysis and therefore may need to be repeated after resource analysis has been completed.

This simple sounding activity may be very difficult to carry out in a way which avoids a mere repetition of the obvious. It is advisable to use some form of structured technique (such as Delphi analysis, see for example Twiss (1992)) in order to break away from conventional and unimaginative thinking. It is also important that such analysis is carried out by a group and leads to some form of group consensus, otherwise individually identified opportunities may be seen merely as optimism or the riding of personal hobby horses and stated threats as plays for extra resources in the game of organizational politics.

The result of all this activity should be a clear statement on the nature of an organization's environment, forecasts on how the environment is likely to change and an assessment on how the organization fits into this overall view.

Analysing resources

This form of analysis is complementary to environmental modelling in that it looks inwards rather than outwards. At its simplest it may involve exploring an organization's strengths and weaknesses, the other side of SWOT. Indeed this basic form of analysis, if carried out systematically for the organization as a whole and also for individual functions, may be all that is required.

However, in the context of operations strategy, there is some advantage in developing resource analysis further by considering such concepts as the value chain and looking at structured ways of auditing resources and the effectiveness of their current use.

The value chain

This way of looking at organizational activities is introduced in Porter (1985). It is a particularly useful concept for the operations strategist as it provides a way of using the value added concept in the context of an overall value creating system.

A value chain is a way of representing a firm which disaggregates its activities in a way which shows how they create value and how they incur cost. This allows systematic linkage with cost advantage and differentiation based sources of competitive advantage. Value chains can also be constructed for a firm's suppliers and its channels of distribution. Thus for a product or service actually delivered to a customer it should in theory be possible to identify all the sources of value and cost. This is most useful in considering issues of vertical integration.

By using value as the basis of analysis this approach is naturally client orientated. The traditional concept of value added is avoided as it treats material costs as in some way different from other costs. The value chain consists of value activities and margin, the difference between total value and cost. Value activities (which are basically the same as transformations in our systems terminology) use purchased inputs, people and technology to perform some function. They use and create information and may have an impact on financial assets such as inventory, creditors and debtors.

Porter recommends that for a particular business unit an analysis is conducted in terms of the following set of generic activities. Primary activities involve the physical creation of product, its movement and the provision of services to the customer. Support activities provide an internal environment for the effective operation of the primary activities. In detail the primary activities are:

- Inbound logistics: receiving, testing, storing and moving material inputs, including routine management and control.
- Operations: transforming inputs into product form along with testing and maintenance.
- Outbound logistics: storing finished goods, physical distribution and order processing.
- Marketing and sales: classic range of planning and promotional activities.
- Service: the traditional idea of service concerned with installing and maintaining the product.

It will be immediately noted that this list of primary activities is most easily related to manufacturing and requires changes in detail, though not in basic concept, if applied in a personal service context. The support activities are more obviously generally applicable:

- Procurement: relates to the function of purchasing all inputs, i.e. materials, energy, equipment and other assets as well as bought-in services. This is a very broad set of activities often spread about an organization but having considerable impact on its effectiveness.
- Technology development: technology is broadly defined to include procedures as well as hardware. Once again its activities may be widely spread beyond the research and development function.
- Human resource management: a total view of the management of people from recruitment through training and payment.
- Firm infrastructure: the general management, finance, accounting and similar activities which are concerned with the firm as an entity in itself.

Working through the details of this approach is the subject of a large book in itself, with amplifications to cover the peculiar circumstances of service management. Yet this approach can be used in a simple and intuitive way to concentrate attention on the value and cost of a full range of organizational activities, while recognizing the contribution made by support activities.

Resources audit

Johnson and Scholes (1989) recommend the use of a systematic resources audit which is similar to the competitor audit described above but can be carried out with far greater thoroughness due to the increased availability of information. The value chain can be used as a basic classification systems but should be augmented by examination of financial resources and intangibles, such as reputation and goodwill. It would also seem appropriate at this point to look at the general health and balance of the organization's products and services, its research and development activities and to conduct an audit of management effectiveness.

There are a number of standard texts on financial analysis using, for example, ratios and trends. These represent a useful and frequently employed check on activities but it should always be remembered that they may reflect creative accounting practices. This is not the place to discuss the morality of misleading investors through legal manipulations of reported accounts but it is perhaps worth noting the stupidity of misleading oneself if data is not also available which shows the 'true' picture.

It is important that an audit of resources not only reflects what is available but how efficiently and effectively it is being used, and the degree of flexibility inherent in its current and future use. Johnson and Scholes (1989) go so far as to briefly introduce a form of 'flexibility analysis' a concept which the operational strategist might adopt and take further using the more sophisticated definitions of flexibility described in Chapter 2.

Expectations, objectives and power

This final part of strategic analysis attempts to confront the political and cultural aspects of organizational life. It is pointless to carry out complex analytical studies of organizations and their markets and yet fail to comprehend the social reality underlying their existence. Organizations have structure, groups, leaders and power struggles. The most elegant analysis and set of recommendations may be impossible to translate into action and result in a given organizational context.

The models we build must reflect the values and expectations of stakeholders, both internal and external, and must take into account their relative power. This requires an imaginative analysis of the specific organizational context which is not a form of analysis likely to be carried out in isolation by the operations strategist, except informally by the street wise practitioner. This is an area of primary concern to senior management but an area where operations should be fully involved due to the involvement of people in all types of operational work.

Many modern 'techniques' of operations management, for example TQM, JIT and job design, have inherent in them particular views on human motivation and appropriate forms of control. In many operations texts the politics of organizations is handled in this coded fashion with fundamental assumptions remaining unanalysed. This can be most dangerous and lead to unexpected opposition to what may appear to management to be rational and reasonable new ways of working.

At a more basic level, inappropriate organizational structures may fundamentally impede progress. One example concerns the most appropriate form of organizational structure for project management. Meredith and

Mantel (1989) provide a useful summary of the debate on alternative forms of matrix management showing the subtle distinctions between project and functionally orientated matrices. If this seems a little too erudite and removed from practical operational experience one should note the painful experiences of General Motors, compared with Honda, as described in Womack et al (1990).

One must also take into account the differing perceptions of a range of managers in the organization. An interesting example is provided by Bowman and Verity (1991), a preliminary paper on research exploring views of corporate strategy in a sample of companies. In one company 'The plot (giving a representation of various managers' perceptions of the actual strategy being pursued by the firm) was revealed to a complacent management group who believed that they had a clear strategic direction, which everyone understood.' The plot showed totally divergent views on the key issues of differentiation and cost efficiency. 'The presentation of the plot shocked the managers and helped to convince them that the strategy of the business needed to be urgently addressed.'

We now carry our ideas of strategic analysis forwards into an exploration of strategic choice and implementation.

Strategic choice

We have spent a considerable time on issues of strategic analysis because if this activity is carefully carried out, choice and implementation may be based on the same set of concepts. We should also remember that our interest here is not a general exposition of corporate strategy but to consider its relationship with operations strategy.

Whilst the choice of overall strategic posture is a general issue, detailed choices will often be functional as will their implementation and such issues are dealt with in Chapters 4 and 5. The contribution of operations will inevitably move from a debate of 'what to do' to recommendations on 'how to do it'. However, some unifying models relating to strategic choice are still of value.

Strategic position and action evaluation (SPACE)

The more ambitious analyst may wish to bring many of the above themes together in a SPACE analysis, an extension of the BCG approach recommended in Rowe et al (1989). This is related to the PIMS studies and uses many factors in order to recommend an appropriate strategic posture for a business unit.

The technical details and scoring systems used in SPACE are described, with examples, in the literature. SPACE is based on the following factors (see Figure 3.4):

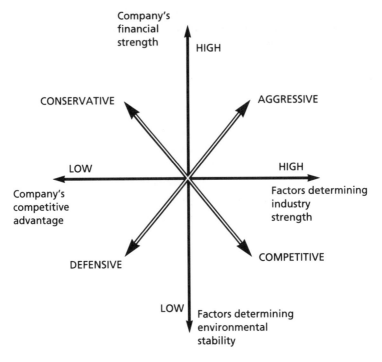

Figure 3.4
SPACE analysis

- *Industry assessment:*
  - Factors determining environmental stability:
    These include speed of technological change, rate of inflation and market characteristics such as price elasticity.
  - Factors determining industry strength:
    Including growth and profit potential, resource utilization and productivity.
- *Company assessment:*
  - Factors determining competitive advantage:
    For example market share, product age and quality, vertical integration.
  - Factors determining financial strength:
    ROI, gearing, liquidity and risk factors.

These factors are scored in ways which lead to a recommendation of suitable competitive posture. The four basic possibilities are:

- *Aggressive posture:* this is suitable where a strong company enjoys a competitive advantage in an attractive, non-turbulent industry.
- *Competitive posture:* this occurs in an attractive industry where a company has a competitive advantage but the environment may be unstable. The company's financial strength is critical.

- *Conservative posture:* in a low-growth but stable market, a company must work hard to ensure its products remain competitive while maintaining reasonable levels of profitability.
- *Defensive posture:* in an unattractive industry without a competitive product and financial strength, a company might wish to follow strategies of harvesting and withdrawal.

Each of the above basic postures makes quite different demands on operations. Indeed it is quite clear that if an appropriate posture is not identified a company's operations might be woefully misdirected and at odds with other functions and the needs of the market. There are a large range of other prescriptive classifications of general strategic direction to be found in the literature. The point being made here is not that one approach is correct but that a company must be clear in a given situation of what approach is actually to be adopted and must ensure that this is widely understood. Unfortunately the need for commercial secrecy or simple lack of attention to internal consultation may lead different parts of a company to be following different strategies or to be reluctantly following a strategy for which no consensus exists.

Having chosen one general approach there are likely to be a number of apparently feasible specific options for carrying it through. An evaluation of their likely consequences is necessary. Johnson and Scholes (1989) list a wide range of techniques for strategy option evaluation, most of which will come as no surprise to the well-read operations manager. Screening techniques are necessary to check whether particular approaches actually lead in the intended direction. These require statements on a range of measures to be used in strategy selection, for example return on investment, market share, development of new technologies and so forth. It is then suggested that a variety of scoring methods, scenario writing and decision analysis techniques may be used to weed out the less appropriate options. It is essential that the operations strategist is involved in the selection of measures used, otherwise it is possible that narrow short-term financial measures of performance will dominate, and real opportunities for strategic operations developments will be lost.

The next stage is the rigorous testing of each option against the selected measures, with an emphasis on gaining an appreciation of the risks involved and likely responses of competitors. This may lead one to consider the merits of producing computer-based simulation models of a business unit in order to forecast likely results of the strategy and to conduct 'what-if' experiments. Such modelling is appealing though likely to require considerable and reliable financial data. An important feature of such aggregate models is their inclusion of data relating to productivity, experience curves and so forth and thus allowing the realities of operations to be reflected to at least a limited extent. A further step in a CIM or a CIB environment (see Chapter 8) is the interfacing of strategic planning models with operational databases. Though this must be a feasible and valuable future direction for the sophisticated enterprise it is likely to be a costly and time consuming methodology and one must be sure that it yields significant advantages. These might well occur in the context of time-based competition in highly turbulent markets where continual replanning is desirable. The limitations on such an approach are then likely to be in the area of its implementation.

It should be noted that the strategic choice methodology described above is rational and objective in tone. The obvious assumption is that the end product is a single agreed strategy. Unfortunately such agreement may be highly elusive. The politics of organizations may lead to different strategies being favoured, quite legitimately, by differing groups of staff. If the result is that decision is delayed or a decision imposed by senior management then the implications must be carefully considered by each function. This is the real world in which operations managers will often find themselves.

Strategy implementation

A project management framework is often a suitable vehicle for a consideration of strategy implementation in operations and it is assumed that the reader will be familiar with the techniques in this area (see also Chapter 9 and Harrison (1990)). It should be emphasized, in line with current think-

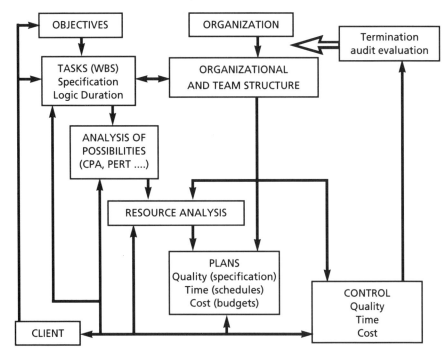

Figure 3.5
Project management framework

ing and research, that the management of change is as much to do with people, their aspirations, working patterns and their motivation, as with formal planning and control techniques. This dual set of considerations is shown in Figure 3.5 which gives an outline map of project management. One should note the need to match tasks with the organizational structure and the need for evaluation at the end of a project to facilitate learning.

Johnson and Scholes (1989) show in detail how resource planning for implementation may be linked with the value chain model. Indeed one of the keys for successful implementation in any project is careful initial analysis and goal setting. The planning stages should not be ignored during implementation but provide a framework for action and for understanding why certain actions are necessary.

A final point should be made here on the issue of corporate planning in general. A fairly traditional and rationalistic view of corporate strategy formulation has been put forward and this type of approach may be criticized as taking an inadequate view of the complexities of organizational life. All too often we find ourselves referring to what 'the company' will do, ignoring the fact that all planning and implementation will be carried out by individuals with a particular place in the organization. Indeed it has often been noted that few organizations seem to actually work in this way.

Writings such as those associated with the 'Excellence' approach (see Peters and Waterman (1982) and Peters (1987)) have a different agenda of issues with an emphasis on decentralizing decision making. However, all approaches to strategic management must address the problem of how an organization can find a coherent direction and concentrate effort in pursuit of that direction. The concepts and techniques described above are only intended as means to that end. However the complexity of operations, the commitment of resources to providing fixed assets and systems and the need to provide concrete and consistent results will mean that the more objective planning methods may well appeal to operational strategists. It should not be assumed that everyone in a company sees things in the same way.

THE DECLINING FACTORY

The concepts of operations strategy apply equally to companies with declining markets as to the more favourable growth situations concentrated on in the literature. Indeed it may be argued that corporate recovery requires as much skill as the management of growth. Even inevitable decline can be managed profitably with care and planning.

In situations of decline, the key policy decisions are less likely to involve location and major new systems. However, continuous improvement (for example through value analysis), quality management, stock control are obviously still important. Similarly action to reduce space through changes in layout may free a resource which might then provide a welcome flow of cash.

A particularly important priority is human resource management, partly because morale may be low in such situations and also because it may be necessary to introduce changes in possibly outmoded working practices. Though the threat of redundancy is hardly a choice motivator, the possibility of impending close may concentrate the minds of management and workers.

Such action will be wasted if not carried out in the context of a well defined corporate strategy. Johnson and Scholes (1989) show a life cycle portfolio matrix which relates competitive position to stages of industry maturity. Thus in an ageing industry, a company in a dominant competitive position may be able to defend its position but others will have, for example, to find a defendable niche, to harvest (that is maximize short-term cash inflow with little investment), or to withdraw.

Each of these has operational implications in terms of volume changes and the dangers of obsolescence. In particular, defending a niche may involve a combination of volume reduction and the development of new product or service features which are specifically valued by the customers in this narrower segment. Such changes may seem contradictory and confused to local management and labour, and the communication of plans and objectives becomes very important in such a situation.

There are other more subtle problems which can hamper the management of declining parts of larger organizations. One example based on a recent industrial project concerns a manufacturing company which was just about surviving but which included a small factory making what was thought to be an outmoded product. Though the demand for this product was steady, factory accounts showed it to be hopelessly unprofitable. Careful analysis showed this apparent unprofitability to be largely due to the factory being given a disproportionate share of group overheads. Unprofitability had become a self-fulfilling prophesy!

In such a case a form of reverse capital expenditure analysis is necessary. The impact on group profits of the positive benefits of closure (i.e. savings and benefits such as the sale of land) must be weighed against the costs of closure, both in terms of short-term finance and the loss of customers. If overheads have to be reallocated amongst other factories in the group then there is no net saving on them. Furthermore a third scenario of development, amalgamation or improvement may bring surprising insights.

THE DESIGN-OPERATIONS INTERFACE

A major breeding ground for ideas in operations management has been the car industry. Historically the Ford experience in the early part of the century, the organizational structure and practices of General Motors and the Toyota approach to the problem of manufacturing with scarce resources in the 1960s have all provided key ideas for manufacturing operations and ideals of efficiency, not always appropriate, for service and office management.

In their recent extensive analysis of this industry, *The Machine that Changed the World*, Womack et al (1990) contrast the approaches of car makers in Europe, the USA and Japan (including Japanese transplant factories). This work centres on the notion of lean production and includes international differences in how factories are supplied and run, how customers are kept happy and how cars are designed.

This latter point is seen to be crucial. A detailed comparison of the design of the GM-10 and the Honda Accord and more general comparative statistics illustrate the vast differences in the performance of the design function and in the effectiveness of the design-operations interface in different regions. Evidently western car makers use twice as many people to develop a car, take far longer to bring it to production and then are far less efficient in overcoming early production problems compared with their Japanese counterparts (see Womack et al (1990), Chapter 5). The competitive advantage inherent in superior management of the design-production interface is so obvious that it must point to a key priority in operations management strategy.

Bennett et al (1992) reviews a number of case studies of design-to-product experience in the electronics industry, once again comparing Europe with Japan, Korea and the USA. They comment:

'...high levels of environmental and technological uncertainty are forcing firms to adopt management approaches which regard design as a strategic, if not the strategic, priority in their businesses.'

They contrast the more *ad hoc* approach of UK firms to Japanese notions of the 'design factory' based on a design culture, high levels of engineering support staff and the systematic use of well developed methodologies for design and implementation. They recommend a balanced portfolio of aggressive and consequential design. Aggressive design involves new knowledge in design and considerable changes in production processes. Consequential design is based on repeat orders and variants; it is less risky though should be very profitable through the exploitation of the learning involved in earlier aggressive designs.

Garvin (1992) includes 'competing on new products and processes' as one of his three main operational strategies (along with quality and productivity improvements). His approach in this area, echoing the discussion above, centres on five issues:

- Learning and experimentation – the concept of the learning organization applied to product and process improvements.
- Management of product and process development paths through research to development and technical design.
- Technology transfer, that is how and when should ideas from research and development be exploited in manufacturing.

- Project management.
- The management of risk, that is arriving at a balanced strategic portfolio of aggressive and safer developments.

Though one could so easily see these issues as the white collar province of designers working with marketing and technical staff, the need for communication with operations is obvious. This relates to two forms of interaction which are explored in the following sections.

Design–operations interface during the design process

Operations involves more than merely the passive implementation of design ideas. It is a source of opportunities through the capabilities of people and equipment. Opportunities can only be exploited if their potential is fully appreciated and this requires communication either between functions or within members of an integrated team.

A frequent finding of studies of project management related to the design function is that a large part of the final cost of the product or service is built in at an early stage in design. Thus reliable cost information is needed relating to all aspects of the future manufacture of a product or provision of a service. This sounds rather obvious but may be hard to achieve in practice due to long design lead times (which require cost forecasting some way into the future) and difficulties in appreciating the problems of implementing new technologies and quantifying the parameters of their learning curves. Later in this chapter we consider some ideas in the area of cost information systems which address this issue.

Certain technical issues of manufacturability and testability must be addressed in product design and methodologies exist in engineering do this. One should also note that the allied area of design quality management is sensitive to the need for integrated design methods through such things as QFD (see Chapter 6). The Taguchi method provides a rather technical way of approaching such issues (for a simple introduction see Taguchi, Elsayed and Hsiang (1989)).

There are two fundamental ways in which one can look at problems of managing the design-operations interface. One is through a consideration of the necessary information flows for this interface to be effective. Such flows may refer to technical and engineering issues, costs, capability, capacity and so forth. The other basic approach is through organizational design, that is through a consideration of which types of organizational structure are most conducive to profitable design and development. Womack et al (1990) is very concerned with this as are standard texts on project management (see Meredith and Mantel (1989) for a detailed discussion with an emphasis on the advantages and problems of matrix and project management structures).

Failures to communicate between design, operations, marketing and the customer are not unknown and this more general problem is considered in all product and service design literature, for instance see Andreasen and Hein (1987) for the former and Hollins and Hollins (1991) for the latter.

Design–operations interface during launch

While we have emphasized the importance of pre-launch management, much literature and anecdotal evidence concerns problems in the handover of products from design and development to full scale manufacturing. To use a common phrase, it seems that products are often 'thrown over the wall' from design into production!

One effective solution is to insist that staff involved in design are also responsible for implementation, that is, they must stay with production until it is proven that the new product cost can be manufactured and is cost effective. This may take some time and is less appropriate if a large design team has been necessary.

Complementary to such hands-on methods is the use of technology, such as CADCAM, to promote design which can be manufactured and to at least partially automate the handover (see Chapter 8). This is also only a part of a much larger problem of the automation of manufacturing through CIM as discussed in Chapters 5 and 8 (see Goldhar et al (1991)).

If, as frequently forecasted, product life cycles become shorter and launches more frequent then problems inherent in the design-operations interface will be exacerbated and the solution often lies in strategic provision of effective organizational structures and procedures rather than trusting to the crisis management capability of operational staff.

At first sight the service sector may be thought to have less problems with this interface. The greater adaptability of the human provider of personal services is obviously of great benefit here but one must not forget that service design sets the basic objectives and procedures for service delivery, and allocates resources, including location, space and technology, which may be far from flexible. In addition the reliance of service on backroom operations, which in turn may be highly technologically dependent, can provide a straight-jacket for the direct provider. Hollins and Hollins (1991) provide a clear methodology for service design which runs parallel to the concept of integrated product design. Also of relevance here is the extensive, if somewhat specialized, literature on the structured design and implementation of computer based administrative systems. These provide the office operations equivalent of the topics addressed above.

FINANCIAL ASPECTS

Though we have briefly touched on some accounting aspects of productivity measurement in Chapter 2, we have yet to examine the many other ways in which operations and finance interact. Some routine data processing interactions will be mentioned in Chapter 8 but our concern here is mainly with the financial implications of major operational expenditures.

Though the literature on corporate strategy contains many references to accounting and finance, the operations management literature is somewhat ambivalent. Hill (1985) is typical of a number of texts which seem pessimistic about the relationship between accountants and operations managers, perhaps partly due to the perception in the UK that strategic investments in new processes and products are often balked by short-term financial perspectives. The view is often also expressed that the accounting function is far too traditional in its approach to management accounting issues in a highly automated manufacturing environment. The view that a gulf exists in many organizations between financial and operations staff is reinforced by observation of many companies where their relationship is poor to say the least.

In the past, many individuals taking operations management or general management courses will have been taught a standard set of principles, often with little critique of their practical application. The spread of competence based programmes has at least required some managers to more fully explore the practical use of management accounting tools. In particular some management accounting writers, for example see Johnson and Kaplan (1987), have criticized the foundations of management accounting and this has been taken up to a limited extent in the operations literature.

The relationship between operations and finance is an important issue for three reasons. First of all the implementation of operations strategies may entail substantial expenditure and the economic implications of this must be fully examined. It is not enough to deplore the use of high discount rates in capital appraisal techniques. The operations strategist must be able to fully debate which financial approach is appropriate in a given situation. Secondly many of the measurement systems in organizations have cost components and a major strategic task is the development of reliable performance indicators to support all operational decision making. It is sometimes said that you get what you measure and if cost and budgeting systems reinforce the status quo then they may provide a barrier to radical improvements. Finally there are a number of organizational issues surrounding the role of staff from various functions in an organization. Having observed financial managers at their most aggressive, one is only too aware of the narrow dividing line between halting unwarranted expenditure and inhibiting sensible improvements. Defining the ground rules for this game should always be seen as an interfunctional strategic issue.

In the ensuing sections we briefly examine the following accounting and finance issues in relation to operational decision making:

- Cost accounting systems with an emphasis on the problems of cost measurement.
- Financial modelling techniques relating operations to organizational financial statistics.

● Capital appraisal techniques appropriate for major operational expenditure.

In each instance we will be concerned only to draw out the underlying principles in each area. The application of techniques is the subject of a number of existing texts. We end this chapter with a case example illustrating some of the real difficulties involved in the practical application of financial techniques to operational decision making.

Cost measurement and analysis

One area which has received considerable attention from accounting theorists in recent years is cost accounting with renewed consideration of such things as activity based costing. Kaplan and Atkinson (1989) provides an accessible introduction to some of this debate though the line of argument below is based on Berliner and Brimson (1988). Their approach is valuable because it attempts to systematically and comprehensively explore a range of issues using a language which will immediately be seen to be of relevance by modern strategic managers. This is in stark contrast to much traditional writing with its narrow focus on, for example, stock valuation. It should however be emphasized that this whole area is continually evolving as ideas become clarified, their practical application is explored and the necessary data capture and analysis technologies further developed and exploited.

Berliner and Brimson (1988) introduce the key aims of cost management systems (CMS) as follows:

● Continual improvement in eliminating non-value-added costs.
● Activity accounting based on functions and tasks.
● Externally driven targets (including target costs) related in turn to learning curves and continual improvement in waste elimination.
  (Target Cost = Sales price at target market share – desired profit)
● Improved traceability of costs to management reporting objectives.

We see here a number of concepts which are familiar to the operations manager. The real problem, however, is designing systems which actually meet these objectives. To this end, CMS uses an explicit framework. It is seen as a management planning and control system with the following objectives:

● To identify the cost of resources consumed in performing significant activities of the firm (accounting models and practice).
● To determine the efficiency and effectiveness of the activities performed. (performance measurement).
● To identify and evaluate new activities that can improve the future performance of the firm (investment management).

- To accomplish the three previous objectives in an environment characterized by changing technology (manufacturing practices).

The above may be further dissected as follows through a consideration of cost accounting issues and then of issues in the appraisal of capital investments:

- Changing cost-behaviour patterns: this includes a smaller direct-labour component, larger equipment component and larger information component (that is related to the cost and value of accurate information) in the cost structure of many operational activities.
- Changing basis of cost allocation and overhead recovery: allocating fixed costs and overheads on the basis, say, of labour hours is inappropriate as a basis for decision making and control in an automated environment.
- Decreased emphasis on inventory valuation: while inventory must be valued for financial reporting purposes, the technicalities of valuation are of little interest to managers in a lean production environment (see Chapter 7).
- Obscured work in progress carrying costs: it is important to separate out the reasons (i.e. the cost drivers) for in-process stocks, in particular if such stockholding is caused by quality problems, unnecessarily high batch sizes or other inappropriate practices.
- Changing basis of depreciation calculation: much traditional accounting is concerned with depreciation but the emphasis often seems to be on tax issues rather than reflecting actual usage of a fixed asset. For example it may be reasonable for depreciation to be based on machine hours rather than fixed time periods though this is not often done in practice.
- The need for timely information rather than period reporting: one curious and rarely challenged aspect of accounting is the production of regular reports rather than timely ones. With manual data processing this may be necessary but should not be with modern real-time systems which facilitate the interrogation of databases, tracking of key variables and management by exception. Unfortunately organizational practice is often slow in responding to technological opportunities, particularly if information is seen as the basis for power and influence rather than decision support.
- The need to provide financial data to design and process engineers: it is widely recognized that much of the cost of a product is built in, often unwittingly, at an early stage of design. Engineers need good cost information which is readily available and up to date.
- The need to control overheads: while so much is written on the allocation of fixed costs, the key issue is to unravel cost drivers and to control such costs. Cost reporting is not the same as cost control.
- The need to improve understanding of cost-behaviour patterns for new technology, that is explicit statements of how costs are related to quality,

flexibility, throughput time and so forth in a range of situations.

- Improved understanding of the appropriate rates of return for a range of investment situations (see later).
- The need for a portfolio approach to project management, that is an avoidance of money being spent on a random collection of small tactical projects.
- An improved understanding of the way in which past technology decisions bind or constrain options for the future. These latter two points are a clear indication of the need for a strategic approach to operations development.
- The dangers of inadequate cost-benefit information: traditional accounting systems (based on absorption costing) are often wrongly used as the basis for appraisal methodologies (which assume marginal costing). There is also often a problem with 'intangible' and 'unquantifiable' benefits, curious notions in the context of accounting modelling but reflecting a real fear that the readily available numbers do not capture all aspects of reality.

Berliner and Brimson (1988) go on to recommend a series of accounting and management principles as the basis for the construction of new systems. A number of these deal with accounting systems' practice and will not be examined here. However, some of their recommendations are so clearly consistent with the themes of modern operations management that their repetition in this context shows that 'accountant versus engineer' battles and misunderstandings are not inevitable if each side gives some consideration to the problems of the other.

Thus principles for the design of new systems include the following recommendations (with some selection and rewording to relate to operational issues):

- Identify costs of non-value-added activities to improve use of resources and recognize asset holding costs as non-value-added activity traceable directly to a product.
- Significant costs (fixed and variable) should be directly traceable to management reporting objectives, that is related to projects, processes or products.
- Separate cost centres should be established for each homogeneous group of activities (possibly a project, a machining cell or a service unit) consistent with organizational responsibility, that is cost centres are defined at a level where costs and activities have meaningful cause-and-effect relationships.
- Costs should be consistent with the requirement to support life-cycle management, that is it should be explicitly recognized that processes often have differing cost patterns at differing stages of their lives and therefore past cost trends may be misleading.

D

- Actual product cost should be measured against target cost to support continuous improvement and the elimination of waste. This is the basis for the aggressive cost reduction programmes used by some manufacturers. Target cost may be defined as above, be based on projected future prices or based on the best practice of other organizations (see the discussion of bench-marking in Chapter 6).
- Genuinely relevant approaches for internal control should be developed as a company automates, that is a real information strategy should be arrived at which properly supports operations management in a cost effective and timely way. This may involve extensive computerization leading to, for example, a paperless operation. Alternatively it may involve simple, decentralized controls such as Kanbans and process control charts. In all cases control and improvement must be encouraged.
- As part of the above one should aim to improve the visibility of cost drivers, that is factors whose occurrence cause cost should be readily identifiable by all concerned. Measures should be few, quantifiable and easy to understand. They should include financial and non-financial factors, though the latter may eventually need conversion to financial terms. Though some organizations act as if the world will fall apart if cost data is widely available (for example through revealing commercially crucial facts to competitors and stakeholders), this must be balanced against the decision making and motivational advantages of employees knowing what is actually going on and being able to take appropriate action.
- The investment management process must be more than a capital budgeting process. It must seek to identify, evaluate and implement new activities or alternatives to existing activities. The approach should be proactive in support of corporate strategies rather than merely concerned with rationing available funds.

The criticisms and proposals shown above, though in some way radical, are still derived from mainstream accounting research. The language of 'cost drivers' and 'continuous improvement' is central to much general management literature and inescapable in operations.

An alternative and far more drastic approach is to reject the whole traditional basis of cost accounting and follow, for example, the prescriptions of Goldratt and Fox (1986) in relating basic measures of organizational performance (such as profit and return on investment) directly to operational decisions. This form of throughput accounting is certainly valuable in challenging preconceived ideas but is perhaps too far removed from accounting standards to expect wide-scale adoption. It does however serve to remind us that management accounting is merely the operationalization of economic decision making in the firm. This, in turn, is only one conceptual model of organizational activity. What is really important is the outcome of the use of cost and accounting systems.

Financial modelling

Most individuals who have taken a management course will have become acquainted with ratio analysis. This straightforward set of procedures is based on financial information in the format of published statements, such as the balance sheet and profit and loss account, and seeks to relate such global data to management issues in a simple way. Thus, for example, the 'stock and work in progress' figure in a balance sheet may be divided into the 'sales' figure to give an indication of the number of times stock is turned over in a year. Such a statistic may be compared with similar results for other companies (for example by using a database of company information) or may be recalculated at differing periods to give a trend.

In addition to conventional forms of ratio analysis, it is often valuable to compute a set of related ratios. An example much favoured by corporate strategy texts is the DuPont formula where return on assets is successively decomposed to show how it relates to a range of factors such as cost of goods sold, inventories and so forth (see Rowe et al (1989)). Hayes, Wheelwright and Clark (1988) show a more idiosyncratic formulation (see Figure 3.6) which is clearly related to operations strategy. This may in turn be related to a simpler version of Gold's model as shown in Eilon (1976).

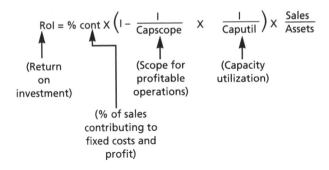

Figure 3.6
Financial ratio analysis

Following these approaches we define variables as shown below:

Sales = total revenue in period

VC = total variable costs, that is purchased materials and variable transformational costs

FC = fixed costs

%cont = ((Sales — VC)/Sales) x 100% = (1 — VC/Sales) x 100%

Thus %cont is the percentage of sales which contributes towards meeting fixed costs and providing profit.

PBT = profit before tax

= Sales – VC – FC
= Sales x %cont – FC

BESales =breakeven sales = Sales such that PBT = 0= FC/%cont

We note that BESales / Sales = FC / (%cont x Sales)

Cap = capacity = Sales level if operating at resource limit

Assets = investment to support this capacity

Caputil = capacity utilization = Sales/Cap

Capscope = capacity scope = Cap/BESales

Thus Caputil, which has a maximum value of 1, measures the extent to which capacity is being used, while Capscope shows the scope which exists for profitable operations. Naturally we want Capscope > 1 otherwise profit is not possible. We also note that:

Capscope x Caputil = Cap/BESales x Sales/Cap = Sales/BESales

and we require Sales / BESales > 1 for profitability.

Now we may decompose return on investment (RoI) as follows:

RoI = PBT/Assets = PBT/Sales x Sales/Assets

= (Sales x %cont – FC)/Sales x Sales/Assets

= %cont x (1 – BESales/Sales)) x Sales/Assets

Thus we have the Hayes, Wheelwright and Clark model:

RoI = %cont x (1 – (1/Capscope) x (1/Caputil) x Sales/Assets

That is return on investment is affected by the following factors, each of which have operational significance:

- Variable costs relative to prices (reflected in %cont)
- The scope for profitable operations
- Utilization of capacity
- Investment effectiveness (shown by Sales / Assets)

Similarly the Gold model (simplified):

RoI = (1 – (VC + FC)/Sales) x Sales/Capacity x Capacity/Assets

The first factor is related to costs and prices, the second is capacity utilization (Caputil) and the third relates to a firm's effectiveness in generating capacity through investment.

Though ratio analysis and its associated models provide a perfectly reasonable method of obtaining a first impression of the effectiveness of company management, two particular problems occur if one delves deeper. The first is due to the necessary aggregation of the data presented and the second concerns the convoluted nature of cause and effect in a company. (We are not specifically concerned here with the further problems caused by creative accounting!)

The first problem is partly addressed through analysis being repeated at differing levels of systems focus. For example if stock holding seems too high, analysis is repeated for different production lines, different product groups, different types of stock (for example spare parts as opposed to finished goods or raw materials) and so forth until a more consistent pattern appears. This is consistent with the approach discussed in the previous section of relating costs to cost drivers and individual responsibilities. The main limitation to such analysis will often be the availability of appropriate data, the point specifically addressed by CMS recommendations.

The second problem relates to the financial dynamics of an organization. It may be illustrated by a simple example. Consider a manufacturing company which in a given period experiences a 10 per cent increase in sales. What are the implications of this trend? Some possibilities are the following:

● More raw materials must be bought but when should they be obtained, when paid for and what is the effect of this on stockholding?
● Other extra costs will be incurred in advance of the extra revenue generated by the sales increase.
● Bottlenecks may now arise in manufacturing necessitating sub-contracting or overtime working.

Though the 'average' effect of these various factors may simply be a 10 per cent increase in many cash flows, the timings of the changes may cause all kinds of problems for the management of cash and working capital. Now while this is a standard management accounting issue it is not easy to comprehend all the effects of a series of similar changes. In particular as commercial conditions require flexible operations, their financial ramifications may be hard to determine.

One approach to this problem which may be particularly appealing to accountants and operational managers is the use of computer based modelling techniques. An introduction to this is provided by Schlosser (1989) which uses a variety of spreadsheet formulations to model problems of working capital management and also investment appraisal. Such models provide the facility for 'what-if' analysis which is valuable both for exploring a given situation and also as a learning tool to improve one's understanding of financial dynamics.

Almost all of the methods described in the financial parts of this chapter may be enhanced by computer modelling. Though such a 'hard systems' approach ignores many of the subtleties of organizational behaviour, it does require clear thinking and teamwork and should be part of the tool-kit of any operational strategist.

A final point to be made here is that operations is both a key source and a frequent user of strategic funds. Funds flow analysis and the provision of funds for investment may appear at first sight to be the province of financial managers. Yet if one criticizes finance managers for restricting capital investment one must also criticize engineers and operations staff for often demanding funds with little appreciation of where they are to be obtained from. In particular would-be spenders may have little understanding of the need for 'baseline funding', i.e. funds which are required merely to maintain ongoing operations, and may not appreciate the risks inherent in seeking new equity and debt financing. Once again computer modelling may be of help in demonstrating the complex nature of company finances.

Capital appraisal

One area of particular concern to the operational strategist is capital expenditure appraisal. Two sets of issues present themselves here. The first is the set of techniques which is available in order to support the investment decision making process. The second is the organizational context within which such action takes place and the use and misuse of investment appraisal techniques.

So vehement has been the condemnation of investment appraisal practice by some writers that one wonders if actual investment decision making is quantifiable and rational at all. Hayes, Wheelwright and Clark (1988) gives examples of the absurdities of company practice and studies such as Marsh, Barwise, Thomas and Wensley (1988) show the complexity of decision making in large and diversified companies. Lumby (1988), a major text in this area, includes a chapter on the use and abuse of techniques, as much due to ignorance as organizational malice. This material is explored in Harrison (1990) where the techniques of discounted cash flow are also introduced in the context of manufacturing management.

In contrast some writers champion financial appraisal techniques, even developing specific software for the appraisal of engineering systems change. Indeed in principle it may be argued that any major change may be analysed in terms of the changes in cash flow it entails, though the measurement of such financial changes may be a daunting challenge.

Though it is not intended here to give details of the main techniques for investment appraisal, an outline of the principle stages in the use of discounted cash flow (DCF) is given below to add focus to the detailed criticisms provided later.

DCF is a methodology which explicitly addresses the relationship between time and money and thus is of particular relevance to strategic investment appraisal. It explicitly separates out the processes of finding funds and allocating them to specific uses which would have to be considered together if appraisal were based on the simulation of an organization's total financial position. That is we assume that a sub-system of the organization is identified and that this sub-system is financed by the organization at some appropriate rate of interest.

Two alternative scenarios are arrived at for the sub-system in question. The first is the base scenario, the status quo, and the second assumes some specific investment action has been taken (for example a new computer system has been obtained, a substantial sum has been spent on training and so forth). The key step now is to isolate the differences in cash flows between the two scenarios, i.e. the incremental costs and benefits of the proposed system change. It should be emphasized that this refers to both the amounts and the timings of cash flows and involves a formidable forecasting exercise up to an often arbitrarily imposed planning horizon.

The next stage is to carry out discounting calculations to reduce these incremental cash flows to a constant time base, that is to compute their present value. This calculation uses the previously mentioned rate of interest which often includes a risk component and which must be adjusted for inflation depending on the convention used when forecasting cash flows. Thus if the effects of inflation are removed from the cash flows then an 'inflation free' discount rate must also be used.

If the net present value (NPV) resulting from this calculation is greater than zero then this individual project is viewed as potentially profitable, though it may then have to compete with other good projects as investment funds are scarce.

A simple example of this calculation is shown in a case study in Chapter 5. The use of the Cumulative NPV diagram is recommended as a presentational device as illustrated using simple data in Figure 3.7.

Whilst logical in conception, this methodology is prone to misuse. Drawing on a variety of sources, in particular Kaplan and Atkinson (1989), the main problems seem to be the following:

1 The use of excessive discount rates: adjustments for inflation are incorrectly made (if made at all) and very high risk components are introduced. Two points are of particular importance in the latter context:

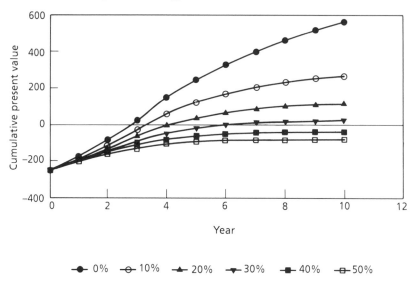

Figure 3.7
Cumulative NPV graph

- Risk assessments should relate to the specific investment under consideration. General assessment of risks, such as that arising from the market, may be constant for all process change scenarios and therefore should not be included. A particularly difficult point is the assessment of risks involved in the base scenario – doing nothing may be more risky than investing.
- Risk is unlikely to be constant in all periods up to the planning horizon. In particular many technological projects may have high initial risk (how much will it cost to make it work?) but may then be very reliable.

These are major problems and perhaps point to the need to reject the use of risk adjusted interest rates and alternatively use a decision theory approach in which probabilities are applied to specific risky events (for example see Bodily (1985)). However, it should be noted that while decision theory and DFC may be used together in this way, the resulting analysis is far more complex to understand and requires a great deal of data, in particular subjective probability estimates which may be very hard to obtain.

2 In practice most of the analysis is often devoted to the new investment scenario and the status quo is assumed to be a constant extrapolation of the current situation. This is often ludicrous. If the current situation consists, say, of old and near obsolete equipment, a lack of investment may necessitate massive subsequent expenditure. Indeed the real base case may be to invest next year rather than this year. Thus the cash flows associated with the base case may be far from constant and risk free.

3 The idea of a planning horizon is not intrinsic to DCF but usually reflects organizational procedures or an unwillingness to forecast. Though understandable this is hardly consistent with the observation that operational systems, equipment and human resource development decisions often provide benefits way beyond planning horizons. Sensitivity analysis of the effects of varying the planning horizon should be a part of all investment analyses.

4 Another damaging organizational practice is the existence of authorized capital expenditure decision limits. This may lead to an incremental approach to expenditure whereby limited projects are undertaken in successive years. If this is done in the context of a well thought out business and technology strategy then all may be well. Alternatively it may result in islands of automation each reflecting the technology available at the time of investment.

5 The underestimation of front-end costs is a common theme in the implementation literature and refers particularly to:

● Delays in the timing of benefits.

● Poor estimation of 'soft' expenditure such as training, programming, data collection, developing new procedures and so forth.

● Failure to understand the possibility of an early productivity decline and the need for a subsequent learning curve.

Another frequent theme in studies is poor estimation of the benefits of investments in operations. In particular failure to quantify the following may be most damaging:

● Reduced inventory (reduced storage costs, administration and working capital).

● Accompanying physical benefits such as reduced floor space.

● Quality and delivery improvements.

● Flexibility and economies of scope (a wider range of operations are now possible with less delay in changeover).

● Organizational learning.

The last point is a crucial one and applies equally to gaining experience in investment decision making itself.

A case exercise relating to investment appraisal, The ZL30 Proposal, is given at the end of Chapter 4. In addition, Case 25 'Cadbury Ltd: A Routine Investment Decision' in Johnston et al (1993) relates a production investment to corporate strategy and the issue of flexibility.

CHAPTER 4

Operations strategy

INTRODUCTION

In the elegantly titled *The Philosophy of Manufactures*, published in 1835, Andrew Ure comments:

> Were the principles of the manufactures exactly analysed, and expounded in a simple manner, they would diffuse a steady light to conduct the masters, managers, and operatives, in the straight paths of improvement ...

Whilst this expresses a somewhat optimistic goal for operational management science, it is in this vein that we consider in this chapter some of the underlying principles, frameworks and empirical results of operations strategy.

Though we have reviewed some of the issues of operations strategy in earlier chapters, it is worthwhile for a moment considering what this area is really all about. In Chapter 1 we introduced the idea of a transformational process as the basic building block of operations. One of the main characteristics of operations in an organizational setting is the multiplicity of transformations that exist and the problems of decision making and control they entail. In operations a very large number of simple parts make up a highly complex whole.

Seen at the tactical level, operations often appear straightforward and intellectually undemanding. Even if they are technically sophisticated (as with some advanced manufacturing processes) or apparently complicated, working in a given operational setting breeds familiarity. Indeed if this is not the case then the systems are quite possibly poorly designed, as simplicity and robustness are usually considered desirable operational features. Yet considered at a broader organizational level the totality of operations is highly complex and difficult to control in a cost-effective manner. Such large scale systems have emergent properties, such as capacity and flexibility, which sound similar to their small system counterparts but which are in practice difficult to characterize and manage.

The working of total operational systems must also be consistent with other functional areas and with corporate policy in general. These are the problem areas addressed by operations strategy. In particular operations strategy uses a vocabulary which is partly derived from corporate planning and partly from operations management. It facilitates the implementation of top-down planning while providing strategic opportunities through operational excellence.

Thus the concepts of operations strategy may seem remote to those working at the ground level. Strategists are concerned with process choice as a fundamental decision on operating principles while day-to-day decisions are more likely to revolve around which job to run on which machine. The former provide the setting for the latter but often in a way which seems opaque and mysterious. Indeed at grass roots level, strategy often seems absent or merely the accumulation of tactical decisions.

Yet however sophisticated or crude the process of strategic planning, however centralized or devolved, the outcome is a working culture, resources for operations and expectations of performance. Trade-offs are made, explicitly or by default, and the results have a major influence on what can be achieved at an operational level.

Key links between strategy and tactics are planning and implementational style. In a rigidly hierarchic situation, a high level planning process results in operational plans, including expectations and constraints, that are to be implemented at another level. Planning and implementation are separated if not divorced. An alternative planning culture (see Chapter 6 on Hoshin Kanri), involving structured consultations at all levels, paves the way for implementation. In particular a more devolved strategic planning process provides greater opportunities for challenging tactical assumptions and working practices and matching them to organizational needs.

OPERATIONS STRATEGY – THE AGENDA

In Chapter 1 we briefly introduced the key policy areas of operations strategy (see Figure 1.1). It is now appropriate to consider in more detail the actual issues to be addressed in operations strategy.

The first set of issues is directly concerned with the transformational processes. They can be summarized as a set of questions as follows:

- *How are the transformational processes defined?*
  We refer here to the focus and scope of individual system models, remembering that systems terminology is a language for describing the world which may be used in differing ways. In soft systems terminology we may ask what are their root definitions.
- *How are the transformational systems linked?*
  An obvious example is linkage by material flows. It is also possible to look at informational links, client movement and so forth.
- *What are the basic operational principles of each transformational system?*
  This is related to process choice and infrastructural needs; for example is

a process based on batch or line principles, is it focused or mixed, is it flexible (however defined)?

● *How is the transformation actually carried out?*

In particular this refers to the mixture of labour and technology used. Further issues revolve around job design and the man-machine interface designed.

● *What are the quantitative limits of the transformational process?*

For a simple transformation this is its capacity in everyday terms, though we should also consider how capacity varies and can be managed. Note, however, the discussion on capacity in more complex systems (see below and Chapter 5).

● *Where is the process located?*

This is also important for warehousing. An interesting problem of location arises when considering off-site servicing. Here the location naturally varies but the service activity must be supported with appropriate resources.

● *How is the process physically organized?*

At a simple level this is a question of layout. One should also consider what arrangements exist for the storage and movement of materials and also for people moving and waiting.

● *Who owns each transformational system?*

We may consider this question either in the legal sense (i.e. which parts of a total system are 'in-house' and which are subcontracted or supplied) or in an organizational sense (i.e. how do transformational processes map onto the organizational structure).

A further set of issues is concerned with the operational infrastructure:

● *How are product and service attributes arrived at?*

We are concerned with questions of how the design function relates to operations in terms of the introduction of new designs (possibly for individual clients) and how changes and improvements occur over the life cycle.

● *How is quality controlled and improved?*

An obvious point considered at length in Chapter 6.

● *How is the flow of materials and people planned and controlled?*

An equally important point considered in Chapter 7.

● *How are the informational needs of operations met?*

This partly relates to information technology, in particular data capture, and partly to other functions such as accounting and marketing.

● *How are human resource needs met?*

In particular addressing such issues as training, motivation and working practices as well as safety and employee well-being at work.

It might have been convenient if each of the above questions could be addressed independently, but in practice they are inevitably interrelated. For instance, capacity may well depend on process choice, technology, flow management and stock holding, productivity and motivation, layout, the effectiveness of quality control and so forth. Thus many of the modern panaceas of operational organization involve general approaches which link decision making and the management of change in several areas, for example:

- Total quality management (see Chapter 6) is a complete approach to matching provision to client need, including procedures, human resource issues, technological capability and relationships between functional areas. It may also be seen as a methodology for promoting organizational change.
- Just-in-time similarly addresses quality and human issues but in the context of material flow management and waste reduction.
- Performance measurement and improvement programmes which, though less well defined, have similar goals of continuous improvement.
- Process choice and capacity management may be more broadly defined and strongly linked to other critical decision areas.
- Time based management, addressing delivery characteristics, flexibility and speed of innovation, which targets important order winning criteria and the operational systems necessary for effective competition.

The answers to many of the above questions lie in the specifics of a given situation, though guiding principles are available in the literature. For instance factory and service layout problems may be modelled using a range of techniques described in most general operations management texts. The major strategic point in layout design is to ensure that it is systematically addressed as part of a drive to cost effectiveness and as part of more general approaches such as JIT which have high profit potential. Other questions are more fundamental and therefore are addressed in the later sections and chapters of this book.

The policy areas listed earlier are not all therefore given equal coverage in this book. This is not to say that in terms of resource usage they are not all potentially important. For instance the location of a factory in the context of a global manufacturing strategy is a major component of corporate strategy and such a decision will be based on factors uncovered by a process of strategic planning (see Chapter 3). The location of one outlet of a retail chain will be based on similar factors at a different level and is covered by standard texts on operations management and on marketing. Neither of these are discussed in detail in this nor the following chapters. Our intention here is to concentrate on issues of real conceptual difficulty in operational planning, thus complementing the existing literature.

MODES OF ORGANIZATIONAL CHANGE

One of the most important characteristics of a good strategist is the willingness to challenge accepted ideas and working practices. This should also extend to the theories of operations management. For instance, there is an almost routine acceptance, not least in this book, that continuous improvement is a good thing.

This may be argued against in the following way. First of all there is a well-known saying that, roughly speaking, 'if it ain't broke, don't fix it!'. Much operational work follows routine and habitual patterns and regularly changing such patterns may be counterproductive. Indeed a frequently used model of organizational change refers to an 'unfreezing' which is necessary before change can take place. Change can be expensive but so can stagnation.

This dilemma may be resolved in a number of ways. The first relates to when a system is 'broke', or rather when it is comparatively ineffective. The key here is a more or less systematic use of bench-marking depending on the circumstances. If we continually ask of each process whether it achieves the same results as the best performer we have some yardstick against which to gauge the need for change. One problem which must be addressed is whether the local actors in the transformational system accept the need for improvement to the same extent as senior management or even agree that a given change will actually be an improvement. The stock controller may be more inclined to keep stock than the financial controller. He may be more aware of the disadvantages of low stock and view drastic stock reductions as leading to a deterioration in service.

The next point is therefore the involvement of all employees in assessing the need for change and then in implementing it. This is well addressed by TQM and similar methodologies.

An interesting alternative mode of change is suggested by the idea of a resilient CAPM system (Maull et al 1990) (see discussion in Chapter 7). Included here is the idea of a series of sprints (discrete improvement projects) as a mode of change triggered by corporate needs.

Perhaps the best general recommendation is for continual learning and systematic performance evaluation allied to an acceptance of change when required at all levels in an organization.

FACTORY, SHOP AND OFFICE OPERATIONS

In Chapter 1 we defined three arenas within which operations are carried out; the factory where things are made, the shop where clients are served, and the office given over primarily to information handling. It was also noted that many organizations had some features of each. In Chapter 5 we concentrate on different types of operations and their settings but it is appropriate at this point to ask how different they really are.

In a conference address (OMA 1990, see Goldhar, Jelinek and Schlie (1990)), Goldhar argued that the manufacturing/service divide is misleading – McDonalds is a factory, while a specialist computer chip manufacturer provides a service. Historically all manufacturing was carried out as a service and the characteristics of the factory of the future are the same as the characteristics of the good service provider.

This is not to say that all operational transformational sub-systems are the same. It refers to the characteristics of the organization as a whole and also points to the pervasiveness of service ideas in manufacturing (for example stockless production mirrors the service situation where production and consumption are simultaneous) as well as manufacturing ideas in mass service situations. Goldhar's main concern is the effective use of computer integrated manufacturing and this in turn relates to a key element in factories, shops and offices – the use of information to provide a competitive advantage.

Operations and other functional strategies

Operations strategy is obviously only one component of corporate strategy and its relationships with other functional strategies must be carefully considered.

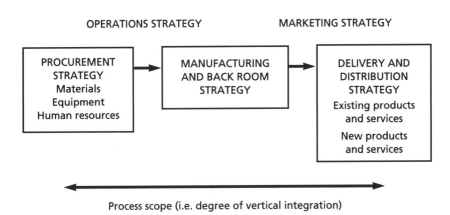

Figure 4.1
Functional strategies – transformations

In Figure 4.1 we show the direct transformational links between procurement, manufacturing and distribution. Each of these can be said to have a distinctive strategy. Procurement may refer to materials, equipment or human resources. Of these the latter is the obvious province of the personnel function. Equipment related to manufacturing has a bearing on manufacturing strategy though its detailed specification is usually an engineering matter. Material procurement, the role of the buyer, is a distinct profession with its own specialist skills including negotiation and the drawing up of contracts. There is obviously a considerable shared interest between these activities and operations but the differences in professional skills tend to separate them in organizations of any size. In strategic terms, however, there must be consistency of planning and implementation in this general area.

Marketing and operations strategy are deeply intertwined and some service operations texts are equally concerned with the marketing of services. Certainly there are areas of operations which lie outside the concern of marketing staff and vice versa but both functions must have a central interest in directly meeting the client's needs through selling and personal service operations as well as through planning future provision.

Furthermore, considering the need to develop appropriate operational infrastructures, Figure 4.2 shows links with other areas of potential strategy formulation. We refer to such strategies as potential because much has been written on the lack of formal planning in some of these areas. Information technology often seems no more than the opportunistic purchase of hardware and application packages. Human resource strategy may only cover recruitment, payment, redundancy and industrial relations with a little training thrown in if budgets allow or grants are available. An organization may well have product designers but no coherent design strategy.

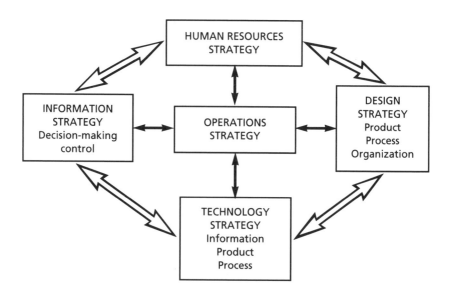

Figure 4.2
Functional strategies – infrastructure

It can be argued for each of these areas that the explicit formulation of strategy is essential in itself and of great value to effective operational planning. A design-led organization will presumably also consider manufacturing viability. A manufacturing company with an information strategy should be in a far better position to evaluate and implement MRP II systems. As operations is one of the major users of human resources as direct transformational agents and as managers, a human resource development strategy should be intimately linked with operational planning, for example through the matching of capacity and manpower planning.

Finally we may note some more subtle, but equally important contextual links. There have been many indicators in Chapters 2 and 3 of the connection between corporate, financial and operations strategies. As the major generator of revenue and incurrer of costs, operations have a great effect on cashflow and working capital management and require sound accounting information for decision making and control. We explore the relationship between organizational design and operations strategy in more detail in Chapter 9, though some reference is made below in the context of process choice. The whole of this activity must in turn be placed in an environmental context.

It is, of course, one thing to state that strategies must be related and quite another to prescribe planning processes which achieve this. The prescriptions of corporate planning texts are of value here but in the final resort it depends on the abilities and enthusiasm of the managers involved. Each functional area has its own concerns and the removal of functional boundaries by adopting some alternative organizational form such as project or matrix management will not remove the need for strategies which address long-term issues in marketing, technology and so forth. Each of these has some relationship with each other but a strong relationship with the practicalities of operations. It is therefore perhaps all the more surprising that this central role of operational strategy formulation has not been more developed in the past.

Frameworks for manufacturing strategy

Explicit frameworks for operations strategy are somewhat predated by those for manufacturing strategy. One of the best and earliest of the latter is in Hayes and Wheelwright (1984) and further developed in Hill (1985). Hill's model was introduced in Chapter 1 and a slightly extended version is given in Figure 4.3 which emphasizes the importance of financial and organizational issues. One key to Hill's approach which has become common currency is the idea of qualifying and order-winning criteria which Hill uses to provide a link between market and manufacturing strategies.

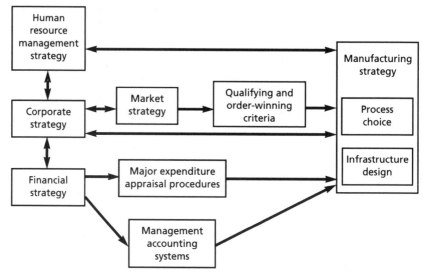

Figure 4.3
Manufacturing strategy framewok

Qualifying criteria are the essential features of a product or service while order-winning criteria provide the basis for customer choice between qualifying alternative offerings. The following list shows some of the possible customer choice criteria which in differing circumstances, or stages in the product life cycle, may be qualifying or order-winning:

- Total price
- Product or service attributes as specified
- Quality of the actual delivered product or service
- Design flexibility
- Delivery lead-time as promised
- Delivery performance
- Volume flexibility
- Speed of quotation service
- Service features
- After-sales support
- Stability of continuing customer support

Though some of the above refer to performance after the order has been placed, it would be rash to discount their potential value in winning or losing further business. This list needs some adaptation in the context of a service provider and if we accept the concept of a service factory then such changes (mainly an explication of 'service features') will be relevant to operational strategy in a manufacturing company and may well impinge on manufacturing strategy itself if extreme flexibility is required (see Goldhar et al (1990)).

The complex nature and engineering content of manufacturing strategy has led to more explicit methodologies being developed which in turn relate to other disciplines. These include the manufacturing audit approach (the subject of a DTI handbook but for a brief description see Platts and Gregory (1990)), DRAMA (see Bennett and Forrester (1990)) and STRATA-GEM (see Maull and Hughes (1990)). This is an area of continuing investigation (see MAESTRO in Maull, Bennett and Hughes (1992)). It is doubtful if a definitive process of manufacturing strategy formulation exists any more than one for corporate strategy, but the above, if nothing else, give checklists and ideas to guide the strategist.

One approach which is less of a methodology than an interesting possibility for any operational situation is given in Small (1990). This includes the idea of 'cash sensitive restructuring', that is the idea of not spending money. In essence one's strategy aims to be self-financing by releasing in its early stages funds which are currently tied up through ineffective operations (for example by reducing stock, space used and so forth). Though this may not be feasible in such an extreme form it points to a partial form of funding and also to the need to ensure consistency between long-term operational and financial strategies.

Generic operational strategies for the future

Even the most cursory examination of general management futurology shows a set of themes which provide a challenge to operations. The increasing globalization of markets and production facilities, changes in Eastern Europe, advances in industrialization in the Pacific Rim, turbulence in financial markets, the privatization of public services and the continuing acceleration of innovation in information technology provide opportunities and threats for most organizations.

Several writers on operations strategy have therefore suggested a range of basic approaches which they feel are more likely to be successful in the future. Garvin (1992) bases much of his approach around the following:

● Competing on quality
● Competing on productivity
● Competing on new products and processes

As tools to achieve advantage in these areas he recommends:

● Development of performance measurement systems
● Exploiting technological opportunities
● Using appropriate organizational forms, in particular project teams
● Developing people
● Sending appropriate leadership signals
● Employing an appropriate working culture

It should be noted that four of the six 'tools' relate to the management of people. This is consistent both with much popular and academic management writing and also with a number of recent mainstream texts on operations management which emphasize 'people issues' at the expense of techniques and procedures. It in turn points to a sensible general prescription for an uncertain future; use a creative, flexible and adaptive resource.

Similar prescriptions are given in Giffi, Roth and Seal (1990) who go so far as to assert 'A manufacturing strategy is a critical component of world class manufacturing... The real winners will be best in strategy implementation'.

Though such exhortations often refer to manufacturing situations, the same advice is also applicable to service and public sector organizations with perhaps the added imperative of implementing strategies which strongly support the direct personal service provider.

PROCESS CHOICE

This is a critical decision in operations strategy but one which often baffles the uninitiated. It is also an area where manufacturing and service concepts, as stated in the literature, are dramatically different. In particular the impossibility of storing a service and the possibility of customer intervention add a distinctive flavour to service process decisions.

However, there are a number of basic principles which may be expounded in advance of the more detailed treatment to be found in the appropriate sections of Chapter 5. Process choice relates to the basic mode of operation of a system. The extremes are project based and continuous processes, with the awkward mode of batch production lying somewhere in between.

A project-based process occurs where a unique item is designed and produced for a specific customer or a unique service rendered. A certain semantic distinction is necessary here because some would maintain that all service situations are different and therefore unique. The same might be said of products but the point being made here is that the organization makes a real effort to explore a client's individual needs and these are substantially different from those of other clients. The organization then makes a product or provides a service which is also substantially different.

Some examples will make the point clear and also show where problems of definition occur at the edges. A commission to design and build an original structure such as a bridge or building is an obvious project, made unique by client needs and the site on which the structure is to be raised. Of course the engineers involved will use past designs and common components as far as possible but substantial original design will be necessary and the whole enterprise will satisfy the commonly used definitions of a project (for example see Meredith and Mantel (1989)). The construction of a series of warehouses to standard dimensions on a level site might be so similar to previous work that standard factory-made components could be used, at a considerable cost advantage to provider and client.

A consultancy assignment may provide an example of a project in a service context. Similarly a surgical operation may be more or less similar to ones carried out previously and therefore require more or less original thought and research.

At the other extreme many common purchased items may have been made by a dedicated system which produces only one thing. At the extreme the chemical process industry and the utilities produce a continuous flow of product. Though automated vending machines may also be very limited in range, and mass entertainment untailored to our individual needs, it is rarely economic for a personal service to be so unresponsive.

Rather more common are highly standardized service situations such as those apparent in retail outlets and fast food outlets where a narrow range of service is both provided and expected. Similarly in manufacturing a production system may well produce a narrow range of items in large numbers, either in large batches (traditional mass production) or on a mixed batch basis as in JIT where some flexibility is possible over a limited range. However, service and manufacturing differ in that the latter has the option of stock holding while the former must either have customer queues or idle periods for the provider if provision cannot be exactly matched to demand.

In manufacturing, and in much office work, tasks are performed in small or medium batches of identical items according to a schedule. Though of obvious appeal, this form of process causes considerable problems of organization and can be costly in terms of stockholding.

All operations would like to combine the advantages of varied provision, customer service and low cost. Manufacturing, service and office operations all use technology in an attempt to achieve some competitive balance of service and cost but the implications of process and technology choice must be fully understood for operations to be profitable.

Process choice – a simple exercise

In order to explore the ideas of process choice further, and also relate them to office situations, the following exercise is suggested. Consider two extreme forms of operation, choosing an appropriate concrete context. The extremes of process type are:

X = A repetitive and standardized form of operations

Y = A one-off tailored form of operations

Typical contexts to choose from might be:

- *Manufacturing:*
  X is the mass production of a common household product
  Y is renovating an old building
- *Service:*
  X is a McDonalds-style fast food outlet
  Y is a college personal counselling service
- *Office:*
  X is the data processing of salary cheques
  Y is desk research for marketing a new product

For your chosen pair of situations in any one type of operation now ask how they differ in terms of the following characteristics (reference may be needed to later chapters and other texts to provide a full answer but much can be gained from an initial use of common sense followed by discussion with tutor support):

- Aspects of the actual product or delivered service.
- Economics of provision in terms of pricing policy and the breakdown of fixed and variable costs.
- Appropriate quality procedures.
- Control of the flow of materials and people.
- Control of inventories and queues.
- Human resource issues; in particular resource planning, job design, motivation, payment, training and industrial relations.
- Appropriate organizational structure.
- Available technology.
- Relationship with the product or service design function.
- Capacity planning.
- Productivity.
- Flexibility.
- Scope for continual learning and improvement..

The result of even a brief examination of such issues should be an appreciation of the richness and complexity of operations and their interrelationships with other functions.

However, the analysis so far has excluded the very difficult middle ground of batch manufacturing and the service shop. The ambitious reader might now like to consider this list in the context of a concrete example from one of these areas, though a preliminary review of the rest of this book along with support from standard texts is recommended.

CAPACITY MANAGEMENT

In sharp contrast to everyday usage, the term 'capacity' has subtle connotations in operations strategy. Whereas we are used to referring to the capacity of a bottle or of an oven in simple physical terms as the amount of some substance which can be held by a container, this notion has limited applicability in an operational context. Certainly it might be convenient to measure the capacity of a warehouse in cubic metres but measuring the capacity of a factory or the local branch of a bank is more complex.

The first point to be made, using systems terminology, is that everyday expressions of capacity usually refer to a stock rather than a flow. While this may be appropriate in our warehouse example, most operational systems are characterized by the transformations they perform and therefore the amount of input that may be transformed in a period of time is a more useful characterization of capacity. Thus the local bank may refer to customers served per day, transactions performed per week or some similar flow related measurement.

Secondly a bottle may be capable of holding the same quantity of a wide variety of liquids, that is the volume of the liquid is critical rather than its other properties (within reasonable limits). Even with a warehouse things may not be so simple. If our stored product is homogenous and easily divisible and handled then we have no problem but warehouses may be required to hold a wide variety of goods each with their own requirements, including the need to retrieve individual items. Therefore a warehouse which might hold 400 cubic metres of paper may be limited to 300 cubic metres of books.

We therefore define the capacity of a system as the limit to the transformational activity of the system. It must, however, be understood that this definition raises more issues than it resolves. These issues are explored through a series of examples below.

The need to handle a variety of flows increases the complexity of determining a capacity strategy. We may explore this through a simple example. Imagine the following two self-service retail outlets:

The first is a local shop selling fruit, vegetables and groceries. It is situated on a busy main road and only five cars may park in the small bay in front of the shop (assuming no delivery lorry is there at the time). Its custom, in addition to such car-related trade, is mainly from a nearby housing estate.

The second is a supermarket on the edge of the same town with a large car park for its almost totally car-borne trade.

Before reading further, you may wish to make a list of the various ways in which the transformational activity of these two outlets may be measured. It is then useful to consider the factors which may limit capacity in terms of these measures of performance.

To measure transformational activity we must first of all consider the objectives of a system. In this instance we might assume profit maximization as one possibility and perhaps maintaining or increasing the number of customers as another. The latter leads us to activity measurements such as the average number of customers served per week. We may then ask what factors limit our ability to handle customers. Some possibilities are included in the following, always noting that the factors mentioned are likely to have differing effects on different customers (for example a single customer arriving in a car will have different operational requirements compared with a family or a disabled customer):

- Factors which restrict the input rate, for example car parking, public transport, the number of trolleys and baskets and so forth.
- Factors which affect the flow of customer's within the shop, for example the layout of the shop including the width of the aisles.
- Factors which affect the customer's ability to obtain specialist service, for example service at a counter where cold meats and other goods are individually prepared.
- Factors which affect the flow of customers from the shop, in particular payment at tills and space for packing goods.

Such factors cannot be seen in isolation from the perceived quality of service. Thus a shop which holds a wide variety of goods may assume that a customer will spend some time in the building and will organize things accordingly, in particular relating to available space. However, if the shop is also to be attractive to a customer with simple needs and limited time, accessibility of goods and fast payment becomes important.

The profit maximization objective leads us to consider not only the number of customers but their spending pattern and the shop's fixed and variable costs. These interact with the provision of capacity in a number of obvious ways. Thus we might consider the possibility of measuring capacity in monetary terms. The most obvious possibility is revenue generated over a period of time and certainly our two examples of retail outlets will differ dramatically in this respect. However, we must be careful to note that revenue is affected by inflation and also by the price of items purchased. The first effect may be removed through the use of appropriate deflating indices. The latter leads to the strange notion that our shop capacity may be increased by increasing our average price. Thus it may appear that throughput of customers is a safer basis for capacity measurement but if each customer makes only one purchase the impact on facilities is different from that produced by a store full of families.

Therefore we might conclude that the volume and mix of customers is important in determining the capacity of a shop. Even this, unfortunately, missed a crucial point – the variations in customer mix and arrival rates at different times of the day and on different days. To set up facilities which will handle the largest number of arrivals may score well on customer throughput but badly on profitability. Some form of 'flexible capacity' is required in this instance.

Thus a more subtle view of capacity is to regard it as a time varying function of operational decision making. In the supermarket example the availability of check-out facilities demonstrates this point. For a check-out till to be available to service customers (in this case a transformation in the ownership of goods and money) two types of resource are required. The first is represented by an area of floor space occupied by the physical paraphernalia of the check-out, i.e. a trolley lane, moving conveyor, electronic till and the information system infrastructure of bar coding and computer technology. The second resource is human, consisting partly of a check-out assistant provided by the supermarket and partly by the customer unloading a trolley and packing the goods. The first of these types of resource is provided on a long-term basis through capital investment and in isolation represents potential capacity. Only when the human ingredients are added (assuming the infrastructure is functional) does real check-out service capacity exist.

Thus potential capacity is provided through the following decisions:

- the supermarket, its management and its information systems that exist as a context for the check-out subsystem;
- capital investment in the physical check-out facilities has taken place;
- staff have been employed and trained in check-out work.

Such staff may be assigned to any one of a number of duties during their working periods. It is only when the operational decision is taken to activate the till by assigning staff is potential service capacity changed into actual capacity. This simple way of working provides some flexibility in total check-out capacity provision. As we will see when discussing service capacity in detail such flexibility is essential in providing an economical service in the context of fluctuating demand. A similar situation may apply in just-in-time style manufacturing. It should also be noted that although the idea of flexible capacity is appealing it may be wiser to attempt to manipulate demand into a smoother and more manageable pattern.

To summarize some aspects of flexible capacity we note the following:

- investment is necessary to provide potential capacity, thus incurring initial fixed costs and possibly some recurring costs in maintaining this potential;
- activating this potential capacity to provide available capacity incurs costs, though these may partly be opportunity costs of diverting resources from other uses;
- as the pattern of demand changes, management must have the capability to deploy capacity to the levels required, that is they must have appropriate information and actually be able to change capacity within appropriate timescales.

We develop these ideas further in Chapter 5 in the specific contexts of manufacturing and service operations where different issues dominate.

CASE STUDIES IN OPERATIONAL STRATEGY

The three case studies given below are intended to show the inter-relatedness of a variety of policy areas in operational strategy with other functional and corporate strategies.

CASE STUDY - ROVID

The following case, based on general experience in a number of company situations, was constructed to show a simple manufacturing situation with a service sub-theme. It is followed by a number of suggested exercises which are best carried out through small group discussion.

Introduction

Andy Schofield has taken up his new post as production manager with the Rovid manufacturing company, a renowned maker of children's plastic activity products. Rovid design, make and sell a range of high quality plastic components which may be assembled by the user as childrens' activity centres. These typically include climbing frames, platforms, slides and so forth.

The basic components of these activity centres are rods, connectors, special fixtures (e.g. plastic channels which form slides) and ground mats. A fairly small range of rods and connectors are manufactured in one colour. These are then packaged in a variety of different ways with particular special features as primary packs for self-assembly by the customer. The company also sell supplementary packs containing only replacement rods or connectors. Components in different packs are interchangeable so the customer may buy several different packs and assemble imaginative activity centres to their own design.

Included within the packs are instructions for assembly, ideas for more advanced structures and safety information on the maximum size of structures which should be built. All the components are very strong and of a high quality.

The ground mats are bought in by the company, repackaged individually or with the primary packs and sold through the same outlets as the other packs. They are of one size and design but may be interlinked to provide a larger play area.

These primary and supplementary packs command a high price due to their quality, both real and perceived by the customer. The quality image presented by the company is reinforced by prestige advertising and by the high standard of the packaging. The packs are sold mainly through outlets in the UK who specialize in childrens' products with an appropriate quality image.

The organization structure of the company

The main duties associated with Andy Schofield's new post include day-to-day responsibility for the company's production processes, for packing and distribution of the company's products and for the planning and control of material flows. The buying of raw materials is the responsibility of another manager who, like Andy, reports directly to the production director, Alan Freeman.

The company has three other directors with executive responsibilities. The managing director, who also keeps a firm grasp on financial and personnel matters, is Alex Taylor. Currently the company is enjoying considerable success as measured by sales growth, market share and profitability. Around half the company's goods are exported, mainly to Europe and the USA. However, this success is beginning to encourage competition both from UK and foreign companies. The company is privately owned, though no longer managed by the original owners whose families nevertheless are still the major shareholders. All finance for expansion and major fixed asset purchases must come from retained earnings.

Technical and quality issues are handled by John Barnes. The placing of responsibility for quality assurance, management services and maintenance in John's department means that communication between technical and production management is of particular importance. Fortunately the stability of the product range and the existing processes means that only a few problems arise. A positive advantage of this arrangement is thought to be the very high product quality levels which the company achieves.

Central to the success of the company are the design and marketing departments under the marketing director, Ian Strong. The marketing department is highly professional in monitoring trends in buyer behaviour and in developing marketing plans and promotional projects to maintain a suitable image of the product with customers. Liaison between marketing and design is excellent. The design department is mainly concerned with the design of promotional material and with producing imaginative new structures which may be built with standard components.

Manufacture and quality control

The manufacture of the rods and connectors is highly automated and based on five fairly small injection moulding machines. Due to the narrow product range, large batch manufacture is possible with high levels of machine utilization. Raw materials are readily available and little labour input is required. However, these machines, working on two shifts for six days a week, provide a bottleneck for the output of the company as a whole. More intensive working is considered to be inadvisable due to the increased likelihood of breakdowns, which are already providing some cause for concern. Company management policy is against sub-contracting the manufacture of rods and connectors. Indeed it is argued that increasing supply might be contrary to the exclusive image of the product. Similarly the purchase of further machines of this type has been rejected on the above grounds and also because of the capital outlay which would be required (around £15,000 per machine).

The production of the special features is based on a variety of fairly old plastic extrusion machines with considerable labour input, scrap rates of around 10 per cent and ample spare capacity.

The ground mats are bought in from three different suppliers who vary greatly as to lead times and reliability of supply. Quality is maintained by making clear to suppliers what is required, determined progress chasing and regular goods inwards audits. Management have always paid particular attention to this area recognizing that shortages and quality problems would affect their profitability.

The packaging department is labour intensive with packaging materials bought from a variety of outside suppliers with the same rigorous quality control as that applied to the suppliers of ground mats. Packaging is the one part of the operation which has problems of variety. It is the part of total operations to which the full range of materials arrive as input and which also has a high variety of outputs, a total of 22 differing packs being sold on a regular basis. Management have been firm in discontinuing low selling lines but consider that market advantage will be lost if the customer cannot buy the choice of components required.

The packs are sold directly to retail outlets who are encouraged to display the eight best selling lines for that locality. The company carries enough stock in all lines to be able to respond very quickly to a specific customer request.

Demand is highly seasonal with peaks prior to Christmas and in the early summer. Though the company uses a discount pricing policy to encourage retailers to buy in relatively large quantities and store on their premises (a policy more successful with retail chain stores), inevitably stocks have to be built up at the factory in autumn and spring. Inventory levels at all locations in the factory fluctuate greatly but are never allowed to fall too low. This is a policy decision stoutly defended by management as essential for maintaining their market position. Data on stock holding is shown in Figure 4.4

Quality control for outgoing goods is extremely stringent, consisting

Year	1986	1987	1988
Turnover	5,780	6,406	7,253
Average stocks:			
Raw materials	628	704	755
Work in progress	318	383	493
Finished goods	738	1058	1371
Spares and consumables	63	104	171
Minimum stocks:			
Raw materials	507	609	676
Work in progress	269	316	372
Finished goods	285	460	542
Spares and consumables	55	97	159

Figure 4.4
Rovid case – stock holding

of an inspection of every pack before sealing for dispatch coupled with sampling audits of sealed packs. The return of any item from a retailer or a customer would be a rare event and would set off a major inquiry within the company. Faults are rarely found at this stage relating to rods, mats or connectors but special features cause continual problems.

Production planning and quality control systems in the company are all manual based on a number of progress chasers and inspectors who are very experienced in handling the problems which may arise. Indeed staff in general are very involved with the company. A strong family atmosphere prevails, particularly in the packing department, which goes well with the quality – related image of the product. Cost accounting and control systems are very simple as management is opposed to bureaucracy and feels it has little need of detailed information other than aggregate costs of resources and rates of flow of materials. The payment system for all staff is a wage or salary (related to a small number of job grades) and a bonus depending on company profitability as a whole.

Future Plans

The threat of competition is continually monitored by the marketing department but in the past rivals have made little headway against the company's product range and reputation. However, a smaller rival UK manufacturer has recently been bought out by a major German distributor of high quality childrens play products. Thus the following contingency plans are currently under consideration:

● The company might attempt to reduce stocks and streamline manufacture in order to reduce costs and prices. It is estimated that a reduction of 10 – 15% in costs might be possible.

- Improvements are always under consideration in packaging and the design of structures based on the standard components.
- It has often been argued in the past that the range of components and colours should be widened. Such changes might be very costly relative to any slight improvement in demand which would result.
- The company could diversify into related plastic childrens' products in order to build on the existing high company profile. Though plans for alternative products are regularly made, they are invariably rejected as less profitable than existing products and a potential source of confusion within the factory.
- A recent proposal from the marketing department has been for the opening up of parts of the factory site as a visitor centre and theme park. A number of visitors already come to the factory shop and space is available for the permanent erection of structures using the company's products. There are good roads leading to the site. The factory itself is modern, the packing process is clean and a reasonable amount of space within the factory is available for visitor facilities.

Exercises (taking the role of Andy Schofield)

1 (One year later.) As feared, the products of Rovid's German competitor are proving a severe threat. In response Rovid's management have decided to widen their product range through the use of a range of colours for all components and a wider range of special features. At the same time, all departments have been asked to prepare plans for reducing variable and fixed costs.

 What response would you make to this new strategic direction, remembering the need to be constructive and plan for future operational effectiveness?

2 Analyse the data on inventory levels and suggest ways in which stock holding costs may be reduced in the light of the above scenario.

3 Rovid's marketing department have suggested that the factory site be opened up as a theme park and visitor centre.

 What are the operational implications of this idea, with particular reference to visitor facilities, movement, safety and overall satisfaction?

4 In response to market threats, senior management have suggested a diversification into related children's plastic products. What operational problems might follow from such a development and how might these be overcome?

CASE STUDY – WILCOX AND SONS

The following case, based on general experience, was constructed to show the relationship between manufacturing and retail and also to give an example of the options open to a design-led company. The task for a group exercise is to role play the meeting referred to at the end of the case.

Introduction

Frank Smith took a deep breath before reaching for the consultant's report sitting on his desk. John Senior from APS Consultants had rung him the evening before and warned him that the report had a mixture of good and bad news. The process of researching the report had been comparatively short, if expensive. What did it contain?

Frank was managing director of Wilcox and Sons, a small, highly prestigious manufacturer of ornamental pottery-based items. The company had been founded over a century ago and had remained independent in the ownership of the Smith family. Its fortunes had fluctuated, being at times supported by the other Smith business interests, but recently things had appeared to be going quite well.

The main Wilcox lines over a number of years had been figurines and groups of figures in rural settings. Despite considerable competition from the major pottery manufacturers the company had survived, mainly due to its design expertise and superb product quality. This was allied to some hard-headed business sense which showed itself in a determined attitude to keeping costs down and avoid misguided adventures into areas of business in which the directors were not totally confident. However, the result of this cautious approach was that the company had remained small and only modestly profitable.

In addition to its factory in Stoke-on-Trent (new premises, paid for by the sale of the much sought-after site of the original works) the company owned three retail outlets, one in the new Potteries Shopping Centre (Hanley) and the others in London and Birmingham. Each outlet was small and though they sold other items of similar quality to Wilcox Ware these were carefully chosen not to compete directly. Wilcox Ware was also sold in other high class outlets alongside the normal range of quality ceramic products.

In the last seven years, the company had been very determined in attracting talented designers, mainly from colleges, and such individuals tended to be skilled in a variety of crafts in addition to pottery design. Alan Parry, the head of the design studio, had decided to experiment with mixtures of pottery, wood, metal and glass in the production of a range of special items for regular customers and these had been very well received. The plan therefore was to capitalize on the skills and the designs that had been developed by marketing such products more widely.

However, the marketing director, Peter Passmore, had been in two minds how to go about this. One possibility was to maintain this new range as exclusive, made-to-order items but the danger was that such items would have to be priced at a prohibitive level. The alternative was to settle on a small range of designs with wider appeal and promote them vigorously, mainly through the company's own outlets.

Either course of action would have considerable repercussions for the management of all functions in the company and therefore a Report had been commissioned from the APS Consultants Group.

Frank Smith opened the report and read the executive summary with mounting concern. After rereading he made a list of points which seemed to capture the flavour of the report.

1 Without sales expansion of some kind, the company was hardly viable due to the added costs of the new manufacturing site and the increased running costs of the sales outlets. The consultants were particularly critical of the levels of inventory in the company which, though not untypical for the industry, could well threaten profitability.
2 Expansion was only likely to be possible at the top end of their existing range of goods or in new ranges such as those involving the mixtures of materials recently developed.
3 There were considerable problems in developing the mixed materials range, not least of which was that if successful, rival firms would be likely to copy the concept. Thus it was important that the introduction and growth of such a product line be very carefully managed.
4 Mixed material products had been made, so far, in the small workshop adjacent to the design studio rather than on the full production line. The processes involved in making such products in quantity were not fully explored. In particular there might well be problems in training the workforce to produce such items and to maintain quality during the early stages of the product life cycle.
5 Crucial to the success of the mixed material range was the way it was displayed and sold in the outlets. The customer was being asked to pay a considerable amount of money for items which, though very attractive, were not traditional. This was somewhat at odds with the highly traditional nature of an industry where successful products might be sold for many decades!
6 Only modest funds would be available to finance this innovation and much of these would have to be spent on promotion (at which the company had an excellent record) and manufacturing reorganization (which might well prove problematic).
7 The APS Consultants Group, when investigating Wilcox and Sons, had sent researchers into the Wilcox retail outlets to gain a cus-

tomer's view of their operational effectiveness. The researchers were highly critical of the day-to-day management of the outlets, complaining of excessive waiting time in the shops, mistakes in ordering items and an impression that service staff, though most helpful, appeared totally in the dark about likely delays in product supply and about the possibility of customization of the standard lines.

8 The company were particularly proud of the quality of their products and, using what was felt to be current jargon, described themselves as a 'total quality management' company. The consultant's report was particularly critical of this, going so far as to suggest that senior management might attend a seminar on TQM to discover what it actually means. Smith felt the consultants had been less than fair in suggesting that Wilcox and Sons were 'inspection orientated' in controlling quality. Wilcox design and manufacturing staff were experienced and conscientious in their approach to work.

So, thought Frank, we will have to make some changes and it's going to be hard to manage. He immediately arranged for the circulation of the report to all senior members of the firm and called a series of meetings at which specific issues could be discussed.

CAPITAL APPRAISAL CASE STUDY – THE ZL30 PROPOSAL

The following case is based on an equipment replacement decision in a large manufacturing company. It takes the form of a sequence of episodes, each followed by short exercises.

Part 1

Frank had just completed one of the regular major overhauls needed on the XK20 line. When purchased, around 15 years ago, this collection of computer linked equipment was considered state-of-the-art. At least Frank's boss, George White, thought so and probably still did. Now it was an expensive nuisance and Frank was determined to change things.

Input to the XK20 line was a motley collection of electronic components which were 'attached' to a printed circuit board. The result was tested and the process produced not only a component but a report on its characteristics. It required little labour for its operation but its input and output materials handling systems caused problems. The latest processes, the ZL30 in particular, saved on materials handling, labour and produced a more consistent output for a wider product range.

Frank had done his homework on the proposed change but knew better than to present a completed proposal to George. Instead he decided to pave the way by asking George's advice. Wandering into the chief engineer's office, and after appropriate social chat, he raised the subject of the proposed change.

George had heard it all before from Frank's predecessors and had tried unsuccessfully on two occasions to change the XK20 line. He reached for a used envelope and with studied nonchalance wrote on the back :

'Cost of equipment, installation etc.   £378,000'

Frank was taken aback, realized he had been outmanoeuvred, and quickly adjusted to giving an exposition of the benefits. Surprisingly George didn't argue but simply wrote them down :

'Annual savings in maintenance and downtime   £39,000
Annual savings in labour costs   £34,000
Annual scrap and quality non-conformance saving £28,000'

'So it pays back in under four years?' he asked.

'Yes, if you accept my figures.'

'I'm not too bothered about that. It will be up to you to justify the forecasts and to carry the can if you can't deliver! I suggest you prepare a capital expenditure paper if you feel so strongly about it. You can sub-mit it to Divisional Finance and we'll see what happens.'

Frank wasn't too keen on the drift of this conversation and he certainly had no intention of writing a paper off the top of his head and launching it onto the sea of corporate politics without preparing the ground.

Analysis 1

Capital Cost = £378,000

Annual Savings =£101,000

Payback in 3.74 years

Discussion 1

1 What strategic, financial and engineering assumptions are made in this form of analysis? What is the value of such an analysis?
2 Suggest other factors which might be taken into account.

Part 2

Frank was welcomed at Divisional Finance like a stranger from a distant land – a curiosity providing a break in the normal tedium of corporate affairs. He eventually found Paul Harris, an alarmingly young looking accountant who specialized in project cost appraisal, and they settled down to a real discussion.

'I'm sure it's a good idea,' Paul commented, 'but you're missing a few tricks in setting out the argument. For a start the payback period is only a rough guide. We really use net present value. As you haven't built inflation into your forecasts we can use an inflation-free rate for this class of expenditure of 18 per cent and a ten-year planning horizon. The cost and benefit estimates are up to you to defend, though I notice you've found no savings in inventory or advantages in energy consumption for example.'

Analysis 2

Discount rate = 18%
All figures in £000

Year	Cash out	Cash in	Net cash	Cum cash	PV	Cum PV
0	378		−378	−378	−378	−378
1		101	101	−277	86	−292
2		101	101	−176	73	−220
3		101	101	−75	61	−158
4		101	101	26	52	−106
5		101	101	127	44	−62
6		101	101	228	37	−25
7		101	101	329	32	7
8		101	101	430	27	34
9		101	101	531	23	57
10		101	101	632	19	76

Figure 4.5
ZL30 case – analysis of proposal

An analysis of the ZL30 proposal is given in Figure 4.5.
Notes relating to Figure 4.5 are given below.
Present value (PV) is calculated for each period as follows:

PV = net cash flow x discount factor

Where the discount factors may be obtained from tables, by using standard spreadsheet formulae or directly calculated (see Harrison (1990) for more detailed examples relating to manufacturing investment).

A graph showing how cumulative cash (Cum) and cumulative present value (Cum PV) grow over time in shown in Figure 4.6. The intersection of the Cum cash line with the horizontal axis (i.e. where Cum cash is zero) gives an approximation to the payback period (which depends on the distribution of cash flows over the year). The intersection of the Cum PV line with the horizontal axis gives the discounted payback period and the final value of Cum PV gives the payback at the ten-year planning horizon. As the latter is positive the investment seems attractive but if the planning horizon had been taken as six years then the Cum PV would have been negative. Thus the assessment of this investment based on Cum PV calculations depends on an arbitrary factor.

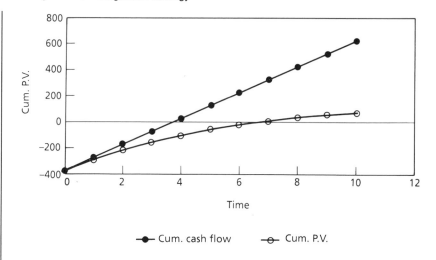

Figure 4.6
Cumulative NPV graph

Discussion 2

Taking the role of senior management, would you accept this proposal? If not, what alternative analysis would you suggest (accepting that something needs to be done about the XK20 line)?

Part 2 continued

On this basis, Frank was able to construct a capital expenditure request which went to the Divisional Finance director's office ...

Part 3

... where, after a long delay, it was thrown out! Not that there was thought to be much wrong with the general principle of renewing the XK20 line. As it was pointed out to Frank (who was now the new chief engineer) the form of the proposal was dull and outdated. First of all any proposal must reflect a comparison between alternative forms of action, in this case between replacing the XK20 line now and replacing it later. Each of these two lines of action had possible sub-themes (what to replace the line with? – when to replace it? ...) and each carried a variety of risks. Suppose the new line doesn't work? Suppose demand collapses for its products? Suppose demand expands for the alternative products which can be made on the ZL30?

Frank's next line of action was to take an in-company course on decision analysis (also attended by Paul Harris) where the workshop sessions concentrated on this particular decision situation.

One of the key points made on this course was the problem of defining the boundary of a system and the need to be creative in considering lines of action and outcomes. It occurred to Frank that one of the greatest possible values of a new system would be its ability to accept pre-packaged component inputs, thus allowing point-of-use delivery of guaranteed defect-free goods from suppliers on a JIT basis. This had strategic implications for the entire company. If carried out uniformly throughout manufacture it could lead to the extinction of the entire goods receiving, testing and storage department.

It had often been said in company briefings that manufacturing operations must be strategy led. This had usually been taken as corporate rhetoric, along with TQM and other fashions. It now occurred to Frank why a manufacturing strategy was a real necessity.

Discussion 3

1 Accepting the points made above, what form of analysis is appropriate for this situation?
2 If point-of-use delivery of components is accepted as a operational ideal in this case, what financial analysis of its costs and benefits would you propose? If accepted as financially viable, how could such a proposal be implemented to ensure that projected benefits actually occurred (for example, what are the critical success factors in carrying out such a change)?

Note: the financial evaluation of point-of-use delivery, as with other similar JIT related ideas (see Chapter 7), is very difficult to carry out in practice. This discussion topic, based on a real situation which caused considerable problems, is well worth exploring in depth.

CHAPTER 5

Manufacturing, service and office management

INTRODUCTION

In this chapter we take two of the main themes of Chapter 4, process choice and capacity management, and use them to illustrate a number of issues in manufacturing and service operations. We then relate these ideas briefly to office management and conclude with two case studies.

In the remaining four chapters of the book, five other major strategic policy areas are explored, that is quality management, materials flow management, technology (which includes information management) and human resource management.

This leaves three policy areas seemingly neglected. However, the link between design and operations, briefly outlined in Chapter 3, is a continuing sub-theme in the section below and in Chapter 8. Strategic decisions on the scope and span of operations (assuming we mean more here than the make-or-but decision and choice of supplier) is a major issue in corporate planning and hence dealt with in Chapter 3. Finally facilities location and layout, though strategic in the sense that major resources are allocated and often fixed for many years, are dealt with in standard operations literature through a series of techniques. Indeed the former is often a matter of regional economics and the latter of engineering and building design, both guided by operational principles. Our concern in this book is more on strategic operational issues that have a major impact on other functional areas and corporate policy directions.

PROCESS CHOICE IN MANUFACTURING

One of the best established models in manufacturing operations is the classification of production systems shown in Figure 5.1. On the horizontal axis we represent the scale of production ranging from single individually produced items on the left to mass production on the right. The vertical axis shows increasing product variety and the five classic forms of production then occupy a diagonal showing the obvious trade-off between scale and variety. This way of showing production organization is fully described in

Hill (1985) where the idea of process profiling is also developed (see also Hayes and Wheelwright (1984)).

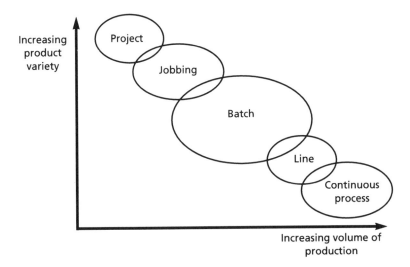

Figure 5.1
Relationship between process forms

Of the five forms, it is mainly the middle one, batch production, which causes confusion. The extremes have obvious applications drawn from everyday life as well as work but batch production may be harder to relate to. In fact it is a very common form of production organization aiming for the economic advantages of mass production with some degree of flexibility. Very many products and services are produced in this way but its emergent properties may be quite awkward to manage.

Of the five archetypical forms, the middle three are given the most attention in manufacturing strategy literature, mainly because developments in automated production systems can be shown as attempts to escape this straightjacket and gain advantages of throughput and variety simultaneously. However, the two extreme forms should not be ignored.

Project management is a major form of work organization encompassing a far wider range of activities than its uses in manufacturing. Some productive industries are largely project based (for example civil engineering) but all organizations have a large number of activities which may be called projects. Indeed for most manufacturers, projects are likely to arise as changes to the production system itself, product developments, organizational restructuring and so forth. A set of 'project management techniques' were developed in the 1950s for the management of large-scale projects but the subject stagnated until recently when three very valuable contributions have come about. The first is an increased understanding of the organizational implications of project work (see Meredith and Mantel (1989) for a detailed discussion of matrix management in project situations, though much general management literature refers to project work). The second is the development of project management software. Finally valuable work has been done on the personal attributes and competencies of the project manager, for example see the cases in Boddy and Buchanan (1992).

Though it is usual to split project and jobbing as two different work forms, one may well speak of the individual work packets in jobbing as 'projects' and much of the valuable theory on how to manage projects applies. For instance problems often arise in engineering design offices when routine and repetitive work is mixed with larger 'one-offs'. Such problems of work structuring can readily be described in organizational theory terms as a mixed matrix of functional and project forms. In carrying these ideas over to service management, a difficult task as we see later, project management terminology seems far more natural then 'jobbing'.

Process industries, where for example highly specialized equipment is dedicated to the cost effective production of very large amounts of standard product, seem separate from other industries but their very success in economic operations makes them an ideal to be aimed for by mass production. Whether this is a valid comparison remains to be seen. In particular it is doubtful whether the comparison with process industries has any particular utility to service management.

Process choice classifications have an obvious descriptive value but the real goal would be to convert them into explanatory theories, to be able to prescribe the most appropriate form for a given situation and to be able to predict the success or otherwise of a particular approach. Underlying this whole approach is the assumption that each form has emergent properties which may be uncovered by observation and analysis and then used as management guidelines. This appears to be accepted as a possibility in manufacturing far more than in the service sector.

Of particular value here is the idea of process profiling, mentioned earlier. Hill in particular has developed a systematic way of looking at the likely organizational implications of the three central forms. Contrasting jobbing, batch and line he asks a range of questions which explore their characteristics. Particularly interesting is the way in which for some features there is a continuum with batch production in the middle while for others the picture is more complex, counter-intuitive and potentially harder to manage.

If we first consider product and market features, of the three process forms, jobbing/project aims at situations with a wide product range and with the customer requiring low volumes, while line manufacture gives a narrow range in large volumes. Batch production fits neatly in the middle, which is hardly surprising as the classification is to an extent based on these characteristics. Hill is also particularly interested in the qualifying and order winning criteria which apply in each case. While these are also related to the stage in a product's life cycle, some generalizations are possible. Jobbing production seems naturally to give design flexibility and unusual product features while delivery performance may well be crucial. Line manufacture aims at low cost and therefore should give price advantages. The picture for batch production is far more confused. On the one hand there are advantages as batch production may be managed to give the mixture required in a given situation (for example some designed variety, scheduled delivery and reasonable cost). On the other hand this may lead to problems of management control. The concept of the focused factory, where in effect batch production is split into mini-lines, is aimed at handling problems of lack of direction, poor control and confusion.

Having mentioned the relationship between process choice and the product life cycle, we should further note that a successful product, as it moves through its life cycle will also require different process forms. Prelaunch test manufacturing may use a job shop (indeed product launch as a whole is often seen as a project) but introduction may require a batch manufacturing environment while the mature product is made on a dedicated production line. When decline sets in, batch production may return. If one accepts the idea that product innovation will be more rapid in the future, with shorter life cycles, then we have a problem in matching needs to manufacturing style in an orderly way.

Of particular concern to the operational strategist is the organizational and financial implications of different production forms. In particular batch production can lead to excessive stock holding, much of it as internal buffers to maintain reasonable utilization of plant and equipment and to give some chance of on-schedule delivery. Batch production can also lead to a form of organizational schizophrenia. Should management be centralized, as in process industries, or decentralized? Is control best established through bureaucratic rules and procedures or the promotion of participation and problem solving? This set of issues is explored in Chapter 7 in the context of the management of material flow but it is of equal concern in the context of quality and cost management.

Another strategic issue highlighted by the characteristics of differing processes is volume flexibility, that is how can the level of output be changed. A civil engineering project construction firm will expect to employ some labour for a given job, to hire plant and equipment and to expect labour flexibility in terms of hours worked as conditions vary. The management of a large chemical process plant may have little option but to close down a plant or build a new one as aggregate demand changes over time. Mass producers of, say, cars make newspaper headlines when they introduce short-time working or lay off workers as the impact on local communities is obviously considerable. Batch manufacturers may use any of these measures with the added possibility of sub-contracting to manage unevenness in demand. In fact the batch manufacturer may have an advantage here in potential flexible capacity always provided this can be managed and controlled economically.

The concept of the focused factory, based on the ideas of Wickham Skinner, was extensively promoted in the 1980s. It is a natural response to the problems of managing batch production to create smaller and possibly temporary sub-systems based on more manageable line principles. A systems view of production is of value here, though the word 'focus' has a subtly differing meaning in each case. We focus our attention on different sizes and levels of system in order to focus our efforts on their effective management.

It should be noted that much of this approach is challenged in Goldhar et al (1991). One objective of computer integrated manufacture (CIM) is to provide combinations of variety and scale of production which transcend this classification. With CIM we can, at least in theory, have tailored individual products produced quickly and in an economic way. This draws attention to a strategic competitive weapon that is perhaps insufficiently explored in the process choice literature, the link with the product design function.

The problem, referred to by Skinner as the innovation v productivity paradox, is well expressed in Goldhar et al (1991):

> Traditional factories ... cast management as a trade-off between innovation and productivity. ... As a product moves from introduction to maturity, the increase in volume requires standardization of the product design and a move from labour-intensive to capital-intensive production facilities to achieve low-cost operations. These 'rational' moves carry a strategic cost. Traditional 'hard tooled' factories with reduced flexibility and slower response time can, however, be devastating strategic weaknesses.

In contrast to this Goldhar et al refer to the advantages of CIM (see also the discussion in Chapter 8):

> ...the CIM-driven flexible manufacturing system is capable of a continuous flow of one-of-a-kind, one-at-a-time products – at a cost and quality at least as good as older factories producing standard products ...

This is, of course, a direct challenge to the standard manufacturing process archetypes. The capability to produce with economic variety is often described as 'economy of scope'. This has several related meanings. To the economist it denotes a saving attributable to a multi-product situation. The marketing manager will be delighted if economy of scope means serving many niche markets with no cost penalty. To the operations manager it may have the limited connotation that the economic batch size is one. If it appears that variety is free, however, then we must beware.

One sometimes forgets the incredibly high levels of complexity inherent in operations. At the level of a small production or service system, such as can be overseen by one individual, decision making and control can be exercised with great effectiveness through human experience and memory. An operational strategy which disaggregates operational decision making into such small cells may be effective if some means of coordinating the interactions between the cells can be found. The just-in-time system attempts to do this through pull scheduling and simplification. Indeed much general management literature emphasizes the value of small teams working in a focused way to achieve concrete objectives. However, much modern manufacture requires coordination of a wide range of tasks.

Traditional factories with limited information systems based on paper, human memory and crude data processing have had to evolve strategies for coping in these circumstances. Buffer stocks, long production runs and other variety reducers (to use the terminology of cybernetic systems theory) allow production to proceed with reduced need for operating information. This is in addition to the other economic benefits of these traditional operating measures (lower aggregate set-up costs and so forth). The overall aim is to achieve regularity and stability of interaction between the smaller, more manageable systems. Thus while operations even in traditional factories may seem difficult to manage at the micro level (production supervisors have been 'thriving on chaos' for a long time!), the macro setting has emphasized orderliness and regularity of functional interaction and strategy. Hence we have long product life cycles and occasional structural change.

With CIM available as a competitive weapon, inter-functional integration and high levels of innovation become possibilities provided the strategic framework to exploit them exists. Almost every aspect of operations is different in such a context. The normal process archetypes give way to high volume jobbing. The design to production interface is in continual use, indeed the design function is now part of operations. Goldhar et al argue that deliberately complicating the product, both to satisfy the customer and as a barrier against it being copied by competitors, may be a necessary competitive strategy. In this case we must 'embed the uniqueness of the product more and more deeply into the manufacturing process'.

We are here moving to the concept of a service factory. Goldhar et al suggest a set of characteristics of such a situation. These may be organized into recognizable themes as follows:

● Factors in the relationship between providers and customers, reflecting total quality management ideals:
  – direct distribution channels between the provider and the customer;
  – flexible, negotiated pricing;
  – high information content in provider and customer relationships;
  – long-term relationships between provider and customer, involving
  – learning by both;
  – customer participation in product design.

● Factors in the relationship between design and production:
  - high variety and customization of products;
  - rapid adoption of new technology in products and processes, including the design process.
● Factors in manufacturing operations and organizational design:
  - integration of physical and knowledge work with managerial decision making;
  - fast response time via short production cycles;
  - use of spare capacity rather than inventory.

We may emphasize this point by paraphrasing a recent American report which characterizes the best factories of the future as having the following features (see Samson (1990)):

● a focus on simultaneous improvements in cost, quality and delivery;
● close links with customers;
● effective use of technology;
● close links with suppliers;
● an organizational structure which addresses issues of flexibility and communication;
● attention to human resource development.

Such features are not conditional on process form; the factory of the future appears to have the best features of jobbing, batch and line simultaneously. This is a most ambitious requirement and perhaps one thing the more traditional literature shows us is that this will not be easy to achieve.

CAPACITY MANAGEMENT IN MANUFACTURING

Whilst in Chapter 4, we have already signalled some of the conceptual difficulties associated with the word 'capacity', we should also note how serious a practical problem this is for manufacturing managers. For instance, in the field of manufacturing resources planning (MRP II) (see Chapter 7 and Vollman et al (1992)) capacity planning is one of the most important components of planning and control software and is ignored at one's peril as many early practitioners discovered.

At the simple level of an individual work unit, capacity is the maximum rate of working multiplied by the available hours. Rate of working depends on staffing, equipment available, training, job design, the quality of incoming materials, the evenness of work flow, the mix of products to be made and so forth. Hours available is affected by the amount of overtime, number of shifts and frequency of equipment failure. All these factors are the result both of managerial decisions and implementational effectiveness. Added to this is a large dose of randomness due to a range of factors ranging from the success of the local football team to the mood of first line supervision.

If this seems complex then we must remember that the capacity of a total production system is not a simple function of the capacity of individual work units. Differing areas may act as bottlenecks at differing points of time. Indeed Goldratt has developed what is almost an entire management philosophy on the concept of production bottlenecks (see Chapter 7 on OPT and other references to Goldratt's Theory of Constraints).

In the context of a CIM-based service factory, and noting the possibilities afforded by organizational flexibility, we see that the effectiveness of inter-functional working and our relationship with suppliers and channels of distribution also affect how much throughput we can achieve.

At a strategic level, factory management must invest to provide potential capacity. Based on a long-term demand forecast and a corporate strategy which includes decisions on vertical integration, choices must be made about labour and technology, process, plant size, number of employees and other infrastructural matters. Some of these may be approached with greater flexibility allowing for contingency planning but others will require hard decisions about very fixed assets.

Factors to be taken into account include the following:

- Likely economies of scale and scope
- Effects of the traditional learning and experience curves
- Fixed plant which is likely to prove a bottleneck
- Degree of automation which is currently available and how this is likely to change
- Possibilities of range and response flexibility
- Facilities location (relative to suppliers) and layout
- Levels of training and preventative maintenance likely to be necessary to maintain capacity
- Possibilities for, and likely effects of, continual learning and improvement

A particularly important point is the key decision about how to handle seasonal and varying demand patterns. Three obvious possibilities exist:

1 Satisfy only a base continuing demand and leave the excess demand to competitors.
2 Invest in capacity to cope with the maximum expected demand.
3 Provide capacity equal to the average demand.

The profit potential of the first strategy depends on the amount of base demand, one's competitive situation and the ability of competitors to erode one's base demand.

The second strategy has obvious cost penalties but may be attractive if the fixed cost of investing in potential capacity is not too great and sufficient flexibility exists to economically activate capacity as demand levels change.

The final strategy requires a further set of decisions regarding the matching of supply and demand in the short term. Possibilities include backlogging orders (make the customer wait), carry stocks, subcontracting or finding some way to provide flexible capacity. A further and very attractive possibility is to manage demand through such devices as flexible pricing (see later on service capacity management).

As stated earlier, a large range of techniques exists in the standard literature on capital investment decision making to provide potential capacity and on ways to manage and control capacity at a tactical level. Further issues for operations management strategy relate to the following:

- the need for adequate systems for capacity management, with particular reference to information systems relating to demands (including timing) and to capacity availability;
- adequate cost information on the ramifications of differing capacity management tactics (e.g. overtime working v subcontracting);
- good interfunctional relationships with engineering, training, marketing and so forth.

OPERATIONS MANAGEMENT IN THE SMALL MANUFACTURING FIRM

The vast majority of empirically orientated literature on manufacturing operations is based on the experiences of large companies. On this base a number of themes, theories, models and techniques have been arrived at. An obvious question to ask is whether the basic theories of manufacturing operations are equally applicable to small enterprises?

Two immediate reactions may be foreseen. The first is to assert that the general operational principles derived from large company situations have an underlying logic which makes them universally applicable. In this case the ideas behind total quality management, stock control theory and so forth are not seen to depend on company size. The second reaction is that small company management is common sense!

The first response, however, does not take into account the reality and stress of small company management, the conflicting demands on limited management resources and the levels and variety of management skills likely to be available. The small company is also far more at the mercy of environmental turbulence and more likely to be made extinct by a single disaster. Whether or not the 'principles and techniques' are relevant, their implementation is often not possible within a small firm environment.

Recent ongoing research at Staffordshire University (early papers include Bell and Gaafar (1990)) and elsewhere has concentrated on in-depth studies of the working environment in small manufacturing companies and revealed differences in most operational factors. Much attention has been given to the organizational and social factors pertaining to such situations and it is within such a perspective that operational planning must be seen. Thus purchasing policy may depend more on to whom money is currently owed than on the formal application of vendor selection policies.

There is little doubt, however, that the careful application of some simple techniques and procedures should be of value in the day-to-day management of operations. Whether time can be spared for the detailed development of corporate and operational strategies is in doubt, particularly as exposure to environmental turbulence might render them obsolete before implementation has taken place. Yet the basic premises of Garvin, say, that competitiveness depends on productivity, quality and new products and processes seem sound provided that Garvin's further prescriptions relating to the importance of human resource development are seen in the context of small firms' culture.

PROCESS CHOICE IN SERVICE OPERATIONS

The classification of manufacturing processes has been established for some time. As we showed above, it may even be becoming counterproductive through not relating to the factory of the future. However it remains a most useful device for describing manufacturing situations and debating their relationships with other functional areas.

A similar classification of service processes has proved more elusive, possibly due to the diverse range of operations it must include. Silvestro, Fitzgerald, Johnston and Voss (1992) explore this problem by listing alternative classifications, each of which captures some key features of service processes. They then go on, guided by empirical research, to suggest a simple classification which we will describe later.

		Degree of service customization and customer interaction	
		Low	High
Degree	Low	Utilities	Computer diagnosis
of			
labour			
intensity	High	Lecturing	Consultancy

Figure 5.2
Service process choice

However, at least one earlier classification which has considerable utility is due to Schmenner (see Lovelock (1992)) and uses the two dimensions shown in Figure 5.2. One dimension is the intensity of the use of labour in providing the service. The other dimension is the extent to which interaction takes place between provider and customer and the extent to which the service is customized. This two-way classification provides a useful heuristic for exploring the differences in service situations. If one takes, for example, public eating establishments then one can see how restaurants, vending machines, fast food outlets and the traditional fish and chip shop each strike a different balance between tailored service and the economics of its provision. A second and very real value of this simple approach is to support an analysis of the implications of different processes for management. Using Schmenner's approach we see that high labour intensity services require care in recruitment, training, welfare and the design and scheduling of work, as one might expect. They also pose problems of control (remembering that service outlets are often geographically dispersed) and the management of growth. By contrast low labour intensity often entails capital expenditure on technology as a substitute for labour and such services may lack the flexibility of human service provision.

Services with high customer interaction and customization may require highly trained staff, be costly and harder to administer and control and pose problems in the management of customer intervention. With low interaction the resulting service may seem cold and impersonal and therefore need a number of measures to be made attractive.

This brief summary does little justice to the strength of even this limited classification in exploring the management problems of service provision. Many of the issues raised are both strategic and also require the management of the accompanying 'office' or back room operations.

Silvestro et al (1992) examine a number of classifications before arriving at a list of dimensions which seems to summarize the concerns of previous writers and reflects key issues uncovered by empirical research. These dimensions are the following:

- Equipment/people focus; similar to the labour intensity dimension used above.
- Customer contact time per transaction; ranging from weeks to minutes in the service system.
- Degree of customization; if high, the service can be adapted for an individual client; if low the client may at most be offered a choice between standard routes and products.
- Degree of discretion; the extent to which the direct service provider can vary the service given without management approval.
- Whether value is added in the front office or back room; it is reflected in the proportion of total staff involved in direct customer contact.

- Product/process focus; depending on whether the emphasis is on what the customer buys or how the service is delivered.

Empirical survey work suggests that these factors cluster to give three archetypes of service provision which are also differentiated by the rate of customer processing:

1. Professional services
These are labour intensive in their delivery, involve long contact time and a high degree of customization and discretion with a process focus and value added by front office staff. A low number of customers are processed by a typical service unit in a day. A typical example is management consultancy.

2. Service shop
A mixed people/equipment focus is accompanied by medium degrees of the other factors. A typical example is a hotel.

3. Mass services
An equipment, back office and product focus is associated with low contact time, customization and discretion. Many customers can be processed in a typical day. Examples include transport and mass retailing.

Such a classification schema has the virtue of simplicity while relating a number of factors. It can easily be associated with a range of management decisions and resource strategies, though it is perhaps counterproductive to proceed further with generalities when the specifics of service situations are so variable.

CAPACITY MANAGEMENT IN SERVICE OPERATIONS

In addition to the issues raised in Chapter 4 and earlier in this chapter, capacity management in a service situation has several further complicating factors:

- Service cannot be stored and therefore stocks cannot be used as a buffer to smooth out problems in the timing of supply and demand.
- Service requires customer presence and thus capacity may be lost through variations in arrival times.
- Service requires customer participation to a greater or lesser extent and therefore processing times and productivity may well vary.
- Capacity and service quality may vary in complex ways.

The latter point relates in part to customer perceptions of the utilization of the server. Thus the apparent absence of a queue may lead to an extension of processing time. Whether the existence of a long queue has the opposite effect is debatable.

If capacity is measured as a limit to the rate of customer processing, then key decisions are how much potential capacity to provide, when to activate it, where it should be located, how customer priorities should be handled and how one can deal with demand fluctuations.

This final point is well known to all service managers and may well provide a permanent preoccupation for first line supervision. Two classic general approaches are possible, to vary capacity or to manage demand.

Variations in capacity are provided in many ways in service situations. Flexible staffing through complex manning arrangements and multi-skilling are possible as is subcontracting. A more subtle approach is to encourage customer participation (for example in a self-service retail outlet) for tasks which may have highly variable processing times. Thus choosing goods in a shop is likely to be more time varying than paying for them. In this regard a supermarket has an advantage over a shoe shop where an assistant is available during fitting, though the latter may be turned to advantage in encouraging purchases to be made.

Demand may be managed through the encouragement of non-peak purchasing through pricing and promotional activity. The development of complementary modes of service (for example automatic cash dispensers) may draw off some peak demand. Customer appointment systems may be tried and if all else fails then queuing may be resorted to. This may be used imaginatively as at a theme park where a long queue for an attractive ride rations demand and also builds up a sense of excitement and expectation. Many queuing situations, however, are intrinsically boring and tactics such as those described in Lovelock (1989) may be necessary to placate the customer.

These essentially tactical aspects of capacity management have been described in some detail so the reader may easily see their strategic implications. For example, the management of demand through pricing requires careful liaison with marketing and good cost information. Flexible manning arrangements have considerable consequences for personnel management. Some approaches, such as giving over a large part of the service process to the customer, are major strategic decisions which, if misjudged, could have highly damaging consequences. However, as with many areas of service management, the right strategy to use depends on the specific situation and not least on customer expectations.

OFFICE OPERATIONS

We have earlier characterized office work as principally involving the transformation of data and information from one form into another. We have also noted that a key feature of operations is that they add value. In some industries the main objective, service provided and source of revenue is information handling. Typical examples include libraries, publishing, education and market research. In other industries a key component of service is information, obvious instances being banking and financial services, consultancy and many aspects of the entertainment industry. In such cases office operations clearly add value as part of a general service.

Most texts on service management contrast front office operations, where a service is directly provided with the customer present, and back room operations. The latter is often not merely an ancillary support but may provide the main competitive thrust of a service provider. If one deals with a travel agent, for example, though the personal skills of the counter assistant and the ambience of the shop are reassuring, the main service provided is the availability of travel information (in brochures and on computer databases) and the potential for actually booking suitable travel. The latter involves a two-way flow of information depending intimately on effective back room operations.

Manufacturing similarly requires office support, though information handling in this context is more general. The commercial department of a manufacturing company supports the interface with the customer, and the buying department similarly deals with some aspects of supplier liaison. Indeed using the Porter Value Chain model, support activities are essentially office based. That is design, programming, some engineering support and management itself are concerned to a large extent with transforming information rather than materials or people.

In Chapter 8 we explore some of the characteristics of office work as described in Zuboff (1988). This book also contains a fascinating account of the development of clerical work on Taylorist principles making it more and more similar to production in a factory and separating it from the domain of the manager where the exercise of judgement and discretion are essential. The former requires 'acting on' skills while the latter relates to 'acting with' others. Thus when discussing office operations we must be clear whether clerical or managerial roles are being referred to.

We will make no quixotic attempts here to characterize or summarize the nature of managerial work. Indeed it is assumed that the reader is already conversant with at least the standard behavioural vocabulary of organizational activity. However, it must be emphasized that back-room support of manufacturing and service operations has both routine, clerical aspects and requires managerial decision making and control. This is of particular importance when modelling information requirements.

Techniques to relate service provision to back-room support are very important and include, for instance, the idea of blueprinting (see Lovelock (1992)). The need for the coordination of managerial control of both areas is also crucial, particularly if the organizational structure of a company inhibits such cooperation.

Process choice, capacity and associated decisions in routine office operations thus seem to reflect similar decisions in manufacturing. For instance,

The Office Factory, Jolley and Patrick (1990), makes great play of the potential of JIT and OPT (see Chapter 7) in an office context. Volume and repetition are seen as the basis for process choice, bottlenecks must be managed, productivity maintained and continuous improvement aimed for. It should be remembered, though, that the ways in which effective operations might be achieved may differ from the factory floor; for instance the telephone is cited as a major reason for clerical non-productivity.

This view of office operations should be tempered in two ways. First of all it applies to routine, 'clerical' work and not to managerial, professional or design activities. Thus attempts to apply traditional productivity enhancing measures and controls to a product design office may backfire. Secondly there are possibly more opportunities in an office environment for the application of TQM methods (see Chapter 6) as office workers continually interact with internal 'clients'. This may, paradoxically, cause problems if empowerment is not controlled and working procedures become highly idiosyncratic.

CASE STUDY – THE NEXT PLATEAU

The following case study was based on interviews with staff in a small engineering company. It reflects the changes in strategy which typically take place as a firm grows and shows how such changes affect all aspects of operations management.

The case study is followed by several exercises which are recommended as ways of exploring the issues raised. Past experience suggests that it is most useful if these exercises are used as the basis for group discussion prior to any attempt to write a formal report recommending actions to be taken. The case was written in 1986 and should be seen in the context of the UK manufacturing environment in the previous decade. The obvious final question is suggested by the title, that is how should company strategy develop in the future.

Introduction

M G Sanders Company Limited (CNC Engineering Machinists) was founded in 1970 by an entrepreneurial engineer working from a shed in his garden. It soon moved to a small site in a Midlands town and five years later moved to its present location. The new building, adapted from a disused brewery, provides ample space. New offices were completed in 1985 giving the company a fresh, smart image at a cost of around £25,000. This is the largest sum spent on any single project other than the purchase of production equipment!

The owner maintains a tight control on cash flow and strategic planning though still has day-to-day contact with operations. The management team is small, its members having worked for the company for several years. All production related managers have the ability to work the computer numerically controlled (CNC) machines if the need arises.

Over the nine years 1976-85 turnover increased at an annual compound rate of around 34 per cent. In the whole of that period, this direct labour increased by only 28 per cent thus showing a dramatically increased use of machinery. For a typical machine, the hourly rate increased by 44 per cent in this nine-year period (with no increase in the last three years). This reflected the increasingly competitive markets in which the company was trading and was obtained by careful improvements in productivity. Information on profitability is not available.

The growth of the company was undoubtedly related to the owner's willingness to take risks in buying new machinery. Company strategy was led by perceived market opportunities and hence by market survival. Finance was mainly through bank overdraft. The direct impetus for change was often an occasion when the company had refused an order because of quality requirements or production capacity constraints.

Company development

Developments over time may be described as a series of production plateaux.

First plateau (1970–7)
The company was a traditional general engineering job shop making spare parts for machines in local industry. This was a limited and declining market.

Second plateau (1978–9)
A CNC lathe was purchased. This was a considerable expenditure at the time. It enabled improvements to be made in quality levels and facilitated larger batch sizes. The mining industry became a main customer.

Third plateau (1980–1)
Having gained considerable experience in using the CNC lathe, the company now purchased two small vertical machining centres. Increasingly customers were manufacturers in the defence industry with once again increases in quality requirements.

Fourth plateau (1982–5)
A major purchase was made of a large horizontal machining centre. The capital cost was almost equal to the annual turnover at the time. For

several months this machine was without work as the enhanced capability of the factory as a whole was emphasized to prospective and existing customers. That is, this machine was bought speculatively and work subsequently obtained. Company staff argue that this is typical of how the real entrepreneur survives and would have been impossible in an accountant dominated company. A five-year payback period was realistically foreseen for this machine. The company had also increased its capacity with smaller, often second-hand, machines and believes it now had a balanced manufacturing base.

The customers

Almost all the work done by this company consisted of subcontracted batches from large manufacturers in defence and similar industries. There was no direct selling at that time to new potential customers, work coming either from existing long-term customers or from recommendations. A wide variety of metal cutting operations could be performed in a typical job-shop environment.

There was a need to continually decide on and review customer priorities. Customer loyalty is crucial but in the short-term business can be very volatile. It is often good policy to maintain a steady flow of work with a customer, even at a loss, rather than lose contact (which is very much on a personal basis with buyers, sales and production staff).

Two important principles of work balancing were held to. One is the importance of obtaining both new types of jobs and repeats. New jobs are essential to maintain company development but require work in programming the CNC machines. Repeats can generate cash while requiring less managerial attention. The second principle is that one machine or machine type must not be tied up producing work for one customer over a long period. Otherwise the company would have difficulty in maintaining the loyalty of its other customers. Certainly the company would not allow one customer to have 100 per cent capacity at any one time and most customers accept this as reasonable.

Quoting for new work can cause difficulty. The cost of preparing a quote can be high and will have to be recovered on other work if the quotation is unsuccessful. After preparing a quote, there is almost inevitably a long delay while the customer himself quotes for the total project. A contract may only then be signed after many months and the now out-of-date prices must be re-negotiated. Thus it is normal practice to quote for a considerable overload in the volume of work. The whole process becomes one of continual negotiation and balancing of the needs of various customers.

Production planning

The production planning system had been designed a number of years earlier but the production situation changed dramatically. The ability to schedule and manage workflow might soon become a serious production constraint. Management had been looking at the possible purchase of micro-computer based manufacturing requirements planning (MRP) systems but many seemed inappropriate. Most material was free-issue from the main contractor and hence the stock control aspects of standard computer packages were thought to be of little use. There was ample space to store work-in-progress. However, a major concern was the frequent need for rescheduling jobs in the factory. There was also a long-term problem with information storage as a job might require repeats some years later and all information and CNC tapes must be retained. The company worked to Ministry of Defence quality standards, which require, a copious quality of paperwork. Two Apple micro-computers were used for wages and basic accounting.

A six-day week was worked with two shifts on most machines. Production planning was very 'hands-on' and could verge on chaos. Scheduling depended on machine availability, operator availability, customer priority and the need to maintain a reasonable cash flow.

The main components of the production support system were as follows:

- Tools – there was a need to improve the forecasting of tool use. This was an area where stock control problems had arisen with crucial and expensive stock-outs.
- Inspection – a vital area due to the high quality requirements in finished products.
- Final finish, packing and dispatch – however automated the machining, this area tended to be labour intensive and could be a major bottleneck if work volumes increased.
- Maintenance – some planned maintenance was carried out with one full-time mechanic being employed.

Routine mechanical maintenance was not seen to be a problem area. Electrical maintenance could easily be handled but electronic maintenance was very expensive. Though the electronic equipment was reliable, breakdowns would be expensive in repair costs and the value of work lost. Eventually the company might have to employ an electronics engineer on site.

Manning the factory

Direct labour was required for the 14 CNC machines. All skilled labour was used with one man per shift. The use of only skilled labour was an important decision. Strictly speaking, CNC machines do not require continuous high skill levels in manning. A setter could be employed for several machines and a less skilled operator the remainder of the time. However, in a small company, the right balance of setters would be hard to find and the use of skilled labour reduces both the number of mistakes made on the machines and also the need for patrol inspection. Mistakes made during machining are expensive as time and material is wasted.

Obtaining a complement of skilled operators was a major problem. The company required five more operators to increase shift working. Unemployment in the area among suitable candidates was low. The company employed individuals with basic skills in machining and the adaptability required in a small company. A newspaper advertisement had produced a poor response. Some success was obtained earlier with three individuals employed on a training grant. This finally produced one operator and one inspector. Fortunately the company was the only one of its type in the town and had no direct competition locally for skilled operatives. Its employees were drawn from up to 25 miles away with associated travel costs. The sharing of cars was arranged by management, particularly if awkward patterns of shift and weekend work were required.

Management emphasized how difficult a problem the labour market for skilled operators could be even with the advantages enjoyed by the company. Operators on the whole were young (maximum age 38) and somewhat variable in attitudes to work and the company. There was a need to match the type of work to the attitude of the operator. For example, if a job might require overtime at short notice, only certain operators were likely to agree. There was a fair level of flexibility in that most operators were primarily competent on the type of machine and could operate others, with the exception of some specialist new machines.

The balance between direct and indirect staff was a crucial issue. The number of indirect staff were strictly controlled. The works manager also acted as first line supervisor, a situation which could not hold in future years if expansion was to continue. One CNC programmer was employed to handle a very variable workload. Two inspectors were employed mainly for those finished goods where certification was needed. The company is about to employ a methods engineer. It was estimated that cycle times could be reduced by 10 – 25 per cent if better working practices were adopted.

Earlier in the year the company had cancelled an annual holiday week due to production changes and management helped operate the machines in order to meet customer demands. Though in the past such activity provided flexibility, it could hardly continue if the business was to grow much further.

Group exercises and points for discussion

(Note: Hill's framework for manufacturing strategy analysis provides a useful background for this case study)

1 For each of the four stages in the growth of the company, identify the following key factors:
    - the main markets being served;
    - the qualifying and order winning criteria for each market;
    - the process form in each case;
    - the principal manufacturing technology in use;
    - the human resource implications in each case.

2 Based on the identified factors, how stable was each 'plateau'? Could the company have successfully remained at an earlier plateau rather than continue with its development?

3 Based on the fourth plateau, carry out a SWOT analysis, that is identify the strengths and weaknesses of the company (in particular related to functional areas such as manufacturing, marketing, administration and finance) and the opportunities and threats present in the environment.

4 Further explore the current (1986) manufacturing process and infrastructure capability of the company with regard to technology, human resource management and design and manufacturing control systems.

5 What are the key operational problems facing the company at the present time? What changes would you recommend to improve the effectiveness of operations?

6 In the light of the above analysis, what future strategic direction would you recommend for the company and what further investment in operational resources and systems might this entail?

FURTHER OPERATIONAL CASES

The following are case studies from Johnston (1993) which relate to specific issues raised in Chapters 4 and 5:

Case 1 – Cadbury World
The operational management problems of a visitors' centre; relates to similar problems explored at the end of the Rovid case.

Case 8 – Royal Automobile Club
Includes problems in service capacity planning.

Case 18 – Holly Farm
Relates to service and manaufacturing capacity management.

Case 20 – Hillingdon Hospital

Service management, with particular reference to capacity problems, in a health care setting. A useful comparison is possible with similar manufacturing problem areas.

Case 24 – Lunn Poly Travel

Issues of service strategy.

Cases 28 and 29 – Huckleberry's (A and B)

Service strategy in a small enterprise.

CHAPTER 6

The management of quality

INTRODUCTION

The word 'quality', in recent management usage, has become over-ladened with a range of meanings and connotations which would have surprised all but the most ardent enthusiast of 30 years ago. The quality control literature of that time was technical, statistical and related to what we would now call a 'conformance' view of quality. The public use of the word was quite different. Before that time it was not considered to be a foolish mistake to equate quality with excellence!

In terms of their organizational roles, quality specialists had a narrow role concerned with enforcing standards. In an organization's system of checks and balances, the chief inspector was the man who would face up to the production director and refuse to pass substandard components or finished goods no matter what problems this caused material flow or customer liaison.

More recent thinking has embraced quality assurance, BS5750 and total quality management. The writings of Deming, Crosby and Juran are as much about general management principles as the narrow technical view of quality control. Quality is everyone's concern; it is 'job one' to use a popular slogan.

Before introducing definitions and concrete examples, some general principles underlying modern views of quality can be stated. First of all, as with all issues in this book, we are concerned with both product and service quality. These two may have some similarities but the differences provide real issues for operations management as well as other functions such as design and marketing.

Secondly, the idea of quality is linked to that other notoriously difficult concept, 'value'. We are concerned, as managers in organizations, with defining what is of value to customers and ensuring its supply. Quality management is a process concerned with every value-adding activity. Furthermore, total quality management (TQM) emphasizes the importance of the internal customer. Every transaction in an organization, every piece of work done or service rendered, should add value in a way which is relevant to some individual, whether an internal or external customer.

The third point is that 'quality', in the way we use the term here, relates to actual products and services. That is, the desired characteristics of products or services are defined through various research and design activities to produce a specification of what will meet reasonable requirements and expectations. At one extreme this will be a complex engineering document describing every product and manufacturing feature in quantifiable terms. It may also at the other extreme involve a service provider, say a medical practitioner or a travel agent, discussing needs and problems with a particular client and then suggesting a line of action.

This design process will be governed by a variety of considerations, including the economics and feasibility of supply. Product and service quality relates, however, to the actual rather than to the designed or intended. The customer experiences the actual product or service and this shapes his or her view of quality relative to expectations, requirements and needs. The important point is that quality is orientated to the experiences of real customers.

While asserting that TQM is relevant to all management, we would not wish to characterize the whole of management as TQM. Thus a customer may be concerned not only with the characteristics of a product but also the timeliness of its delivery. It is a matter of semantics whether the latter is termed a quality or a delivery issue. In a factory with a traditional organizational structure, 'quality' and 'delivery' are likely to be the responsibilities of different individuals. A personal service, however, may involve one provider and the two issues are intertwined. A simple approach may be to refer to the extent to which actual delivery meets its reasonable expectations as 'delivery quality'. This leads to a series of conjunctions such as 'design quality' (what is intended by the designer), 'product quality' (what a real customer actually gets in product terms), 'service quality', 'delivery quality' and so forth. Perhaps it would be easier to emphasize that for all activities and artifacts we should be concerned with how to match up reality to reasonable expectations. The process which addresses this issue is TQM.

DEFINITIONS OF QUALITY

Garvin (1988) includes an extensive discussion of the definitions and dimensions of quality. His five definitions may be briefly summarized as:

- Transcendent quality: an indefinable condition of excellence
- Product-based quality: related to differences in product attributes
- User-based quality: the capacity to satisfy user needs and preferences; fitness for use
- Manufacturing-based quality: conformance to requirements design or specification
- Value-based quality: excellence for use in a given situation for a given price.

Our line of argument most closely approximates his idea of 'user-based' quality and therefore we should consider his warning that individual preferences vary widely and any actual product or standardized service cannot hope to provide a precise match in all cases. We have, however, in our discussion emphasized 'reasonable' expectations. Product and service characteristics cannot be separated from price or from the alternative offerings of competitors. This moves our attention to value-based quality. The idea that we try to do our best for a 'customer' (that is an internal or external recipient of our services) given their actual situation and constraints of cost and price is most appealing but places great demands on operations in terms of flexibility and information requirements.

To a large extent, however user-driven we may be, generalizations about customer characteristics, decisions, trade-offs and compromises are necessary thus leading to specifications of the required characteristics of products and services or informal standards based on past practice. The issue for quality assurance then becomes one of whether an actual offering conforms to specification or standard, 'manufacturing-based' quality in Garvin's classification. This is a very familiar idea to quality practitioners. Indeed if we can rely on a specification as the operationalization of customer needs and expectations we are in a good position to use the tools and techniques of quality improvement to ensure that such standards are met, consistently and at minimum cost. Indeed for product and standardized services we shall assume that this is possible, with the warning, however, that customer expectations are a moving target and the currency of standards and specifications must be maintained. More personalized services are a different matter as we discuss later.

Having summarized Garvin's definitions of quality. It might be appropriate at this point to list his 'dimensions of quality'. These are performance, features, reliability, conformance, durability, serviceability, aesthetics and perceived quality. As well as providing a useful checklist these dimensions have a strategic use in market planning. Garvin discusses the situation where one wishes to compete against a market leader. A direct attack emphasizing the same quality dimensions as the brand leader may fail due to the combined effects of customer loyalty on demand and the experience curve on supply. He quotes the example of Yamaha (as a piano manufacturer) competing against Steinway through an emphasis on the reliability and conformance of pianos made on an assembly line rather the uniqueness of the more individually produced competitor's offerings.

One unusual aspect of the quality literature is that it is very personalized in reflecting the often trenchant views of key individuals, often referred to as the gurus of quality. The evolution of quality ideas is well summarized in Dale et al (1990) as a progression from inspection to quality control (often with a highly technical statistical bias) to quality assurance (with an emphasis on procedures and quality manuals) to TQM. The writings and consultancy of Philip Crosby, W. Edwards Deming, Joseph Juran and others have pushed practitioners along this evolutionary road. Common messages from the gurus include the importance of prevention rather than reworking, the need to spend time and attention in defining and measuring costs of quality, the possibility of zero defect production and above all else the importance of people in ensuring high quality production. Deming's 14 points include such advice as 'drive out fear', a recognition that quality improvement is not merely a technical exercise but founded in good general management principles.

A considerable emphasis must be placed on the implementation of quality improvement initiatives and the maintenance of good TQM practice. One puzzling feature of quality management is why the excellent advice of the gurus needed to be given at all. Why do so many organizations seem to have an inbuilt resistance to such ideas? The answer may lie in the transient nature of motivation, in the conflicting objectives which face managers in many situations, in the need for integrated and coordinated teamwork or in a lack of belief that consistent good quality is really achievable. To counter such barriers the gurus all give great emphasis to structured, organization wide implementation strategies for achieving sustainable improvements. We return to the practicalities of implementation at the end of this chapter.

TOTAL QUALITY MANAGEMENT

As we have mentioned total quality management (TQM) on several occasions above, with the suggestion that this idea represents current state-of-the-art quality management, we should perhaps here define what is meant by this term. Kanji (1990), in the first article in the *Total Quality Management Journal,* defines TQM in the following terms:

Quality – is to satisfy customer's requirements continually.
Total quality – is to achieve quality at low cost.
Total quality management – is to obtain total quality by involving everyone's daily commitment.

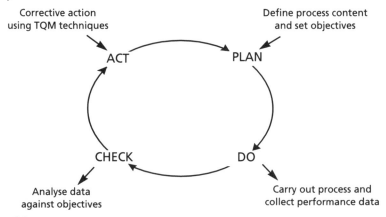

Figure 6.1
Plan-do-check-act cycle

Thus he describes quality as a process of continuous improvement ('Kaizen' in Japanese). This is embodied in the plan-do-check-act cycle (see Figure 6.1) which may be applied both tactically as a framework for the solution of specific quality problems or for the organization as a whole. The meaning of the terms in the cycle are:

- Plan – defining a process context and setting objectives
- Do – carrying out the process and collecting performance data
- Check – analyze the data against the objectives
- Act – take corrective action using TQM techniques and assess future plans.

This defines a feedback control system with the possibility of modifying current operational objectives, a key point in seeking continuous improvement.

Kanji emphasizes the strategic nature of TQM and the way this approach impinges on organizational culture and ethics. He also includes an impressively long list of TQM techniques. In another substantial text on TQM, Oakland (1989) lays special emphasis on the internal customer and goes on to detail a large and organizationally comprehensive set of TQM techniques. Indeed one of the great strengths of the TQM approach is this marriage between the strategic vision and the practical details. TQM copes equally well with issues of inter-functional cooperation as with the engineering technicalities of design and manufacturing. Perhaps this is why many organizations are finding this approach to be of value far beyond the limited objectives of cost cutting and short-term reduction of customer complaints.

QUALITY AND PRODUCT DESIGN

In the previous section we have emphasized the interfunctional nature of quality management and in particular the importance of design. Oakland (1989) and Dale et al (1990) include substantial discussion on suitable techniques to ensure that designed products are appropriate to customer needs whilst at the same time capable of cost-effective and consistent manufacture.

Burn (in Dale et al (1990)) sets out in some detail the ideas and methodology of quality function deployment (QFD), defined as:

> A system for translating consumer requirements into appropriate company requirements at every stage, from research, through product design and development to manufacture, distribution, installation and marketing, sales and service.

Quality functions deployment is concerned both with the full design cycle for a product and also with the product's life cycle itself, the continuing ability of the product to be attractive to consumers. A further objective is to counter any tendency for the engineer/designer to be overconfident and casual in making assumptions regarding customer needs. Similarly QFD is concerned with manufacturability and with cost. Thus we are here describing a genuinely strategic and interfunctional approach.

Oakland (1989) describes seven tools for quality design. These range from brainstorming aids (the affinity diagram) and logical analysis tools to the matrix diagrams used to inter-relate and analyse different tasks, functions and characteristics. Such techniques will perhaps be most familiar to marketing specialists working in the area of product development. Process decision charts are now used to translate the priorities uncovered by this analysis into the manufacturing and delivery systems.

Burn and others summarize this process as the 'house of quality', an integrated approach which moves systematically from customer needs and competitors' products to process and production planning within one rather large diagram. The choice between such specific techniques is a matter for the individual organization, but the underlying strategic principle is the use of a formal procedure which institutionalizes communication between all the principal actors in product design.

A more technical approach, with similar objectives but different emphasis, is the robust design methodology associated with Genichi Taguchi. A straightforward account is given in Phadke (1989).

Taguchi has a somewhat idiosyncratic, though appealing, definition of quality as 'the loss imparted by the product to society from the time the product is shipped' (see also the discussion in Cullen and Hollingum (1987)). Thus all manner of product problems from repair, inefficient operation and pollution to scrap costs become part of quality loss according to this definition. This 'Green' definition can hardly be faulted from an environmental perspective. It also has the advantage of concentrating attention on both design and manufacturing aspects of product quality. This reduces to what Phadke calls the fundamental principle of Robust Design, '..to improve the quality of a product by minimizing the effects of the causes of variation without eliminating the causes. This is achieved by optimizing the product and process designs to make the performance minimally sensitive to the various causes of variation'.

Taguchi concentrates on the ways products are made, the ways they are used and how they deteriorate over time. The techniques used are somewhat complex and statistical in nature but have the desirable strategic feature of encouraging a logical company wide approach to meeting customer requirements at minimum cost. The ideas inherent in the approach are also applicable to service contexts though their complexity and emphasis on quantifiable characteristics must be a barrier to their wide adoption outside the engineering profession.

While discussing product design issues it is opportune to mention the considerable impact which computer aided design and Manufacture (CADCAM) systems have on quality. Buxey (1991) discusses this specific issue, linking Garvin's dimensions of quality (augmented by the possible customer requirement of tailor-made products) to this technology.

There is nothing subtle or obscure in the quality benefits of CADCAM. Computer aided design (CAD) software often includes such elements as finite analysis, simulation and other engineering calculation packages which should make feasible the design of more sophisticated products, lead to fewer calculation errors and to designs better tailored to customer operating conditions. Information processing errors in transferring designs to manufacture should be reduced and the component technologies of computer aided manufacture (CAM) should enable better decision making in process planning and production flow planning and control. In addition automatic measurement and testing equipment (ATE) may be incorporated in computerized machining processes to monitor the key characteristics of machine performance and products on a real-time basis so that immediate corrective action may be undertaken as deviations from optimal performance occur.

Recent CAD systems may also include sophisticated product visioning capabilities so that essential product characteristics, such as size, colour, surface texture, may be electronically 'seen' in realistic contexts. For example the aesthetic and practical details of ceramic products (ranging from fine china to bathrooms) may be assessed by designers and customers.

Japanese manufacturers are reputedly obsessed with the collection and use of quality-related data. The plan-do-check-act cycle depends on it. At the heart of CADCAM and computer integrated manufacturing (CIM) systems is the effective handling of data. Thus CIM and quality management are fully complementary activities. Attention to quality (including data quality) is essential to CADCAM and CIM while on the other hand CADCAM directly addresses the quality management issues raised in this chapter (see for example Iijima and Hasegawa (1990) and Dwyer (1990)).

SERVICE ISSUES

In a survey of recent experiences of USA based service providers, Moores (1991) notes that the costs of non-conforming services may be as high as a quarter of sales turnover. Of particular worry is research findings that whilst 94 per cent of customers experiencing poor service would not complain about it, 91 per cent would not return but would relate their dissatisfactions to an extensive network of friends. These facts taken together show why service providers in competitive markets take service quality very seriously.

F

Much popular management literature actually addresses this subject, possibly as the reader as a consumer can most readily empathize with the message of service improvement. Indeed if we take the TQM idea of internal customers seriously, then service quality is an issue in all our daily transactions.

Though much quality literature seems dominated by manufacturing concerns, the quality gurus are broader in their concerns. Deming (1986) contains ample, if anecdotal, references to service quality covering medical care, teaching, banks, hotels and many others. His comments emphasize not only the great variety of service situations but the volume of transactions, and accompanying paperwork. Thus both front office and back room aspects of service quality are important.

One obvious point of interest, however, is the customer's perception of service received through direct contact with the staff of service providers. This may be a routine bank counter transaction, a medical consultation, service in a restaurant and so forth. It may be routine or personalized but the situation is assessed by the customer in terms of satisfaction given. In addition the customer may participate, as in a supermarket, and may certainly offer continual feedback to the service provider. Thus the behaviour of front-line staff is clearly important. This is emphasized by Moores:

> Empowering those at the sharp end to be able to respond constructively and imaginatively to customer concerns begets its own particular brand of creative thinking.

Indeed service provision has a number of potential advantages through direct customer feedback (if encouraged), participation and staff motivation (if fostered). One attractive model of service quality concentrates on the following factors:

- Professional judgement and competence of the service provider. Is the customer receiving a good service in terms of options on offer, advice given, care in relating the service to their needs and so forth.
- Behaviour of the direct service provider, i.e. courtesy and so forth.
- Processes and procedures which are in operation.

It is amusing to note occasions when these are unbalanced. A cold but efficient service may be appropriate in some instances but not in others. Similarly we are all familiar with the friendly but hopelessly muddled shop assistant. In a much quoted list Parasuraman et al (1985) discuss the determinants of service quality (included here with brief explanatory comments):

- Reliability – the correct service is provided every time
- Responsiveness – providing prompt and willing service
- Competence – the server has required skills and knowledge

- Access – contact is easy
- Courtesy – the service is polite and respectful
- Communication – the service is well explained in understandable terms
- Credibility – the organization and direct service provider are trustworthy and believable
- Security – freedom from physical danger; confidentiality is assured
- Understanding – taking care to learn a customer's specific needs
- Tangibles – facilities, appearance of personnel, quality of materials used.

This wide range of service quality issues, in addition to product quality concerns, demonstrate the need for service quality missions, visions, strategies and concrete plans. At one level, service strategy is easy to outline:

- Find out what the customer wants
- Decide how best to deliver the service
- Develop your staff to perform the delivery effectively
- Monitor the result in terms of customer satisfaction.

Not surprisingly this is far harder to carry out than to state. A useful further model from Parasuraman et al (1985) defines quality as gaps between perceptions and expectations, the service equivalent of non-conformance. The authors define no less than five potential gaps which must be filled:

- *Customer expectation v management perception:*
  Service providers do not understand which aspects of a service are valued by customers.
- *Management perception v service quality specification:*
  Service provision managers know what is required by customers but fail to specify it, possibly because they feel the requirement is unreasonable or too expensive to provide.
- *Service quality specification v service delivery:*
  The specified service is not delivered, possibly a failing in staff training and monitoring.
- *Service delivery v external communications:*
  The provider has promised, through media promotions, more than can be consistently delivered.
- *Expected service v perceived service:*
  The actual service delivered appears to have fallen short of expectation. This may be due to poor communication at the point of service, possibly as the customer has erroneous views on what is possible.

This rather complex set of possibilities is simplified in the model shown in Figure 6.2. It will be seen that the model applies equally to product and service situations while drawing on service concepts. Obviously this cross fertilization of ideas is valuable within the general TQM philosophy.

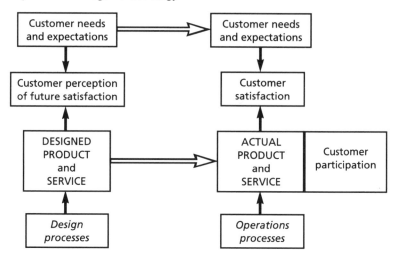

Figure 6.2
Service quality dynamics

As with manufactured goods, a mass service provider in particular may well develop extensive procedures for quality assurance (for example based on ISO 9004-2:1991 (E)). Similarly a providing organization may make use of the same range of quality improvement techniques. It is important that the application of such procedures fully recognize the specific nature of service quality, in particular the fact that customer expectations are constantly changing.

PUBLIC SECTOR ISSUES

A recent government fashion in the UK is the issuing of 'Charters' relating to the level of service provided by public bodies such as the NHS, BR and education. The idea that a public body should define the level of service it intends to provide and then be held accountable is obviously welcome though naturally raises a number of issues such as the process by which such standards are set.

Coote and Pfeffer (1991) analyse the meaning of 'quality' in a public service context and extend the concept in a new direction. They identify five generic meanings of 'quality' of which the first three are well known and briefly mentioned below:

- Traditional approach conveying the notion of prestige
- Scientific approach of conformance to standards
- Managerial or excellence approach measuring customer satisfaction.

The fourth meaning departs somewhat from these ideas by defining the 'consumerist approach' as follows:

...quality is achieved by empowering consumers. While the 'excellence' approach expresses the desire of providers to satisfy customers, the consumerist approach expresses the desire of customers to be satisfied. It casts the customers in an active role and seeks to increase their power to the point where they – as 'sovereign consumers' – hold sway over the decision-making of the providers.

This is related to the consumer movement and consumer related legislation. It uses the political language of rights and power rather than the economic language of competition, though obviously the two are related.

The authors then go further and speculate on the possibility of a fifth approach, referred to as the 'democratic approach', as being more suitable in a welfare situation. This embryonic concept emphasizes openness, participation, planning as well as empowerment. It recognizes that some public service situations we are both customers and providers.

These latter approaches are at the very least useful in reminding us that just as we have to be careful in applying product quality concepts in a commercial service situation, we also have to be careful when taking the further step into the public sector. Service providers are already sensitive to the effects of customer participation in service delivery. Here we are examining the implications of customer participation in service planning and objective setting.

An interesting example of such a situation is provided by higher education. What is the meaning of 'quality' in a university context? Some possibilities (reflecting the Coote and Pfeffer approaches) include:

● Academic excellence
● Conformance to specified attributes of the curriculum
● Meeting the needs of students.

However there are other stakeholders in this situation; past students, funding bodies and the local community for example. Do their perceptions of quality differ from current staff and students? To what extent should students and staff, as current actors in this transformational drama, be empowered to change key aspects of the situation in order to 'improve' some aspect of quality, possibly at the expense of another. Most universities in fact have well-established and democratic mechanisms for quality management but one wonders how capable they are of managing change in the current environment.

STRATEGIC QUALITY MANAGEMENT AND BENCH-MARKING

A number of studies, not least of which is the influential PIMS approach, have shown that profitability is positively correlated with quality. Traditionally managers have been all too aware of the costs of producing high quality goods (if less aware of the real costs of non-conformance – see below). It appears that in the right circumstances the revenue from high quality manufacture and service provision can exceed cost.

Garvin (1988) addresses the strategic advantages of quality explicitly both in terms of cost saving and as a competitive weapon to increase market share. This may refer to any of the dimensions of quality mentioned earlier. He specifically explores the 'correlates of quality' in the following terms.

Conventional thinking suggests that price and quality should be positively correlated. The simple argument is that higher quality goods are more expensive to make and therefore sell at a higher price. Yet the situation is far more complex. Consumers have imperfect information on the actual quality of a product or service and may even use price as an indicator of quality before purchase and be unwilling to change their minds after. Thus higher price is the cause of a perception of higher quality, a curious and statistically awkward state of affairs. More detailed studies suggest that price is related to different dimensions of quality in different ways depending on the circumstances. Explorations of the relationship between advertising and quality reveal a similar complex picture. Perhaps consumers are as adept as marketing professionals in playing this communication game.

It is possibly counterproductive to even ask if quality and market share are directly related. If we choose features and performance as our favoured dimensions then the resulting high price will tend to lead to smaller volume, though whether this is the same as smaller market share depends on the definition of a particular market. There may be no reason why improved conformance or superior aesthetic design should lead to higher costs and hence the potential for using these as a market share enhancing weapon exists. A company may not choose to do so, however. It may prefer to charge a premium price and more directly affect short-term profits.

The relationship between cost, productivity and quality are discussed in the next section which concludes that low cost, high productivity and high conformance quality make a perfectly feasible trio. The upshot of this argument is that no automatic correlations should be assumed between these key strategic variables. The discussion depends on organizational objectives, on the choice of quality dimension and the effectiveness of operations management in delivering expected benefits.

An interesting and highly important issue in this competitive process is that of bench-marking. Ideas surrounding this approach and a case study of its application to Royal Mail are to be found in Jackson (1990). She defines bench-marking as:

- measuring your performance against that of best-in-class companies;
- determining how the best in class achieve those performance levels;
- using the information as the basis for your own company's strategies and implementation.

An extended case study of the use of total quality management at Royal Mail is to be found in Bank (1992).

This process of systematic measurement and comparison is not only applied to products and services but to all internal and external transactions, a true use of the TQM philosophy. Its most diligent use appears to have been by Japanese companies ('dantotsu' – strive to be the best of the best) with more recent converts including Xerox, IBM and so forth.

The term bench-marking covers a range of situations. Bench-marking may be competitive (related to products and services in comparison to competitors) or related to processes. Process bench-marking may involve comparison with similar processes in other organizations or comparison between similar processes in different parts of the same organisation. External process benchmarking, the focus of the Royal Mail case study included below, may involve comparisons with direct competitors or may be generic, that is involve comparison with similar general processes in any industry.

Bench-marking is another example of a structured approach involving the whole organisation and being sustained indefinitely. It is thus intended to yield strategic and lasting benefits. Its implementation is not without problems and costs, though added benefits might well include improved motivation and a widening of the vision of employees.

Key problems of implementation include empowerment, ethics and maintaining impetus. If bench-marking is devolved down an organization then the discovery that improvement is possible will only lead to frustration is implementation is blocked. Thus thought has to be given to the degree of autonomy allowed in making changes and the need to disseminate good practice throughout an organization.

As bench-marking involves the gathering of potentially sensitive data, some thought must be given to the boundary between legitimate enquiry and industrial espionage. It is obvious that the mutual sharing of commercially non-critical information between organizations is preferable where a long-term bench-marking strategy is in place.

Maintaining impetus is a problem bench-marking shares with all quality initiative, indeed it is a fundamental problem in the management of organizational change. It is addressed at various points in this book though with no pretence that a magic solution exists.

HOSHIN KANRI – ACHIEVING MAJOR ORGANIZATIONAL CHANGE

Whatever the rhetoric, it is all too easy for quality improvement to become a tactical, shop-floor issue. It is not enough for senior management to support TQM ideals for others in the organization. They must practise it at a policy level. Following Wood and Munshi (1991), Hoshin Kanri is 'target and means control', or policy deployment. It may be viewed as the application of the **Plan-do-check-act** cycle at an organizational level (see Figure 6.3):

> Management has a responsibility to innovate and bring about quantum leap improvements from within the organization itself. Hoshin Kanri is a systematic method for focusing the activities of an organization on critical breakthrough areas.
> (Wood and Munshi (1991)

It is complementary to the more routine applications of quality improvement programmes. Indeed Hoshin Kanri and daily control are the two fundamental improvement cycles of TQM.

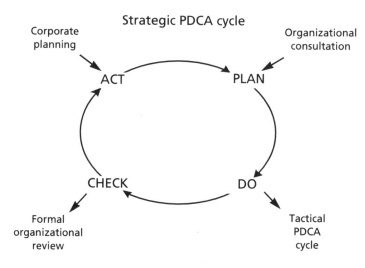

Figure 6.3
Hoshin Kanri

Working on an annual cycle (though a shorter cycle might initially be more appropriate), we begin with an extensive and formal review (**check**) of organizational achievements, learning and problems in the context of changing environmental factors and customer needs.

The next stage is a revision (**act**) of corporate direction and long-term plans. The result is a 'future action' framework which, in distinctive Japanese style, is modified by organizational consultation through a deployment stage (**plan**). This is a critical feature of this methodology:

> A salient feature of Hoshin Kanri is the extent to which the targets and means initiated at the corporate level are extensively modified through 'bottom-up' feedback. The traditional 'top-down' approach is forsaken for an approach which allows the creativity of lower management to contribute to final plan formula-

tion. This involvement of lower management also results in full 'ownership' and understanding of the plan at all levels.
(Wood and Munshi 1991)

The final implementation stage (DO) now integrates tactical quality improvement (PDCA) actions with this strategic approach. As one might expect, continual monitoring and adjustment must be carried out and the results fed back into the next cycle of Hoshin Kanri.

This elegant linking of strategic and tactical quality planning gives some substance and a set of planning procedures to what may otherwise be a facile phrase, quality is a strategic issue!

COSTS OF QUALITY

One of the major conceptual breakthroughs in quality management has been the insistence that great care and attention be given to the measurement of the costs of poor quality. We have already mentioned the Taguchi definition of quality which, via the concept of 'loss to society' formally places quality in an economic context. However, the operationalization of this economic idea is far from easy.

If we begin from a simple view of quality costs we can easily identify the following:

- The internal costs of scrap, rework and retesting due to the production of defective product.
- The external costs of warranty work and replacement of faulty goods sent to the customer.
- Appraisal costs (inspection, testing and audits).
- The administrative costs associated with the above.

With care the above may be quantified, though it should not be assumed that reliable data always exists for this to be a trivial matter. It requires little imagination to arrive at a further set of possible costs:

- Loss of sales and goodwill due to faulty goods being put on the market, and also due to extended delivery lead times caused by quality problems.
- Prevention costs (planning, training, reporting and so forth).

Some care should be exercised here in that prevention costs are intentionally incurred and thus we are here in a decision making rather than a cost recording situation. This, however, is by no means the end of quality economics. There are a wide range of indirect costs incurred by non-conforming processes (see Figure 6.4):

- Downtime (including that of associated processes) caused by quality problems.

- Loss of capacity due to quality problems, and the need to build excess capacity into the planning process if poor quality is routinely expected.
- Excessive lead times due to quality problems, and the use of excessive lead times as a buffer in case of future quality problems.
- Excessive stock holding as a buffer against quality related delays. It is quite likely that if high stock levels are held for this reason, a fair part of such stock will also be obsolete.

The costs of quality
Basic costs
Scrap, rework and retest
Warranty work and replacement of faulty goods
Appraisal costs (inspection, test and audit)
Administration costs
Derived costs
Loss of sales and goodwill
Prevention costs
Systems costs
Downtime
Loss of capacity
Excessive lead-times
Excessive stock-holding

Figure 6.4
Cost of quality

Interestingly one notes that cost may be incurred not only as a direct result of actual non-conformance but in the routine expectation of future poor performance. Though one can hardly blame production planners for acting rationally in the face of past experiences of schedules ruined by rejected batches and machine overhauls, this is a particularly unfortunate situation. Any type of buffer held to ameliorate the effects of poor quality manufacture not only condones but hides the problem thus leading to a self-reinforcing cycle of poor quality, productivity and service. This is in addition to the very considerable costs of excessive stock holding.

We can therefore see why JIT manufacturers (see Chapter 7) place such an emphasis of TQM. One of the costs of poor quality is that man-ufacturer is excluded from the potential vast benefits of just-in-time production.

The traditional view of quality economics is that there is an optimum trade-off between prevention and rework which is somewhat short of zero-defects. This view often fails to fully appreciate the indirect costs of quality. Thus more recent references emphasize extensive systems for routinely capturing quality costs (e.g. see Oakland (1989)) as well as non-financial measures of performance (e.g. of vendors) and reporting on these on a regular basis. This information is then fed into regular planning and action cycles.

However, comments above on JIT, and our discussion on financial aspects of operations in Chapter 3, suggest that an alternative decision making framework is possible. Indeed quality issues should be part of other decision agendas. Andreou (1991), Berliner and Brimson (1988) explore ways in which direct non-conformance quality related actions are non-value adding activities (adopting strategic management frameworks such as Porter (1985)), should be reported via activity based costing systems (including a careful identification of non-conformance cost drivers uncovered using quality improvement techniques) and directly related to business performance measures such as return on investment and (quality) project net present values.

There is always a danger that extensive cost gathering is not linked to decisions and actions. Fortunately TQM has a number of action-based improvement cycles that can make good use of such data. What must not be ignored is the importance of this data for decision making and improvement projects in other spheres of company activity, in particular design and material flow planning.

QUALITY IMPROVEMENT PROGRAMMES

Our discussion above has concentrated on fundamental issues and the ways in which our whole conception of quality affects operations. Most texts on quality quite rightly place equal emphasis on the techniques, procedures and motivational requirements for quality improvements. Though it is not appropriate here to describe these in detail, a typical list would include (see Bank (1992)) flow charting of a process, measuring and data gathering, statistical analysis, capability studies, statistical process control, use of problem solving tools (brainstorming, Ishikawa diagram, Pareto diagram for instance), quality cost analysis and other similar tried and tested techniques. This activity should always take place in the context of formal team-based quality improvement programmes which in turn must be fully supported by senior management. The latter point is critical. Quality improvement activity crosses the boundaries of organizational responsibilities and often results in criticism of existing practices. Real support from the top is always necessary to support quality improvement teams and resolve organizational problems.

A further set of useful techniques is to be found in Oakland (1989) in the context of TQM practice. He recommends a set of questions to be applied in any customer-provider situation to tease out customer needs on a continual basis. These might be used as part of a formal quality improvement programme but are perhaps most valuable when they are habitually used on a day-to-day basis. There is nothing sacrosanct about the techniques mentioned here. Large organizations often put together their 'this is how we do things here' procedures involving methods of investigation which are particularly appropriate in a given context. Whilst not wishing to inhibit innovation, the re-invention of the wheel seems wasteful of time and resources and the strategic management of quality improvement programmes involves some hard choices on the most cost-effective way to proceed. Industry as a whole is some way along the TQM learning curve and it seems appropriate to tap into the experience of others in planning one's own programmes. Perhaps some form of bench-marking of other organizations' best quality management practice is a good starting point for senior management.

Many employees and managers know of quality management ideas mainly through attempts to gain BS5750 or ISO 9000 accreditation. Though providing motivation and a concrete goal to aim for it appears that such a 'big bang' approach may be counterproductive, particularly in small firms, and detract from the ideal of continuous improvement by all employees. This is of course not the intention and quality manuals should on the contrary ensure that continuous improvement takes place. The real issue here possibly revolves around organizational culture and the management of change. The main strategic priority for senior managers is to decide on the most appropriate approach in a given context and whilst this may include BS5750 for commercial as well as motivational reasons real attempts must be made to develop a TQM working culture in all organizations.

CONCLUSIONS

Whether we are referring to a product or a service, TQM is a management process driven by customer needs, requiring information and necessitating routine and creative decision making and control. Though we have explored the 'what is quality' question, the real operational focus must be on continually satisfying customers within economic constraints. We must add value for customers, or to use a more recent phrase particularly suitable for educational situations 'create value with the customer'.

All texts on quality management emphasize the importance of communication in this context. Indeed a systems view of quality related information flows is most useful. In a product situation these are illustrated in Figure 6.5 but this in turn must be seen as dynamic and involving the concepts explored earlier as shown in Figure 6.2.

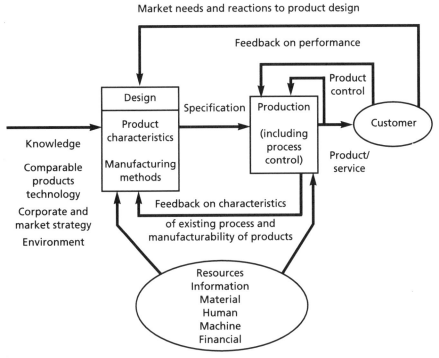

Figure 6.5
Communications model of product quality management

A number of strategic issues have been discussed above but in addition we might note the following concerns as fundamental to operations strategy:

1 How broad and variable (over time and between individuals) is the range of customer expectations? It is important to know whether a particular customer is likely to reasonably expect, for example, a short list of standard product features competently delivered or a tailored personal service. This has considerable implications for process choice and the extent of interfunctional working (for example between production, sales and design).

2 What is the time scale of satisfaction, that is for what length of time must the customer be supported?

3 We have used the word 'quality' as an attribute of a product or service. Yet in everyday language, and advertising, it is often attached to the producer or service provider. This is not merely a public relations exercise when operations are visible, have a large service component or when their future depends on loyal and well informed customers.

4 TQM literature sometimes seems naive in assuming the 'customer' is readily identifiable. Marketing literature is more sophisticated in this respect and perhaps in many cases TQM could be sharpened by some form of stakeholder analysis or use of soft systems methods (see Chapter 1) to explore the underlying rationale for a given transformational system, particularly in public sector situations such as health or education delivery.

CHAPTER 7

Materials management systems

INTRODUCTION

We now move to an area of operations strategy which has, over the years, caused considerable problems for management. One of the most obvious priorities from the customer's point of view is that manufactured goods should arrive when required, or at least when promised. This requires careful management of the flow of materials by the manufacturer. Now this might sound straightforward to the inexperienced but the sheer complexity of manufacturing logistics and shop-floor operations coupled with the unfortunate opportunities for delay and confusion which exist in any manufacturing system make timely delivery a considerable challenge. Our everyday experiences of delays in receiving promised household goods demonstrates that this challenge is often not met with great success.

In this chapter we explore four dominant methodologies in planning stocks and flows of materials (see Figure 7.1), with a particular emphasis on manufacturing companies where these issues are often critical. It is assumed that the reader has some familiarity with the systems under discussion, either through practical experience or prior studies in operations management.

SSC Scientific stock control	MRP MRP II Manufacturing resource planning
JIT Just-in-time	OPT Optimized production technology

Figure 7.1
Production management systems

It will be evident from the above that most of the material in this chapter relates to manufacturing. The parallel problem in managing personal service systems is controlling the flow of customers, with a particular reference to queuing systems. This somewhat technical subject is dealt with in most standard texts on operations management, though the reader might consult Lovelock (1989) for a more 'psychological' approach to queue management. Our discussion of scientific stock control is largely applicable to non-manufacturing concerns and the potential for using JIT and OPT in offices and retail outlets is obvious.

KEY IDEAS IN THE MANAGEMENT OF MATERIAL FLOW

All texts on operations and production management spend time on this area, traditionally under the heading of stock control but more recently examining popular topics such as JIT, MRP and OPT. Much of the traditional approach, therefore, is either highly mathematical or consists of expositions of packaged 'philosophies'. Both may be misleading in stating the results of specific mathematical analyses or company practices without exploring the assumptions on which they are based.

We can hardly ignore the details of important methods of stock and flow management but our strategic perspective leads us to attempt at least to summarize the principles on which the differing approaches are based. This will be done prior to an exposition of the individual methods in order to focus attention on fundamental issues and the main strategic decision of which approach to adopt in a specific instance.

The key ideas which affect systems design for planning and controlling material flow are presented as a set of questions in the following sections.

Uniformity: are all parts of the material flow system handled in the same way?

A common recommendation in stock control literature is to apply a Pareto analysis to prioritize items so that those with a high value of annual usage are controlled more tightly. Though one can appreciate the common sense advantages of this, a low valued item may be critical to a product and, if in short supply, may delay delivery.

A more sophisticated variant of prioritization is the identification of bottlenecks and their regions of influence in OPT. Areas of production which directly affect the flow of goods to a bottleneck resource are treated differently from those which may be managed independently of any bottlenecks. A practical example of this is seen in many manufacturers of ceramic goods where a continuously operating kiln must have a carefully timetabled input. The physical management of material inputs and outputs associated with such a facility can cause considerable problems and tend to dominate flow management.

Aggregation: what size of system is being managed as an integrated whole?

Scientific stock control makes a virtue of systems disaggregation. In fact the use of stock and other buffers to decouple decision making and control in differing parts of a logistical chain is a perfectly reasonable approach provided one understands the trade-offs involved. MRP on the other hand makes a virtue of the central planning of stocks and flows throughout a large system.

Buffering: how can individual sub-systems be separated so that variations in one does not affect others?

There are a number of ways of decoupling systems so that they may be managed in isolation. We refer to these as systems buffers and they have the further advantage of helping us overcome the effects of uncertainty in demand, capacity, quality and so forth. Typical systems buffers are the use of stocks of materials, inflated lead times, spare capacity used only on an emergency basis and so forth.

It should be said immediately that the intentional long-term use of such buffers is totally at variance with the JIT approach. The experienced JIT practitioner will know that in the short term they will be unavoidable but the evolutionary aim is to eliminate the need for them through better quality control, preventive maintenance, flexible workforce and so forth.

Underlying this debate there seems to be a suspicion that buffers are just too convenient a device for making life easy for day-to-day management at the expense of the company as a whole. The Japanese attack on such practices is based as much on ethical as logical considerations. Buffers allow us to avoid the evils of Muri, Muda and Mura (excess, waste and unevenness; see Schonberger (1982)) which should be faced up to and eliminated rather than condoned. Goldratt and Fox (1986) argue a similar point by showing how synchronized manufacturing (i.e. OPT) working with low inventory has wide ranging beneficial effects which more than outweigh the inconvenience of minimal buffering.

Visibility versus data-base management: how can the system be viewed?

Early manufacturing systems were directly controlled by workers, supervisors and managers. 'Management by walking about' is not a recent invention. The increased bureaucratization of Ford-style production led to the possibility that planning and control decisions could be based on paper, and, more recently, computer records. This entails an accurate data model of a production unit where the essential features for material flow control may be measured and communicated to managers/controllers in sufficient time and with sufficient accuracy for good decisions to be made. This is the basis of computer aided production management (CAPM).

It is not surprising that CAPM is much concerned with data validity. Indeed modern data recording devices such as bar coding are particularly useful in such contexts. There is an obvious danger, though, that management becomes remote from key issues and events in the workplace and manages by what is measurable (stock levels, recorded times for example) rather than by what is important. This, however, should not be interpreted as a drawback of CAPM but rather as a warning on management style.

At the opposite extreme, JIT-style approaches work with direct management of flows by local supervision using pull scheduling techniques. Whilst examples of company success are most persuasive in showing the benefits of this approach, which incidently fits in well with modern approaches to leadership and involvement by management, one must ask what is the real scope of individual vision. How much of the total picture can the shop-floor-based manager see? In particular, how much of the customer and his needs is visible? Once again this should not be taken as a drawback of JIT but as a challenge. Might some combination of electronic databases and direct visual control, allied to TQM concepts of client interaction, provide an excellent model for effective manufacturing management?

Learning: how can the system learn and improve?
To put the argument in a simple and blunt manner, do we expect material planning and control systems to be designed by experts (from within an organization or external consultants) and implemented with the expectation that they then produce the required performance; or do we think such systems will evolve over time through a process of trial and error?

We are concerned here with how an organization learns to control its material flows (i.e. what systems to use and what performance to expect), whether systems implementation should be revolutionary or evolutionary, who is empowered to change a system's operation and the extent to which the 'design space' for such a system is closed on initial implementation or is open to future action and adjustment.

Integration: in what ways and to what extent should the system be integrated?
The vision of some CAPM specialists is that such a system will plan and control all aspects of manufacturing and distribution operations – a totally integrated system. Though one may see many potential advantages in this approach, some critical points must be addressed.

The first, quite simply, is what is meant by integration in this context? Many studies have recognized the potential difficulties of defining integration in CAPM, for example Waterlow and Moniot (1986). In a slightly more general context (Integrated Manufacturing) Voss (1989) extends their work in suggesting the following five 'dimensions' of integration:

- Strategy (manufacturing, markets, finance and so forth)
- Material flow (inter-site and within sites)
- Technical (compatible hardware, software and so forth)
- Information (common data definitions and entry)
- Organizational.

Strategic integration has been extensively discussed in the last decade, a useful UK based guide being Hill (1985). In such work, CAPM is seen as one possible facilitating technology for the manufacturing infrastructure. More recently the work of Gregory and colleagues in developing a systematic approach to manufacturing audit explicitly considers the role of CAPM:

> Even when the implementation of CAPM is technically perfect, CAPM rarely improves business performance significantly unless the controls are operated for the good of the business overall ... Manufacturing audit should always precede significant changes to CAPM systems in a business.
> (ACME 1990 p.25)

Material flow and technical integration are at the heart of CAPM systems design. Similarly information integration is at the heart of computer integrated manufacturing (CIM) and it should be noted that Browne et al (1988) see CAPM very much within a CIM perspective. Not only does CIM require a fast and effective material flow planning and control system but the automated data capture of a CIM system is particularly valuable for ensuring database validity in CAPM.

Organizational integration, despite its categorization by Voss, receives relatively little attention. In a CIM context the problems are critically analysed by Ebers and Lieb (1989). One particular point which is strongly made is that:

> ... CIM is a technical solution to an organizational problem. To be successful, both administrative and technical innovations must proceed at a balanced rate.

In more detail a particular problem occurs when CAPM/CIM are naively implemented:

> One problem in CIM implementation ... is that as a company searches for economies while automating, it reduces organizational slack (spare capacity) and thus removes the system's buffering which previously absorbed uncertainty. The increased systems' coupling which is the objective of CIM reduces the total sys-

tem's ability to cope in the face of environmental turbulence and data inaccuracy. There is a greater risk of inappropriate data being used as less human filtering takes place.
(Ebers and Lieb 1989)

Though the above issues have been selected as particularly pertinent to material flow management, it will be evident to the reader that fundamental issues addressed throughout this book are always present, i.e. what operational process has been chosen, what does the customer want, what do we expect of the people who are part of our operational system and so forth. It is for this reason that we are concentrating so much attention on flow management rather than dismiss it as a set of arcane infrastructure techniques.

THE BASIC METHODOLOGIES FOR MANAGING MATERIAL FLOWS

It would be nonsense to ignore accumulated wisdom and practice in this area and not to consider existing approaches in detail. Indeed this has already happened in the previous section. We now outline the four approaches which seem to underlie current thinking. For ease of exposition these will be discussed as separate entities, though in practice companies adopt unique and idiosyncratic mixtures.

Scientific stock control

It should be obvious that stocks and flows together are essential features of systems models in this area. By comparison environmental systems, demographic and manpower planning models illustrate the interplay of these features. It is curious therefore that traditional production management theory from the early part of this century should give such an emphasis to stock control. Perhaps this orientation reflects an accounting view of the firm where the measurement of stock value is an important task in constructing accounting statements. Yet the holding of stock is not usually seen as a value adding activity!

Stock control tended to be viewed separately from production planning and control, the latter usually including the control of work in progress but not major inter-process stocks. Queuing theory models and complex scheduling algorithms were often recommended for production planning in its tactical sense. Aggregate production planning involves strategic decisions on stock levels which we will consider later.

Scientific stock control (SSC) has as its basic unit of analysis an item of stock held at a particular location. This stock may be held for a number of reasons though the most obvious are the following:

- Decoupling production processes within a firm or decoupling the firm from its environment either at the input (raw material stocks) or output (finished goods) stage.
- Counteracting seasonal fluctuations in supply or demand.
- Securing economies of scale in supply, distribution or manufacture.

The approach is usually to set up some more or less elaborate system for forecasting demand (often based on a statistical analysis of past usage) and then to attempt to control inputs in terms of amount and frequency with the objective of cost minimization for a given level of output service. Costs are usually seen as those incurred by holding stock and those incurred by ordering stock. The level of sophistication of the resulting prescriptive formulae then depends on the simplifying assumptions made in the analysis. Standard texts give the details of this approach (e.g. see Silver and Peterson (1985)) and therefore we will concern ourselves only with a critique.

A typical SSC model for stock replenishment might include the following factors:

- Decision variables:
  - Order quantity
  - Re-order level
- Forecast variables:
  - Demand average, variability and pattern
  - Lead time of supply
- Constants:
  - Holding cost per unit
  - Ordering cost
  - Shortage costs
  - Price schedule (which may include quantity discounts for large orders).

One notes immediately that no mention is made of quality, human factors, organizational structure, strategy and so forth. SSC theory is neutral in such terms, though the implementation literature may contain some common sense advice. This may well be an unsatisfactory position as illustrated in SSC Example 1 below. In this example we show an occasion in which such a limited approach is not satisfactory.

SSC Example 1

A company manufacturing a range of pharmaceutical products has a central receiving and storage point for raw materials. In the mid-1970s order processing and administration for this facility was carried out manually but supposedly in line with a strict set of procedures. A manager was given the task of computerizing this system, but being of a cautious disposition he began by observing the operation of the system. The following are some of the points noted in this investigation:

1 The formal procedures were not logical, not complete and often not used! If they had been used mechanistically then one alarming effect would have been that goods received but later returned to the supplier having failed quality checks would have remained on the books. Staff operating the manual system made a number of routine adjustments to make the system work, but were not motivated to write these down as formal changes to the procedure.

2 A statistical analysis of ordering behaviour over a period of time showed that excess stock was held for a number of lines but stock levels tended to come down as the manager was carrying out his study. The reason for this was a matter of speculation though one possibility was worker reaction to being observed.

3 One particularly expensive and disruptive stockout occurred during the study period. This was particularly puzzling as statistical analysis of supply and usage in the period showed no problems. It appeared that when stocks of one particular item were becoming low, demand accelerated causing a stockout and the costly obtaining of emergency supplies, which turned out to be unnecessary! Investigation showed that supervisors on individual product lines, fearing a shortage, withdrew material from stock earlier than strictly necessary. Though the central store ran out of this material, the factory as a whole had plenty. The 'stockout' was a phantom!

This investigation demonstrated to company senior managers the need for a materials control systems strategy rather than a local computerization of a manual system. They proceeded to investigate and implement an MRP system. In 1990 a further study in this company addressed the lack of effectiveness of a series of MRP and data processing systems. This later project demonstrated the need for a business and operations strategy to properly define the objectives of future CAPM developments.

The next point to note is that great care must be taken when relating decisions to forecasts based on past data and past decisions. SSC Example 2 explores the reliability of lead-time data in this context.

SSC Example 2

A junior manager in a large office has been given the task of setting up a simple ordering system for office consumables. Following a standard textbook he attempts to define a re-order level for a particular high usage item. Examination of historical data for the supply lead time shows great variability which would entail high buffer stocks for his system. Yet a casual conversation with more experienced colleagues suggests that these items can be obtained at very short notice by the simple expediency of a phone call.

Investigation reveals that the recorded lead time is more a measure of clerical inefficiency than supplier delay. If stocks are low and the order is vigorously expedited, items will arrive almost immediately. If stocks remain adequate, nobody chases up the order and little happens.

It is unwise to trust data unless you are fully aware of the intricacies of the measurement and recording process which produced the data and the human situation in which the measured phenomenon occurred.

Decision making in SSC

The decisions made in SSC are on the basis of trade-offs relating to costs which are essentially considered to be constant. A common equation used is the EBQ formula, much derided by JIT practitioners. In this case a cost balance is struck between holding and ordering costs leading to the prescriptive formula:

Economic batch size = square root(2*Co*D/Ch)

where D is average demand, Ch is the holding cost per unit per annum and Co is the ordering cost per order occasion. The latter may be a machine set-up cost if this formula is used for in-process or finished goods stock.

Now the holding cost is mainly dominated by the cost of capital (though it is often not clear whether an average or marginal cost has been used) along with some notion of warehousing and other storage costs. The latter will of course be an average despite the fact that warehouse costs are largely fixed. Ordering cost is similarly an average despite the fact that administrative costs are likely once again to be fixed for a company in the medium term. The problem is that the cost balance (Co/Ch) depends largely on average historic costs with no incentive to take action to reduce costs.

An alternative view of this formula is to note that dramatic reductions in ordering cost (and in particular machine set-up cost) will allow far smaller batch sizes to be economically feasible. That is a different view of the same economic model (Co is a factor to be reduced rather than a constant) leads to a quite different prescription. Yet this model was traditionally used as a prescription for batch sizes rather than a vehicle for expressing key relationships in a system. The real problem may be that most practitioners simply do not understand the mathematics of the model and hence can only use the final prescriptive equation. One may argue that this was not the intention, and operational research specialists might well be able to use such models more imaginatively, but it is probably naive to expect anything different.

Thus whilst SSC models many important relationships between systems factors, its basic language is worryingly close to the limits of the comprehension of most practitioners. Therefore it is either applied mechanically or its use is firmly in the domain of the expert, who may have a less than realistic grasp of the full system under consideration.

Factory-based uses of SSC are still valid if related to other ideas we explore below. Its use in retail and distribution is perhaps less controversial. Similarly its use in controlling ordinary items of administration consumables, for example, might be beneficial where everyday practice is wasteful and JIT not felt to be justifiable (but see below on office JIT).

One final phenomenon we might explore under the heading of SSC, though its effects are evident in other revolutionary systems changes, is the implementation problems of transient systems behaviour as shown in SSC Example 3.

SSC Example 3

A major manufacturer in the early 1970s sought to computerize their raw materials ordering system. This was carefully carried out by technically highly competent staff in line with a business plan giving target cost savings and service performance levels. After the system was implemented, senior managers were most alarmed to note that stock-related costs were rising rather than falling while stockouts still occurred.

Management were nearly at the point of turning off the new system and reverting to the old when a detailed analysis revealed the following:

- The new system had automatically re-ordered stock for a wide range of items where existing stocks, though technically too low, were in no real danger of stockout. In the short term this increased administrative and stock holding costs.
- Items which were held in excessive quantities were unaffected by the system; excess stock would eventually be used up but the system could not affect this process.
- Though new order quantities tended to be lower than existing ones, early orders placed by the system were often for high usage items where this effect was less noticeable.
- Though immediate orders were placed for items in danger of stockout, these were not always timely due partly to small delays caused by system implementation.

Reassured that things were basically under control, the system was allowed to continue in operation with some small adjustments. Gradually stock holding costs and administration costs fell and stockouts became respectably rare. The short-term excess cost was a transient systems effect which should have been predicted. The company had taken care in prescribing technical and long-term business performance levels but had failed to note the impact on cash flow of short-term systems effects. Lessons learnt in this instance were fully analysed and reflected in future systems implementation procedures.

Control of spares stocks

The experienced reader might have noted that one important category of stock not mentioned so far is spares, whether for customer or factory use. Much cost is involved in carrying stocks of spares in many industries, and in writing them off when obsolete. Though some attempts have been made within SSC to develop models of spares stock holding, most practitioners would agree that the key issues here are ones of design standardization, product reliability and the possibility of manufacturing spare parts with short lead times. That is the key strategy is one of stock avoidance rather than control. Perhaps this is an appropriate comment with which to end this section.

Materials requirements planning

Having noted that scientific stock control often suffers from a lack of consideration of system-wide effects, we now move to a methodology which fully embraces the need to centrally plan stocks and flows in a manufacturing facility as a whole. Several terms have been used to define this general area, in particular the acronyms MRP, MRPII and CAPM have some prominence. The terms 'production management systems' (Browne et al 1988) and 'manufacturing planning and control systems' (Vollmann et al 1992) are also used in this context but also tend to include JIT, OPT and other approaches. We will therefore adopt the term 'computer aided production management' (CAPM) as the general term to describe integrated computer-based approaches associated with MRP-style ideas though often moving beyond them.

To increase the confusion still further, the acronym MRP has two related meanings. General interest in the basic formulation of material requirements planning (MRP) dates from the early 1970s and was strongly influenced by APICS and by software suppliers. At its simplest, MRP aims to maintain a valid schedule of customer delivery dates through the use of a computer-based planning and control system. It differs from scientific stock control by considering within-company demands as dependent on the demand for finished goods, which is rather obvious in principle but surprisingly difficult to organize in practice. Thus the approach is one of centralized planning, requiring comprehensive databases covering a variety of entities.

In Figure 7.2 we show a basic closed loop MRP system and the following activities and databases will be observed:

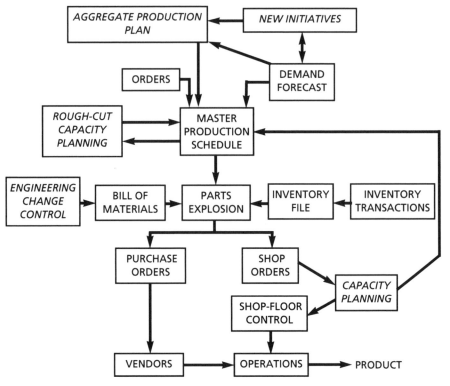

Figure 7.2
Materials requirements planning system

- Aggregate production planning: the overall matching of forecast demand and supply for a substantial period into the future (say, one year) and the setting of basic plans which define the companies intentions in terms of capacity adjustment, stock holding and so forth. This activity must be fully integrated with marketing and financial planning for the same period.
- Demand management: forecasting demand relating to all categories of product (e.g. including spares and field service stocks) and managing the relationship with specific customers with particular reference to order promising and monitoring changes in requirements.
- Master production scheduling: the master production schedule is a time-phased set of customer requirements, that is a list of dates at which particular amounts of differing product must be shipped to customers. It represents an agreement between customers and production regarding what is realistically planned to happen. If customers order products with a required supply lead-time less than the manufacturing lead-time then some finished stock will be required. This is provided for in the system by including some make-for-stock

orders in the schedule, though these should obviously be carefully controlled.

- Rough-cut capacity planning: this provides a basic check on the feasibility of the master production schedule by using average load factors (related to the proposed product mix and volumes) to predict the impact of a given schedule on resources. This is done with less precision than possible with capacity planning, which uses the more refined output of the MRP process. It does, however, provide an early warning of gross over or under utilization of available capacity.

- Material requirements planning: this is the stage in the process where the requirements listed in the master production schedule are broken down, using the bill of materials, into time-phased requirements at all levels of sub-assembly. These are compared with existing stocks and thus the need to manufacture and buy in parts is determined, once again with an emphasis on timing.

- Bill of materials: this database provides information on the materials required to make particular finished goods in terms of amounts and lead-times. Data is usually arranged in hierarchical form. That is a given product is divided first into major sub-assemblies (noting the time needed for bringing these together to form the final product). Each sub-assembly is then itself broken down, and so on until one arrives at bought-in components whose supply lead-times are noted. It is generally recognized that MRP is of most use when complex products requiring many levels in their BOMs are being manufactured.

- Inventory file: a database giving information on the amount and location of all components and finished goods in the factory. This database has to be far more accurate than is normal in most pre-CAPM systems. CAPM essentially depends on knowing where everything is at all times and thus entails very high levels of discipline in data recording, an activity which can be made far more effective by the hardware and communications parts of advanced manufacturing technology systems.

- Capacity planning: this uses the very detailed information provided by MRP to analyse the impact on resources and facilitate the production of detailed schedules and purchasing needs. This may include a simulation of the operation of a factory to predict the likely effect of delays and changes to existing plans.

- Production activity control: this controls the release of work onto the shop floor and its subsequent movement, with a particular emphasis on the loading of facilities. Effective activity control in a classic MRP context is highly dependent on timely data gathering (e.g. through bar coding) and discipline in following plans and schedules. One possibility here is the use of visible controls and pull scheduling (i.e. components of JIT) to control shop-floor activity while remaining in a CAPM framework. This, however, has implications for the data flows from the shop floor required to facilitate other CAPM components (such as capacity planning and inventory control).

● Purchasing: similar to PAC but dealing with outside suppliers. This can easily become a major problem area if long and erratic supply lead-times exist. Once again JIT principles may be useful in managing this area without compromising the CAPM framework.

A particularly important issue here is the frequency with which the MPS is changed and the implications of such changes being fed through the system. In theory MRP seems eminently suited for handling such alterations to plans but in practice care must be taken not to make the whole system unstable. This usually involves a freeze on replanning orders in the near future.

More recently CAPM systems have been expanded to become complete planning and control mechanisms giving rise to the new term 'manufacturing resource planning' (MRP II). MRP II is conceived as a wide-ranging, closed-loop business control system, designed to carry out detailed planning and monitoring of plans. This is done by integrating all the related business and transaction aspects of manufacturing, including MRP, capacity planning, inventory control, product costing, shop-floor control, finance, marketing, engineering and human resource management.

Manufacturing resource planning is a 'top down' system which depends heavily on a valid MPS, efficient data feedback and highly disciplined staff. In a recent report on a workshop comparing production control methodologies (Waterlow and Richards (1988)), the assumptions underlying MRP II and the organizational implications of its use are listed in some detail, including the following questionable assumptions:

● Lead times at all stages of manufacture and supply can be specified and preferably the aggregate lead time is less than the required product delivery lead time.

● Organizational structures are capable of adapting to a centralization of materials management and all relevant functional managers will use the MRP II system as the central business planning and control system.

The second point has considerable implications for education and training in an organization. At the simplest level, all staff must be comprehensively trained in the use of the system. Such training may not, however, affect basic attitudes regarding the planning and control of materials flow, and senior and middle management may find that the discipline of an MRP II system conflicts with their habitual freedom of action. An extensive literature exists pointing to the potential problems which exist with the human parts of this rather mechanistic approach.

The 1990 edition of the *Industrial Computing Sourcebook* (BPICS 1990) lists, for the UK, around 80 vendors of 120 major software products under the general CAPM heading. The software and support costs of a system can range from £400 (based on a personal computer) to £0.5M, the latter not including the substantial disruption costs of major systems implementation in a large company.

In view of the size and sophistication of the CAPM industry it is somewhat alarming that opinions differ as to the value of CAPM. Stevens quotes a recent report in the *Financial Times*:

> It has been estimated that only 11 per cent of UK MRP II implementations have realised their full potential and that the rest are realising only 10 per cent or less of the benefit available.
> (Stevens 1989)

Alternatively a report in the BPICS journal of a user survey asserted that 90 per cent of installations met their objectives (Little and Johnson 1990). Such evidence is of no more than anecdotal value in the absence of rigorous definitions of success and agreement on objectives and sampling procedures, but the point is well made that success, or its absence, is a factor of concern and worthy of investigation.

Material requirements planning is unusual in having its own class system. Class A represents an excellent user who is achieving considerable benefits from the system as shown by answers to a self-administered standard questionnaire. At the other extreme a Class D user is often characterized as a company where the only people using the system are data processing staff, i.e. genuine benefits are not apparent. As Browne and colleagues (Browne et al 1988 p132) perceptively comment:

> Many systems are *installed*, as opposed to *implemented*, i.e. the formal system is not the real system.

Statistics on the prevalence of each class are not readily available, and may be coloured by the publicity to be gained from being in Class A, or to be avoided by admitting to being Class D. Two surveys in the early 1980s suggested that in the USA around 10 per cent of users were of Class A and 60 per cent belonged to Classes C or D. As MRP began to be used in the USA in the early 1970s with somewhat later adoption in the UK one may draw one's own conclusions about its current success rate in this country.

Certainly successful users exist as evidenced by companies who claim Class A status and encourage visits to their plants, thus opening themselves to potentially searching investigation by critical specialists. Similarly the regular series of articles in the British Institute of Management journal (see *Management Today* Nov. 1990) on 'Britain's best factories' contains illustrations of successful MPC, usually in the context of general excellence of manufacturing operations and engineering. Indeed an interesting point is whether CAPM can be of high quality in isolation from other engineering systems in a company.

We can therefore hardly avoid the question 'why do MRP installations often not live up to expectation?'. Voss (1986) has developed a CAPM chronology showing how the initial enthusiasm of the early 1970s in the USA turned into doubt (usually expressed as problems with 'implementation') and then to a consideration of alternatives. We postulate that the following are the reasons, real or perceived, for CAPM failure:

1 Lack of discipline in use: workers, production schedulers and managers may be the most obvious recipients of blame. This must in turn cast doubt on the user-friendliness of the system, the clarity of its objectives and value, associated training and other features of the total (rather than the narrow technical) system.

2 Poor implementation: another soft target, particularly when implementation was carried out by 'outsiders'. The real problem may well be an artificial split between the set of activities included under the heading 'implementation' and those under 'operation'. This is one area where JIT methods have a profound advantage.

3 The operational principle of CAPM is inappropriate in a given instance: central planning of all stocks and flows may not be a good idea. The decision to use CAPM must relate to process choice amongst other things.

4 Other systems attributes are not compatible: it should be obvious from the discussion so far that CAPM is far more likely to succeed in a very well-ordered engineering factory with extensive data automated recording and a tradition of stable and disciplined operations. If other systems (for example quality assurance) are chaotic, CAPM is an unlikely change agent.

5 Not part of the strategic plan: CAPM systems emphasize certain priorities (e.g. planning deliveries in a complex batch production environment) and these must reflect business strategy.

Brown, Harhen and Shivnan (1988) also make the interesting observation that many installations are only partly computerized. Thus, in a survey published in 1986, and consistent with earlier studies, it was found that only 61 per cent of MRP users had computerized the MPS, 42 per cent had computerized capacity requirements planning and 52 per cent had computerized production activity control. While even a glance at the pages of the current trade press will show determined attempts by computer systems vendors to change this situation by offering ever improved variations on MRP/JIT/OPT, it is interesting to speculate on whether partial computerization might provide at least a short-term stable system. However, any attempt to move towards CIM or CIB must be based on comprehensive databases or materials related information will not be widely available to support decision making throughout an organization.

We end our discussion of CAPM with some discussion of recent research on its implementation in the UK. In 1986 the ACME (Applications of

Computers to Manufacturing Engineering) Directorate of the Science and Engineering Research Council established their CAPM initiative. This set of 16 projects involved an investment of around £2.5M. A recent ACME newsletter succinctly states the problem addressed as follows:

> Why do CAPM systems fail? Largely because requirements change over time. The research team developed a methodology that places the definition of a CAPM solution in the context of the changing business needs which it has to support.

The initial study of the ACME/CAPM initiative (Waterlow and Moniot 1986) makes a number of points on the inadequacies of MRP installations in a survey of companies. For example, the master production schedule is central to MRP as an agreed plan for factory output, and yet:

> The existence of a computer-based master production schedule was no guarantee that its content had been debated between sales and production.

Many systems were set up by outside consultants based on some investigation of users' perceptions of their needs:

> For decision making assistance, a manager's perception of what he needed changed with experience, events and with the development of the CAPM system.

> Companies with a successful integrated CAPM system had generally invested heavily in internal education courses for staff at all levels. Although these courses were regarded as crucial, anecdotal evidence implied that the real understanding of a CAPM system came from its practical use over an extended period.

Finally a warning is sounded that even 'successful' implementation can hide fundamental problems:

> The reports on the few companies in the sample which had achieved full CAPM integration and some integration of CAPM with other business functions indicated that the global scale of such systems can be incomprehensible to staff, especially middle management.

One might optimistically hope that management could live with an incomprehensible 'black box' system if it were fully competent in achieving its objectives. Yet few contemporary specialists would assert that CAPM can be used on 'automatic pilot'. Therefore if management are expected to use the system imaginatively they must be able to at least form a conceptual model that closely relates to its working idiosyncrasies and be able to influence those workings to improve performance.

This study, and a later workshop (see Waterlow and Clouder Richards 1988) provided the impetus for extensive research, much of which was reported on in ACME (1990). Though some of this work was of a technical nature, the majority surveyed current practice and proposed methodologies for the audit, design and implementation of CAPM. This work is reflected on earlier in our discussion on manufacturing strategy.

Of particular interest in the ACME studies was the way in which both technical and organizational issues were seen to be at the heart of CAPM implementation difficulties. Three examples will be discussed here to illustrate the way in which organizational problems were addressed. The first is a contribution to ACME (1990) from Bessant and Lamming which addresses organizational learning, in particular 'double loop' learning in a CAPM context:

> This research provides detailed case study evidence to support the hypothesis that successful integration of CAPM is closely related to the ability of an organisation to 'learn'.

> ... the ideas of Argyris and Schon on 'single and double loop learning' are a useful construct in analysing CAPM implementations. Cognitive mapping has emerged as a possible tool for assisting organizations move from single to double loop learning.

> Factors generally associated with successful CAPM (e.g. participative design, readiness to change procedures, cross functional cooperation) are engendered from the outward looking adaptive behaviour which is characteristic of double loop learning.

Newell and Clark (1990) provides additional information on the work of researchers at Aston Business School who led the second ACME/CAPM project. This was also concerned with organizational learning in the context of 12 case studies of CAPM innovation. Of particular interest here is the distinction made between 'automating' and 'informating' technologies (following Zuboff 1988). The latter are identified with integrating technologies which:

> ... demand a reshaping of the organizational boundaries and a shared vision of the future.

The third example of an ACME/CAPM project centres on the notion of a resilient CAPM system (Maull et al 1990). This work is highly prescriptive and recommends a strategy-led implementation methodology. An audit and 'vision building' set of activities lead on to a communication of a mission statement and a series of sprints (discrete projects) with a 'performance ratchet' to encourage continuing incremental improvements. This approach has marked similarities to JIT, in basic structure at the very least.

Thus we can see that current research has fully accepted the need for an organizational perspective in CAPM design and implementation and shows a broad-based approach in borrowing concepts from other areas of management research. Whether such research will translate into effective company practice remains to be seen.

The just-in-time approach

Though of comparatively recent origin, the just-in-time approach has generated great interest amongst manufacturing managers. One reason has been the stunning successes reported by some companies in implementing JIT. Schonberger's book on *World Class Manufacturing* describes some of these including order of magnitude improvements in lead-times and stock holding performance. More recently Womack et al (1990) have shown how Lean Production has changed the global car industry. Such changes have the potential to alter radically the competitive balance within particular industries.

At first sight the idea of eliminating stock entirely (except of course for work literally being processed) seems nonsense. How can one allow for the inevitable fluctuations, delays, breakdowns and so on in a supply and manufacture chain except through keeping some safety stock? Yet the ideas which accompany JIT (typically worker involvement in process improvement, product simplification, preventive maintenance, improved quality management) seem natural and hardly new. Is the key some aspect of Japanese culture which somehow makes these ideas more potent? Or do the Japanese and their more successful imitators simply work harder and more intensely on actually doing the things others talk about?

One of the earlier books to popularize this approach (Schonberger 1982) puts it as follows:

> The JIT idea is simple: produce and deliver finished goods just in time to be sold, fabricated parts just in time to go into sub-assemblies, and purchased materials just in time to be transformed into fabricated parts ... Like perfect quality, absolute just-in-time performance is never attained, but rather is an ideal to be pursued aggressively.

One subtlety must be grasped from the start. JIT is a process for improvement as much as a final goal. Unfortunately, in a world where words sometimes seem as important as actions, some companies have seized on JIT as a sign of merit. Others use it as a signal that they intend to insist on unrealistic supply flexibility. The JIT improvement programme must proceed in a logical sequence. In particular 'supplier JIT' is only feasible after 'in-company JIT' has been achieved. If a company's use of raw materials really is fluctuating, unpredictable and erratic then a supplier has an impossible task in providing JIT performance, except by maintaining stocks of finished goods in a warehouse adjacent to the user's factory!

The basic elements of JIT are waste elimination, total quality control (TQC) and the development of human resources. Indeed the more one studies this approach the more one appreciates the deep interrelationship between these factors, in total contrast to SSC and CAPM. The first of these is often wrongly seen as merely cutting stock levels, but in fact waste may also occur as scrap, queues, set-up times, materials handling and movement or machine downtime. The linkage between JIT and TQC is so fundamental that they must be examined together when discussing operational management.

The development of human resources is central to the Japanese approach. The logic of JIT does not imply the importation of a Japanese working culture but the development of an appropriate mode of operation for achieving waste reduction and TQC. There is no reason to believe that employee problem solving, flexibility of working practices, imaginative engineering, good communications and so forth are intrinsically the product of an Eastern culture. Japanese companies have found ways of doing the things in ways which are natural to them and Western companies must do likewise if they want to achieve the same results.

It can be argued that some elements of the JIT approach are relevant to any operational situation. However, the logic of JIT may mean that it is only fully applicable in particular manufacturing situations and to explore this we must consider a typical implementation path in some detail. Following a popular prescription we divide implementation into several stages which must occur in the correct sequence.

Stage 1 JIT

This involves the systematic application of a series of concurrent changes designed to simplify and improve the manufacturing situation in preparation for the more dramatic techniques to be used. Typical activities are given below. It will immediately be noted that there is nothing specifically 'JIT-ish' about most of these recommendations and to some extent Stage 1 JIT is simply a reminder of good manufacturing practice.

- *Product simplification:*
  Pull scheduling and direct shop-floor control require comparatively simple product structures and routings.
- *Total quality control:*
  The total quality system should be improved with an emphasis on process control.
- *Preventive maintenance:*
  Equipment breakdowns and malfunctioning must be dramatically reduced. Then problems which do occur can be given immediate attention. This will demand very high standards of engineering consistency.
- *Set-up time reduction:*
  This is given a very high priority, in total contrast to SSC and CAPM. One researcher records an instance of a 17-minute set-up on a major machine being reduced to eight seconds at minimal cost and mainly through the efforts of shop-floor staff working on a systematic produc-

tivity improvement programme (see Voss (1987). Such improvements have value far beyond the saving in productive time on the machine.

● *Layout:*
Hardly a new topic for the production engineer but one given renewed impetus. A recurring theme in JIT literature is the use of group technology to identify families of products and components followed by dramatic changes to plant layout with the objective of reducing the distance material must travel to an absolute minimum, even if this involves the duplication of some facilities.

● *Small machines:*
The idea is that through the use of a number of small machines in place of one large machine, compact layout and product focusing are possible. It may also be easier on such machines to utilize in-house innovation skills to reduce set-up times and improve material and tool handling.

Two points should be noted here. First of all the outlay in terms of capital expenditure in Stage 1 JIT is comparatively small and may easily be recouped in terms of tactical benefits occurring and organizational learning. Stage 1 JIT is a useful reorientation device for all personnel and helps to promote pride and interest in the workplace.

The second point is that though the above list was drawn up with manufacturing management in mind, rereading it in the context of service or of office management raises a number of interesting issues. Work simplification, TQC and layout improvements are of obvious value in any work environment. Similarly set-up time reduction, reinterpreted as job design to facilitate moving quickly from one set of activities to another, will be recognized by any office manager as highly desirable. Finally if the use of small machines seems a distinctly manufacturing issue then consider the spread of personal computers, i.e. flexible small machines which may easily be moved to a new location and adapted to a new set of tasks.

Stage 2 JIT

Stage 1 activities will bring benefits when applied in a number of situations. They also, when applied as a totality, prepare the way for a number of more radical changes which would otherwise have been difficult to implement but now have the potential for dramatic improvements in operating performance. These Stage 2 changes are more distinctively 'JIT-ish' in nature, are more demanding in implementation but in the right situation give enormous potential for improved performance.

● *Multi-functional workforce:*
The effective operation of Stage 2 JIT requires the re-allocation of workers from areas of low demand to areas of high demand at very short notice. Similarly workers are expected to contribute to problem solving

and systems fault recognition as a normal part of their working lives. Job grades, payment schemes and training must match these objectives.

● *Problem visibility:*

A fundamental tenet of JIT and TQC is that problems must not be hidden but should be highlighted in order that preventive action can be taken. This might involve the use of charts displaying all the key features of an operational system and the acceptance that when a problem occurs the relevant operator has the authority to stop production and demand immediate expert assistance.

● *Enforced improvement:*

This is the interesting idea that management continually reduces the assets needed for manufacturing and so creates problems which must be solved without increasing other assets. Typically the assets reduced may be machines, labour, buffer stocks, space and so forth, though care must be taken with the sequence of reduction. The traditional black humour of the workplace may suggest that this is a normal form of management! However, JIT-style enforced improvement is carefully planned and provides considerable support for the problem solvers.

● *Pull scheduling:*

One objective of JIT is to achieve a continuous flow of material based on short lead times and very small batch sizes. A key idea in facilitating this is pull scheduling. This is the discipline that no manufacturing or transportation action takes place at any stage in a production process until an instruction to manufacture or move an item comes from the next stage down the line (i.e. through some KANBAN mechanism). It should now be obvious why the changes listed in Stage 1 were necessary. This type of production control requires simple products, simple manufacturing methods, short lines, good communication, flexible workforce and no breakdowns!

● *JIT purchasing:*

Having made all the changes listed above, a manufacturer will have achieved a smooth flow of goods based on a controlled range of material requirements. It is now possible that a close relationship with a supplier could be managed to the mutual benefit of both parties. The ways in which this may be achieved are particularly well described in Womack et al (1990).

As will be evident from the above description, the implementation of JIT is a continuing process over a long period of time. One danger is that the environment is too unstable or the needs of the customer too varied to allow the simplification entailed by JIT. Thus the choice of how much JIT is relevant to a given situation is a key strategic issue. Few would argue with its desirability but its universal practicability must be questioned.

One obvious linkage is with the concept of focused manufacturing which sees simplification as a strategic issue in the total design of a manufacturing facility. A tightly focused plant may be capable of JIT operation but, being orientated to manufacturing a small range of products or parts, may have a short life. Thus one important issue is whether JIT may be subjected to more accelerated implementation.

Now much of the discussion above relates to the conversion of a traditional plant to a JIT-style facility. Obviously a company experienced in the JIT approach will be able to set up a new plant on JIT lines in far less time. Yet the problem remains that a plant may not be sufficiently simple in operation, for a variety of reasons, for JIT in its full sense to be used. The next section describes a methodology for approaching an operational situation where severe bottlenecks exist, i.e. features which acutely affect throughput and necessitate more centralized planning to maximize the flow through the bottleneck.

Optimized production technology (OPT)

The most recent of our four main methodologies is optimized production technology, sometimes referred to as synchronized manufacturing. This approach is chiefly associated with E.M.Goldratt and popularized through his book *The Goal*, a novel based on a few months in the life of a production manager. OPT links together a number of useful ideas for improving material flow with a clear view of how such improvements may affect a company's financial performance (see Goldratt and Cox (1986), Goldratt and Fox (1986) and Goldratt (1985)). The breadth of approach is therefore a very attractive feature of this methodology.

A controversial aspect of OPT is the use of expensive software as part of the consultancy package offered by consultants trained in this approach. Details of the software are not generally available. However, there is much good advice here which can be used without the more technical aspects of OPT, particularly if the bottlenecks in a factory are easy to identify.

The OPT approach is also relevant to the setting of objectives through the use of the concepts of throughput, inventory and operating expense. OPT is particularly innovative and ambitious in its linking of business and production decision-making and control systems. At this level it provides an indicator of what might be achieved if one is willing to rethink such basic areas as cost accounting in conjunction with materials management. A similar questioning approach to the concept of cost and the measurement of financial performance is found in some recent approaches to quality assurance.

Thus one may view OPT either as a set of ideas or as a computer-based finite capacity scheduling package. The latter may be seen as complementary to MRP. It differs, however, in deriving lead-times from schedules which are set with reference to due dates and priorities.

Some discussion is necessary here on the nature of production lead-times. The time taken for a 'product' to pass through a manufacturing unit is made up of a number of components, of which time taken undergoing actual material transformation (e.g. cutting, bending, etc.) and assembly may be a small proportion. In the traditional factory, particularly where large batches are being made, most of the lead-time consists of waiting and queuing time. Therefore the use of historic lead-time data (using averages as a predictor of future lead-time) may simply institutionalize the expectation of long lead-times including excessive idle time. There is no natural mechanism within SSC and CAPM to counter this beyond the occasional purge on levels of work-in-progress inventory and arbitrary setting of new target lead-times.

The JIT approach takes this issue very seriously. Waiting time and idle time represent waste and many of the JIT techniques (in particular reducing set-up times and pull scheduling) are aimed at drastically reducing lead-times. OPT makes lead-times a central issue. They are variables in the system rather than constants. However, for the logic of OPT to work, a distinction has to be made between situations where bottlenecks affect flow and situations where they do not.

A bottleneck is a resource constraint which directly affects throughput. OPT concentrates on maximizing the flow of materials through bottlenecks, schedules for other facilities being derived to support the bottleneck flows. Indeed, provided the bottlenecks are efficiently handled, other facilities may be approached on a JIT basis in order to keep non-essential inventory to a minimum.

Some of the practical details of OPT are summarized in the '9 Rules of OPT' (see Goldratt (1985)), rules which are of value for the management of material flow in any context. These rules emphasize the importance of bottlenecks, the derivative nature of lead-times, and the need to be flexible in setting the sizes of process batches and transfer batches. Thus OPT differs from the other methods in the agenda of issues it considers to be important in managing material flow.

THE ORGANIZATIONAL RELEVANCE OF CAPM AND JIT

It is now an appropriate point to consider a fundamental question – what is the real purpose of implementing a CAPM system?

The most simple response is that it does a job and therefore provides benefits, i.e. an investment in hardware, software and training allied to continuing expenditure on user salaries and consumables produces quantifiable benefits. Now in this instance the costs are very evident and therefore one must ask if the benefits are sufficient and likely to occur. In particular the benefits must be in excess of those likely to occur with current practice or alternative strategies, i.e. stock reduction is only a benefit if it is caused by the CAPM investment and would not have occurred otherwise. This clear and logical approach stands or falls on the evidence of implementational success, which in turn suggests that benefits do not automatically occur, hence the relative failure of Class C and D users. One may indeed respond that such failure is to be blamed on incompetent implementation and poor management but this misses the point. Provided installation is correctly carried out (which should be possible in most cases) and a reasonable level of commercial skills exist in the company, then according to this line of reasoning benefits should occur.

If, as the evidence suggests, failure is quite likely then one must look for the cause. In particular as this is a relatively mature technology, it is not sufficient merely to blame failure on poor software or a lack of knowledge in the business community as a whole on how to use CAPM.

One possibility, using cybernetic terminology, is that MRP lacks sufficient intrinsic variety to act as a control system in a turbulent environment. Early case studies of success emphasized the importance of working in a stable commercial setting. A typical symptom of MRP problems is a lack of coordination between different users, particularly between different functions. However it may be that in such cases each user *was* responding to the peculiar challenges of his own environment and this caused operational incompatibilities which could not be resolved by the system in the time-scale available.

An interesting comparison is with the implementational strategies recommended for JIT. Here an emphasis on, for example, quality improvement, lead-time reduction and training a multi-skilled and adaptable workforce provides an inherently more flexible manufacturing context. Furthermore an emphasis on variety reduction and on product and process simplification reduces the range of variables to be controlled. The intention is not to attempt to control a high variety, dynamically unstable situation but to simplify the situation to the extent that very simple controls (such as pull scheduling using Kanbans) are adequate to meet customer requirements at a low cost.

The comparison between the fundamental roles of MRP and JIT is illustrated by a quotation from Lubben (1988):

> Because MRP systems try to anticipate and follow rapid changes in the production schedule, they tend to encourage complexity as opposed to encouraging stability. Thus, the users of MRP systems attempt to resolve a complex scheduling problem by using an increasingly complex control system. The end result is the development of an unnecessarily complex manufacturing system that is not self-limiting and that continues to increase in complexity.

This may be caused by the use of MRP (a planning tool) as an execution tool. Some companies are maintaining MRP as a planning tool, and it works well.

The implication is that the strength of CAPM is in its potential as an integrated planning environment. Control of the flow of materials is best achieved by JIT-style simplification and problem solving.

There is a further dimension to this comparison which is of interest. JIT practitioners go further than a quiet stability and pursue competitiveness through setting ever more dramatic goals. This in turn makes JIT systems once again hard to manage but the strategy for regaining control is the use of human inventiveness both for day-to-day management and for finding ways towards strategic improvement. This may involve new working practices or new technology but there is no assumption that a final plateau of stability will be gained. If the environment doesn't provide challenges then enforced problem solving will!

An important point to note at this stage is that one should avoid any characterization of JIT as rampant shop-floor entrepreneurialism. As Klein (1989) reports, JIT is a disciplined procedure promoting responsibility in process change. She quotes a team manager at an engine plant who asserts that under an enlightened but pre-JIT management:

> I was told ... I wasn't to do anything just because 'that's the way it's done', I was told to do things the smartest way I could.

Klein contrasts this with JIT developments at the plant:

> Under JIT and statistical process control (SPC), this 'entrepreneurial' spirit is limited; ideas are still encouraged but have to be tested under SPC guidelines ... displacing worker trial and error with more scientific methods may have a negative psychological effect.
> (Klein 1989)

However, JIT in its pure form is mainly applicable to situations of repetitive manufacture and CAPM has the ambitious goal of providing a planning and control environment for a far wider set of manufacturing situations. Thus moving back to CAPM we may ask if the positive ideas of JIT have an interpretation in an electronic context of central planning.

The first point is the need to attack inadequacies in the manufacturing situation and to simplify where such action will not reduce competitiveness. This in turn entails the existence of a valid competitive manufacturing strategy. One problem with CAPM and the often isolated nature of its in-company adherents is that such fundamental actions may be beyond their scope.

The second point is to form an alliance between algorithmic and judgemental problem solving, that is allow decision makers to use CAPM as a decision support system. Unfortunately this simple prescription hides a considerable problem, with implications for staff development and organizational design. Very many factors and individual actions affect the total business performance of a CAPM system. Not only can one action have a wide range of results in terms of product delivery performance, stock levels, resource utilization and so forth, but similarly one measurable result (e.g. a specific customer receiving his goods on time) may be affected by a wide range of decisions.

Imagine therefore a manager contemplating a schedule change. How can an extensive analysis of databases be carried out to track down all repercussions of this action? This is the point where the logic and structure of CAPM is most useful in performing 'what-if' analyses.

Drawing once again on a comparison with JIT, a third point is the continual improvement of the CAPM system itself in structuring information when acting as a decision supporter and also in its more routine capacity of expediting existing decisions. One possibility which is receiving some interest is the development of an expert systems approach to CAPM which gradually takes on board the judgemental inputs of staff, though once again the competitiveness of the environment and its effects on operational stability must be considered. Perhaps as the system takes on board one set of judgements, the human operator is freed to think up the next!

It may seem obvious in this context that the human operator is involved in this process of change. Experience to the contrary leads Schumacher to assert that:

> ... failure to involve everyone not only leads to a loss of credibility of the system but also contributes to the Achilles heel of MRP II approaches, namely their inability to cope with sustained improvement potential with respect to either capacity or throughput rates.
> (Schumacher 1988)

CONCLUSIONS

We summarize our discussion with a series of models based on the four key production management systems under consideration and contrasting their approaches. The underlying assumptions of each methodology are shown in Figure 7.3. It can readily be seen that these systems are not simply alternatives but radically different approaches which must be matched to a given context with some care.

In Figure 7.4 we show their interrelationships which once again brings into sharp focus their differences. The differences should not, however, preclude their being used together in suitable situations if they comple-

SSC	MRP
Rational short-term decision making	Computer-based integration
JIT	OPT
Continuous improvement through simplification	Schedules based on maximizing flow through bottlenecks (simplified accounting)

Figure 7.3
PMS – philosophy

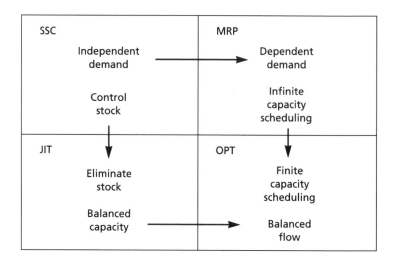

Figure 7.4
PMS – relationships

ment each other. For instance in MRP style contexts it may be convenient for some stock items to be controlled as if independent from the majority. There is also an argument that the long-term objective of OPT is the elimination of bottlenecks thus becoming a form of JIT.

One way in which the methodologies differ to a considerable extent is in their implementational paths. These are briefly summarized in Figure 7.5 and the human resource implications of each are very different. While

MRP tends to be implemented through a series of dramatic changes led by experts, JIT has a quite different approach involving actions by many staff over a long period of time.

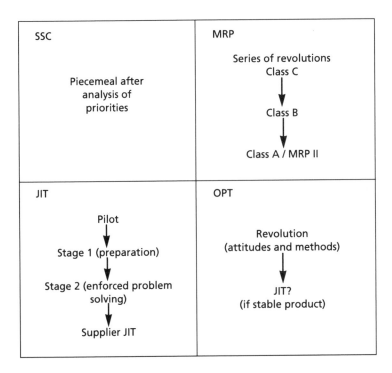

Figure 7.5
PMS implementation

It is of course a strategic decision for any given manufacturer which methodology to apply, or rather how best to concoct a system using principles and techniques discussed above to meet a particular need. Two points should be noted at this point. The first is that differing systems may well be appropriate for differing parts of a factory, following our earlier discussion of focusing and manufacturing strategy. The second is that material flow control systems cannot be seen in isolation from organizational structure or from other information technology systems.

CHAPTER 8

Technology strategy

INFORMATION TECHNOLOGY IN THE OFFICE

At a number of points in this book we have referred to the competitive advantages inherent in the use of technology, in particular information technology (IT), in operations management. In this chapter we extend and summarize some ideas in this context, commencing with applications in the environment of the office. Inevitably this chapter will contain a broad range of applications and comments on their operational advantages. The strategic ramifications of these developments are usually obvious in terms of potential benefits and systems' development costs. It goes without saying that the implementation of such systems must take place within a well-defined corporate and operational strategy.

Office operations is an area which has been transformed by IT, a change which is familiar to us all, if only through the ubiquitous personal computer. However, office uses of IT predate factory and service applications as the orderly routine of office life seemed an obvious target for programming. Early data processing examples are well known, including payroll and commercial applications common in the 1960s. Information technology has grown from such simple beginnings into one of the major industries of the latter part of this century.

Office operations are dealt with in a number of ways in textbooks, with the final picture often lacking in coherence. The study of organization and methods pre-dates computer technology and carries the general methodologies of work study into the office environment. Much of the attention in this context now centres on the design of data processing systems as traditional office tasks such as typing, filing and accounts preparation have been replaced by work processors and suchlike. This is not merely a direct substitution of electronic technology for machines and paper. Information technology provides opportunities for productivity and new services way beyond their obvious benefits. Allied to more effective data capture (via bar coding and document scanning), communications, data handling methods (for instance through data base management systems) and presentational devices, the computer promises benefits way beyond our current organizational capabilities for exploiting them.

In a text on current thinking in information systems planning, Ward, Griffiths and Whitmore (1990) refer to the 'three eras' model of systems development:

- The Data processing (DP) era from the early 1960s to the present, concerned with promoting operational efficiency in information processing.
- The Management information systems (MIS) era from the mid-1970s onwards, where the goal is to satisfy managers' information requirements, thus improving their effectiveness.
- The Strategic information systems (SIS) era from the late 1980s onwards, where the goal is to improve competitiveness by using IT to change the nature of the business.

The last of the three is the most ambitious and is obviously consistent with a number of themes in this book. Strategic information systems have a number of features which contrast with earlier 'eras'. They are intended to be:

- based on integrated networks
- widely available for users
- capable of innovative and imaginative use
- related to and driven by business strategies
- flexible in operation

An example of the strategic use of office automation is provided in a newspaper article on a Danish hearing aid manufacturer, Oticon (see Toksvig (1992)). At the headquarters of this company, paper has virtually been banned. The shredder is continually in use, important data being stored electronically. The building has a comprehensive computer network where staff can interact with databases as required.

Yet the most notable part of this example is the changes to human work and organization. Staff are encouraged to be extremely flexible in the tasks they perform, to work in continually reforming teams and to be pro-active in their approach to work in this company. The paperless office is not an end in itself but part of a total approach in freeing staff from organizational and informational constraints in the way they work.

Ward et al (1990) provide a number of similar examples and more are given below in the section on service uses of IT. However, we now move to a more radical view of the effects of office automation. Going beyond standard IT texts, some more behaviourally-orientated research explores the implications of current systems developments. An example is Zuboff (1988), *In the Age of the Smart Machine*, which is based on research in both production and office contexts. Two of Zuboff's many ideas are of fundamental relevance to operations management. The first is the concept of 'informating':

... information technology is characterized by a fundamental duality that has not been fully appreciated. On the one hand, the technology can be applied to automating operations according to a logic that hardly differs from that of the nineteenth-century machine system – replace the human body with a technology that enables the same process to be performed with more continuity and control. On the other, the same technology simultaneously generates information about the underlying productive and administrative processes through which an organization accomplishes work. It provides a deeper level of transparency to activities that had been either partially or completely opaque.

Zuboff refers to the latter use of technology as the capacity to 'informate' rather than automate. Such informating supports management to a level far beyond traditional automation, though much of the rest of Zuboff (1988) charts organizational inadequacies in dealing with this new opportunity.

The implications of this simple idea for individuals and organizations are considerable. If activities are potentially visible, who is allowed to see them? What actions are permitted in response to knowledge gained? Who is empowered to change processes and procedures? What is the effect on the traditional role and responsibilities of management? Zuboff's work addresses these problems, with conclusions which are of considerable interest for designers of management information systems as well as more routine data processing:

> Information technology essentially alters the contours of reality – work becomes more abstract, intelligence may be programmed, organizational memory and visibility are increased by an order of magnitude beyond any historical capability.

A simple example of informating applies to the control of text preparation and data handling in an office. The productivity and quality of office work done at a computer keyboard may easily be checked electronically. In this way the work becomes observable and transparent. But what is the effect of this on motivation? What organizational dysfunctionality will result from the ever-present Big Brother (and Sister)? Most important, how can such technological opportunities be translated into real competitive advantages rather than merely reinforce traditional control procedures?

The second of Zuboff's concepts which seems to have real implications for operational management is the distinction between 'acting-on' and 'acting-with'. Much craft knowledge is 'know-how', that is literally knowledge that comes from repeated action and experience and translates into an ability to perform future tasks effectively. This is referred to as 'acting-on' and is typical of much operational work, including traditional office-based clerical tasks. Managerial and professional work is somehow different in the way 'know-how' is obtained and used. Words such as judgement, power and influence enter into descriptions of managerial work which is more political and unstructured than other organizational roles. This is referred to as 'acting-with'.

Now, the informational requirements of 'acting-with' are quite different from those of 'acting-on', which partly explains the difficulties which data processing specialists have when asked to develop management information systems. Any system design methodologies which commence with a logical and exhaustive analysis of data inputs and outputs grind to a halt when confronted with the senior manager whose needs, beyond basic financial and operational data, are endlessly changing and who fully understands that information is power. Yet almost all systems models used in operations management are simple and unitary and assume that 'acting-on' is taking place. If operational strategy is taken as a genuinely top management area of responsibility then it is equally based on 'acting-with' skills.

The following quotation from Zuboff (1988) refers to the problems facing managers in an information rich environment:

> The shifting grounds of knowledge invite managers to recognize the emergent demands for intellective skills and develop a learning environment in which such skills can develop. That very recognition contains a threat to managerial authority, which depends in part upon control over the organization's knowledge base ... Managers who must prove and defend their own legitimacy do not easily share knowledge or engage in inquiry ... New roles cannot emerge without the structures to support them.

Though our discussion began with a consideration of office IT, it has ended with a challenge to the very core of managerial practice and organizational structure. If we limit our consideration of office operations to routine tasks then a factory analogy is suitable, as discussed in Chapter 4. If we widen it to management and strategic information systems then we move far beyond the boundaries of operations management strategy.

A final point which should be noted in the context of managerial uses of technology is that communications technology is possibly of more direct relevance to much managerial work than the desktop personal computer. For many managers, the portable telephone and the fax machine offer more possibilities than spreadsheets and databases. This relates to the extent to which much managerial action involves communication rather than text handling. This in no way detracts from the potential uses of IT for management but rather serves to remind one of the interpersonal nature of managerial work and the wide range of information sources the manager actually uses. It is noticeable that current electronic offerings for the busy executive are very portable, user friendly and always include a diary and clock showing times at differing parts of the world! Perhaps in the future they will also incorporate a usable phone and language translation facilities.

INFORMATION TECHNOLOGY IN SERVICE OPERATIONS

The image of service operations as small scale and technologically crude is totally out of date. Retailers, distributors, transport, hospitals, banks and so forth use technology as essential features of their competitive strategies and rival the best manufacturers in the extent to which technology is integrated throughout their businesses.

Apart from office uses, which have been dealt with above, the service sector also uses technology as the basis of service provision. Typical examples here are transport and cinema entertainment. In the latter case improvements in service quality, such as wide screen and enhanced sound, are based on technological developments. Alternatively a new or alternative service is made possible by technology, such as the use of computer based diagnostic equipment in medicine.

The above refer to ways in which technology is directly used in the service encounter. Technology may also be of value in processing customers' materials, such as dry cleaning. It may also provide information for the customer as in the case of a travel agent. At one stage removed it may improve customer service real-time control of the service environment (for instance in a theme park) or through staff training by simulating service situations.

Service uses of technology – an example

An example of the ways in which different levels of technology may contribute is given by considering a hypothetical remote booking office for a large theatre or entertainment complex. In the past, booking operations might have been conducted as follows:

- Source of information – leaflets on future shows
- Booking mechanism – available tickets from block held at this office
- Payment – cash or cheque

A modest use of technology would allow the following:

- Source of information – regularly updated chart showing shows for which tickets were still available
- Booking mechanism – database of seats available at this office with telephone used to check availability of others if necessary
- Payment – credit card

We may envisage the following as possibilities for a busy booking office:

- Source of information – continually updated display
- Booking mechanism – networked database with a decision support system to guide choice based on a specification of needs and automated ticket printing
- Payment – direct debit of bank account

The essential point to note here is that each use of technology provides advantages both for the customer and the user. Each is also based on a mixture of data processing and communications. The latter example is obviously the more costly to install but provides considerable potential benefits, one of which is the possibility of totally automated booking or even adaptation to provide a service from the client's home via television and telephone.

Expert systems in service operations

Murdick et al (1990) provide considerable further detail of service uses of technology along with a classification of computer-based information systems and a consideration of the use of expert systems in service provision.

The use of expert systems in medical diagnosis has long been a subject of speculation and research. As we describe below in a manufacturing context, such systems attempt to use knowledge culled from experts in a given area to solve recurring problems for the direct benefit of the client or as an aid to effective management. In a service context they have the potential to:

- aid decision making at locations where the expert is not available;
- make consistent decisions where the underlying logic can be examined if necessary;
- make decisions quickly at any time with the same high levels of quality;
- provide assistance in confidential situations or where an impersonal service might be preferred;
- be used as a training device for service providers through simulation of service situations;
- provide cost effective service and increase productivity.

The above list of possible advantages is highly attractive to many service providers and developments in service based expert systems are listed in Murdick et al (1990).

Fundamental changes in the way a service provider does business may be based on technological advances. The implications of IT for one form of service provider are described in Thomson (1992), an article with the heading 'Case of the vanishing banks'. As repositories of at least some of our money, we would prefer banks not to vanish and fortunately, for the customer at least, this article only refers to their high street manifestation, the local branch.

Some banks are already exploring the possibilities afforded by telephone handling of transactions. The operational implications of this affect both personal service and back-room activities. Obviously the telephone is a medium for the exchange of information only. Material products must be handled by other delivery systems, the postal service or cash machines.

Also the lack of face-to-face contact must be compensated for by effective security checks to counter fraud, theft and straightforward mistakes.

A major potential disadvantage is the lessening of opportunities for selling financial services, though it is not always evident that bank staff make the most of such possibilities. Similarly some customers will still feel the need for face-to-face service when discussing very important personal matters. Indeed in many ways a change to tele-banking is a trade-off between some potential service disadvantages and back-room operational advantages in cost saving and productivity.

In a more general context, the back-room advantages of modern computing are obvious in terms of the automation of routine information processing. Service advantages may exist if the database technology could also be used to informate, that is provide added value through the quality of information on hand during the service encounter.

A simple example is provided by the experience of attempting to obtain service from one of the power utilities in the past. This involved a visit to a local shop where a harassed assistant would attempt to contact the service engineers who had, of course, just left to carry out some calls and were unavailable for either action or discussion unless the emergency was life threatening. In contrast a telephone call would now be promptly answered by an employee working a computer with current information on customers and service engineer availability, in theory at least.

Hospitals have long been seen as potential users of IT. The possibilities were seen from a patient's viewpoint and summarized in Sarson (1992). A picture of repetitive record-keeping emerges with handwriting competing with printout in a context where existing information technology could bring considerable benefits. Sarson conjures up a picture of a doctor decision support (DDS) package where electronic versions of X-rays, patient test data (and, in this modern world of health care, presumably costs) coexist and are accessible on high resolution screens at any point in the hospital where they are required.

This surely is not too far-fetched for a service provider which can currently cope with computer based diagnostic high-tech and high levels of personal care in the same operating environment. The organizational implications of IT in health care provision is a vast subject in itself and may perhaps provide indications of problems and solutions for other operational areas, though cross-fertilization of operational ideas with other sectors seems rare.

TECHNOLOGY IN MANUFACTURING OPERATIONS

The use of machine technologies in manufacture were at the root of the Industrial Revolution. Whether machine-based factories were a good or an evil depends on one's point of view but Ure (1835) has no doubts on the matter:

Manufacture is a word, which, in the vicissitude of language, has come to signify the reverse of its intrinsic meaning, for it now denotes every extensive product of art, which is made by machinery, with little or no aid of the human hand; so that the most perfect manufacture is that which dispenses entirely with manual labour.

Advanced manufacturing technology (AMT) is the generic term given to a range of systems which have been developed in recent years and have dramatically changed manufacturing processes and the design interface for many companies. Though the picture is endlessly changing we can summarize some of these developments in ways which show their likely impact on operational strategy in a manufacturing enterprise. Further details are contained in Harrison (1990) which is concerned specifically with the management of AMT.

AMT relates to the physical transformation of materials, their movement, inspection and storage. Individual technologies in this area include computer numerically controlled (CNC) machines, robotics, automated guided vehicles (AGV) for moving materials and automated test equipment (ATE). These may be grouped together, physically and through computer control, to form flexible manufacturing systems (FMS) and in total given the acronym CAM (computer aided manufacture). Seen in isolation, CAM has much the same aims as other manufacturing technologies, that is to cost-effectively improve productivity and quality and to provide a stable and predictable manufacturing environment to ensure that delivery promises are kept. This is achieved through the substitution of capital for labour to an extent that led some to foresee lights-off factories as a possibility in the near future.

There is a further strand to the justification for such technology seen in the use of the word 'flexible'. Setting up such equipment to manufacture a different product is largely computer controlled, substituting programming for the machine setter. This, coupled to such notions as SMED (single minute exchange die) which promote response flexibility, gives the possibility of small batch production or even a mechanized form of JIT. Thus CAM has ambitious aims, indeed is an organizing principle for manufacturing as much as a collection of equipment.

Advanced manufacturing technology is also concerned with product design through CAD (computer aided design). CAD has moved on in recent years from two-dimensional draughting systems to three-dimensional modelling and to systems which allow the visualization of the final product in a range of different environments. Thus, for example, manufacturers of baths and washbasins can now produce graphics showing their products in a variety of colours, styles and configurations in a customer's own bathroom. The result can be viewed from a range of angles and quickly adjusted to customer taste. The result of such experimentation can then be quickly costed to produce a quotation thus fully involving the customer in key design choices. The concept of the service factory comes to life through such examples, though for many manufacturers both organizational and economic barriers remain which inhibit its adoption.

Computer aided design can then be linked to manufacture through CAD-CAM systems. Though mainly engineering issues are addressed in CADCAM, this is the key link for many industries such as electronics, enabling very complex designs to be downloaded to production in a short time and with a minimum of mistakes. Such systems gain considerably in effectiveness if then linked to CAPM (see Chapter 7) and implemented in the context of general improvements in the management of production and quality. They are often accompanied by changes to workforce organization to team or cell-based workgroups.

If CADCAM is linked to other factory based systems, such as costing and human resource planning, we have some form of computer integrated manufacturing (CIM). A goal for many system designers is even more comprehensive integration into computer integrated business (CIB). Figure 8.1 provides a diagrammatic reminder of the linkages mentioned above. CIM may be seen as the ultimate form of manufacturing system with overwhelming potential advantages or as a rigid, over-expensive and unmanageable albatross. Certainly it addresses most of the standard sources of manufacturing competitive advantage, i.e. productivity, quality, speed of innovation and so forth. Its organizational implications are increasingly being charted and associated issues, such as effective costing systems, being addressed. Whether an individual organization can bring together all the pieces of the jigsaw into a coherent whole is a challenge that many organizations are addressing world-wide.

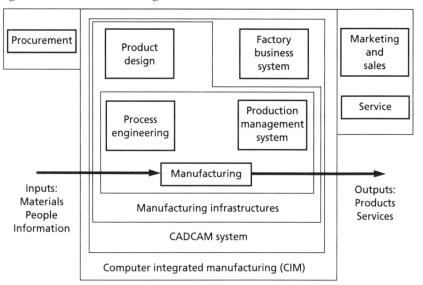

Figure 8.1
Computer integrated business

Three major points should be noted in the use of AMT and CIM. The first is that such technology as a total system is very different from the mere sum of its parts. In systems terminology it has emergent properties, some of which may be referred to by common operational terminology such as productivity, flexibility and so forth. It should also be noted that the behaviour of such systems may be hard to predict and control. An interesting analogy here is provided by computerized share trading systems whose very reactiveness can lead to apparent instability. Engineers therefore are very concerned about problems in the control of large, integrated manufacturing systems and operational managers should note this when, for example, scheduling work in MRP II systems.

The second point to note is that manufacturing is becoming very sophisticated in its use of materials, equipment and systems. Newer developments such as bio-technology will perhaps mean that operational staff will require a more substantial scientific training in order to comprehend design and manufacturing processes.

A final point to address is the portability of CIM between different organizational settings. Though the engineering aspects of CIM are product and material related, there seems little reason why developments in one area of work cannot, with ingenuity, be adapted to others. Certainly many problems remain in the widespread use, for instance, of robotics partly due to the difficulties of programming visualization systems. However, a large amount of research in such areas of computing has been underway for some time. Along with reductions in computer processing costs and increases in speed, the possibilities inherent in this technology continue to grow. Diffusion in computer innovation has always been a strong point in this technology and hence the progress of the last thirty years seems set to continue.

Problems in the diffusion of CIM seem more related to organizational and human resource issues. However fast the physical and programming technologies develop they must be translated into business action and this is where technology and operational strategies come together under a corporate planning umbrella.

The central control of manufacture is a powerful image which has been in existence for a long time. For instance Ure (1835) considers it a central feature of the manufacturing enterprise:

> The term Factory, in technology, designates the combined operation of many orders of work-people, adult and young, in tending with assiduous skill a system of production machines continuously impelled by a central power.

This idea of a central power continues in modern usage as a metaphor for organizational control which can inhibit the consideration of alternative structures. Goldhar et al (1991) have no inhibitions in recommending the benefits of CIM. In surveying trends in manufacturing since 1980 they identify the following factors:

- Shorter product life cycles
- Greater product diversity
- Fragmented markets
- Widespread alternatives
- More rigorous quality standards and expectations
- Sophisticated customers.

It is argued that the conditions that formerly supported economy-of-scale logic are gone. In their place, conditions now support and reward factories that exhibit economy-of-scope and strategies that utilize flexibility, and this leads us to consider the value of CADCAM, CIM and so forth as enabling technologies.

They do, however, note that many firms have considerable problems in implementing such systems and quote the following:

- Islands of automation only give first-order benefits (labour and inventory saving) but incur second-order disruption costs.
- Automated shop-floor and old MRP systems are overwhelmed by design implications.
- Design and distribution are not capable of translating manufacturing advantage into market place.
- Inadequate market and business strategies to realize advantage.
- Organizational structure and systems cannot handle the new flexibility.

Benefiting from new technology requires new business strategies, different organizational forms, revised administrative procedures and above all else needs top-down commitment. The result should be the factory of the future, which according to Goldhar et al (1991):

> ... is best defined as a system with a high level of flexibility, plus a very short response time in all aspects of its operations. ... This factory will have many of the characteristics of a computer-based information system. Indeed, it can be conceptualized as a computer-based information system with associated peripheral devices such as machine tools, robots, and other production devices in place of the familiar printers and plotters of office computers.

Factory operations using CIM are similar to those in an office. They are also like a process industry in that most transformation costs are fixed; the only variable costs are materials, energy and small amount of variable labour. This also implies that setting up the factory is crucial. We must use past experience and simulation in imaginative ways in order to avoid early and costly mistakes. The learning curve applies in a different way. We do not learn by mere repetition through cumulative production. We have to learn from our cumulative experience with different products. We need to indulge in learning from innovation rather than burying our mistakes.

Thus CIM is seen as a powerful enabling technology but will not produce commercial advantages unless business and operational systems exploit its potential. Operations in this context has characteristics of manufacturing, service and office.

Benetton as an example of IT use

The Benetton organization provides an example of the fusing together of manufacturing, service, design and office operations with information technology as a key strategic ingredient. As described in Belussi (1989), the company (which was only formed in 1965) is based on a network of manufacturing subcontractors and franchised outlets, Benetton itself only employing perhaps 10 per cent of the workforce needed to make and distribute its products.

It uses an integrated production planning and distribution system to eliminate warehousing. Stock is displayed on the shelves of outlets and replenished through a complex demand forecasting and ordering exercise based on IT networking. Thus information technology is a key source of competitive advantage in enabling a form of world-wide JIT to be used, so essential with fashion products where obsolescence is an ever-present danger.

A comprehensive CADCAM system is used to design new products, automatically allowing for a range of sizes, and then to download the designs to production machinery in appropriate factories followed by the automating of the dispatch and distribution functions. Thus IT is the enabling technology for product design in a company which aims for very short development cycles.

Thus Benetton provides an impressive example of computer integrated business allied to strategic flexibility, countering any charge that comprehensive integration leads to inflexibility.

Expert systems in manufacturing

Though a consideration of modern developments in software engineering appears to take us some distance from our central theme of operations strategy, it is important to note possibilities which have the potential to change the balance between the use of people and automation.

Knowledge-based systems have potential for supporting human decision making and also in some cases for replacing it. The uses of expert systems in medical diagnosis are well known but their potential use in manufacturing planning, alongside more conventional automation, is also receiving a great deal of attention.

These developments are explored at some length in Kerr (1991) which shows how manufacturing planning and control systems may be viewed as relational databases and highly sophisticated decision support systems put in place, if possible incorporating expert knowledge in scheduling and process planning.

The purpose here is not merely to replace human decision making but to improve the total system. An example given by Kerr is the thinking time needed for scheduling and problem solving. In a complex batch production environment considerable time may be required to plan what to do next in the context of rapidly changing priorities. This in itself is a disadvantage if 'time-based competition' is the goal. The use of JIT, which devolves much decision making to the shop floor, has to be accompanied by product and process simplification and pull scheduling so that continual decision making is feasible. An alternative approach, avoiding excessive time buffers, is to invest in real-time decision support systems which facilitate the very fast evaluation of alternative courses of action.

The need here is not only for highly advanced software but also for organizational responsiveness. This includes adequate cost management systems which along with engineering and commercial systems provide the necessary information for an effective response to be made in a turbulent environment.

An 'engineering systems' model of technology developments

There is an ever present danger that the systems models of engineers and computer specialists will not be comprehensible to business specialists and yet at the same time be inadequate in reflecting the social and economic world in which business is conducted. Certainly attempts have been made to relate, for example, soft systems methods to engineering problems but more context specific models are also of value. One example, developed by sociologists interested in technology and organizations is the 'engineering systems' approach described below in the context of its use in showing the changes over the years in the implementation of CAPM systems.

Our previous discussions in Chapter 7 showed the need for a more comprehensive systems model reflecting all aspects of CAPM implementation in a historic framework. In carrying out such an analysis one must avoid the trap of assuming that the potential benefits of contemporary systems were available 20 years ago.

Drawing on Clark et al (1988) and Rose (1990), the concept of an engineering system provides a useful characterization of the changes which have taken place in MRP in its 20 year history. In Figure 8.2 we show a typical MRP installation for the early 1970s. The technology would be a mainframe computer with customized software in order to cope with the complexity of even a small installation. In the engineering systems model, the term 'architecture' refers to the systems principles in operation and would in this instance include as fundamental the MRP basic logic. Early literature on MRP emphasized the integrative benefits of this approach (with perhaps insufficient concern regarding types of integration) and in particular emphasized discipline.

PRIMARY ELEMENTS	
Architecture	*Technology*
MRP logic	Mainframe
Integration	Customized software
Discipline	
SECONDARY ELEMENTS	
Dimensioning	
Use of consultants	
Design the 'right' system and implement efficiently	
Appearance	
Line printer output!	
Standard formats	

Figure 8.2
MRP in the 1970s

The term 'dimensioning' refers to the customization of the system to a particular organization and would in all probability, in the 1970s, be carried out by consultants in line with the idea that a system was being designed to do a job and the key imperative was that it be 'correctly' operated.

The term 'appearance' might seem out of context in an engineering system but includes ergonomic design and the clarity and usefulness of screen outputs. These are important in encouraging users to interact with the system. It is doubtful if standard forms produced by line printer would have this effect.

By contrast Figure.8.3 characterizes the possibilities for CAPM in the 1990s. Technology now allows for access to the system to be widely distributed and appearance may emphasize accessibility (through user-friendly screen output design), the highlighting of specific problems, and exception reporting on issues defined by the user.

In line with the recommendations of ACME consultants, and current recommended practice in operations management, dimensioning/customization may be based on a strategic corporate and manufacturing audit of the company and a subsequent 'pick and mix' approach to a wide variety of well-understood approaches to manufacturing control.

PRIMARY ELEMENTS

Architecture   *Technology*

Strategic flexibility (resilience)   Networking
Continuing improvement   Modular software
Links with TQM, product design, MIS, etc

SECONDARY ELEMENTS

Dimensioning

Strategic audit
'Pick and mix' from MRP II, JIT, OPT, etc

Appearance

Accessible for all functions
Problem visibility
User-designed outputs

Figure 8.3
CAPM in the 1990s

The fundamental principles (architecture) for systems development in the 1990s should at the very least include the following key features:

- Strategic flexibility (resilience)
- A philosophy of continuing improvement
- Genuine integration with total quality management (TQM) initiatives, design and so forth.

In particular, in a modern system there is no reason why the 'design space' (i.e. scope for modification and improvement) of the system should be closed off at the point of implementation.

In Figure 8.4 we illustrate how an informating cycle might draw on CAPM (or any other operational) databases to improve formal decision making systems as learning takes place through the continuing adjustments of individual informal models. We have previously commented on the desirability of such learning and Zuboff's studies clearly point out the organizational problems inherent in such an approach.

Thus we have seen a challenging approach for the improvement of CAPM systems through continuing learning and noted the grave potential difficulties both through the past record of CAPM implementational failures and the studies of ACME researchers and others. The need for a

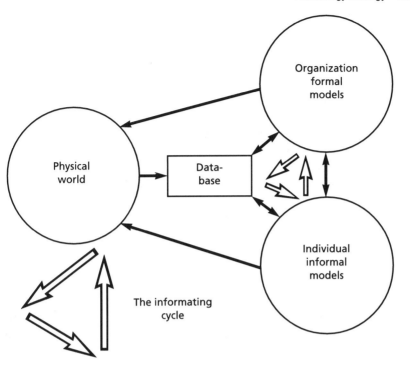

Figure 8.4
An informating cycle in CAPM

clear strategic direction is evident, if only to avoid the fate envisaged by Schumacher (1988):

> MRP II can ... act like a gigantic iron corset around the enterprise and suffocate the initiative of local managers.

TECHNOLOGY STRATEGY

There is a substantial overlap between operations strategy and the management of technological innovation. Though the latter often concentrates on product innovation and naturally relates to marketing strategy, the links with operations are considerable and were mentioned in Chapter 3 in the context of the design-operations interface.

The management of technology is also a key issue in the direct development of the technological infrastructure for operations. Research and development (R&D) may equally refer to process and administrative systems as to product design and ideally relates to them all. The management of this whole process is considered as a coherent discipline in itself in such texts as Twiss (1992). Many issues in technology strategy are similar to those in operations, for instance the financial evaluation of major capital investment projects and methodologies for project management. Technology strategy, however, is also centrally concerned with technological forecasting for product development and with the management of the R&D function.

Thus once again we see similarities and differences between approaches which nonetheless have a central core of common interests and objectives. One area in which this common concern is evident is the management of relationships with equipment vendors.

The continuing relationship between users of technology and suppliers is a very important topic in technology management. In the context of manufacturing operations and the use of advanced manufacturing technology (AMT) this is addressed in Zairi (1991) who advocates a strategic approach by both parties.

Based on empirical investigation in a variety of manufacturing contexts, Zairi postulates that in practice users appear to adopt either an offensive or a defensive approach. Typical of a defensive strategy is a piecemeal approach to capital equipment purchase often based on a need to replace or upgrade existing equipment. The business goals are typically to provide additional capacity, improve productivity levels and to maintain share in a low growth market.

Offensive strategies by AMT users are seen to be based on the integration of the following key elements:

- Manufacturing and marketing strategy
- Human resource strategy
- Financial strategy
- Supplier appraisal.

The result may be the pursuit of productivity as with the defensive approach but it may also include flexibility, shorter product life cycles and comprehensive integration.

Suppliers of AMT also vary in terms of their basic approach. A policy of selling standard products requires a particular approach to promotional activities often aimed at the defensive user. To use Porter's generic competitive strategy model, such an organization may well aim to be a low cost supplier. On the other hand a supplier may aim to differentiate and in systems purchasing situations this may mean the development of a long-term relationship with clients emphasizing joint learning and the pursuit of complementary strategies.

Thus innovative and differentiated suppliers may find natural partners in offensive users. This is not to discount other relationships but the synergy of a well-matched approach where both partners are strategically proactive may be considerable. Of course a technologically sophisticated supplier may offer a complete service to a less experienced user but the latter is likely at least to have a well-developed business plan in order to make such a relationship profitable.

Another feature of this situation is the networks which exist as users have a number of suppliers and vice versa. Similarly suppliers of systems may act as coordinators and project managers for a number of subsystem vendors. The overall effect of all this activity is the diffusion of learning, often amongst competing firms. The company which most effectively uses this potential knowledge has found at least one piece in the complex pattern of competitive strategy.

CHAPTER 9

Human resource development

INTRODUCTION

A full exposition of all the human resource issues in operational manage-ment would be a massive undertaking. In this chapter we assume the read-er has a working knowledge of the principles and practice of the manage-ment of people in organizations and we provide a few pointers to specifi-cally operational issues where a strategic approach to human resource development is necessary.

However, we first return to the systems terminology introduced in Chapter 1 and note that most operational systems have features which, to do them justice, require modelling as complex/pluralistic or complex/coercive systems. We might do this through soft systems methodology for instance and the resulting debate is likely to produce a rich variety of systems' characterizations.

Effective operational management, however, must deliver coherent strategies and procedures which are capable of being understood and acted upon by a wide range of people. This assumes simple and unitary underly-ing models. Operations strategy must bridge the gap by providing mean-ingful, sophisticated analysis as well as operations prescriptions.

This is usually done by attacking complexity through the disaggregation of operations into a range of sub-systems and addressing specific issues such as layout, flow control and quality. Similarly plurality is addressed through unifying concepts such as TQM and project management which attempt to organize, persuade and motivate others into the acceptance of a working culture which promotes operational effectiveness while accepting differences in objectives and priorities.

The latter raises a key issue, the extent to which operations depend on local experience or on expert knowledge. Are effective operations due to the profound knowledge (to borrow Deming's phrase) of a range of actors deeply concerned with actual operational provision or due to the applica-tion of sound theories by managers and specialists? Recent approaches seem to favour the former, provided 'profound knowledge' does not become merely the routine and emotional acceptance that only the *status quo* will work.

Yet it is widely known that many technological opportunities are available whose workings are difficult to understand and whose implementation will upset the *status quo*. Goldhar et al (1991) comment on the increasing scientific basis of manufacturing operations and the implications of the scale and complexity of computer integrated manufacturing (CIM) systems are not easy to comprehend. The provision of professional services, with their emphasis on human intervention and discretion may seem a different world to CIM but the service factory depends on such joint working of people and computer systems. Such systems will not come into existence merely by the continuation of current ways of working. They are new and different and require imaginative innovation and implementation. They are also risky and will not work if people do not make them work.

It is also a prime responsibility of the operational strategist to provide direction. Operations must be consistent with corporate planning and once again such consistency will not arise by chance or inertia. Yet a totally top-down approach which ignores local knowledge and the need for consensus, though possibly necessary in extreme situations, may be costly and unsuccessful in practice, quite apart from its effects on the quality of working life.

Thus a key question in strategic operational design is the balance between autonomy and intervention. Operations is not only about productivity and effectiveness but also concerns motivation and organizational structure.

HUMAN RESOURCE ISSUES IN MANUFACTURING

A great deal has been written about human resource management in the context of manufacturing industry both by management specialists and by social scientists. A useful framework is provided by Kinnie and Staughton (1991) which has the added virtue of relating such issues to Hill's model of manufacturing strategy (as introduced in Chapters 1 and 4, see Figure 4.3 which extends Hill's model to include both financial and human resource strategies). In the context of case studies based on seven manufacturing companies, Kinnie and Staughton discuss the following key issues, the following extended discussion being based on a variety of source materials:

● Education and training
● Pay systems and structures
● Staffing arrangements.

Education and training is often characterized at the first budget to be cut when an organization is short of cash. A more enlightened view sees it as a powerful vehicle for change in an organization. The latter view does, however, assume that developmental programmes are consistent with corporate strategy and closely related to other changing features in an organization. This requires a level of planning and careful implementation way beyond that which was painfully evident in many traditional manufacturing companies.

Most providers of management training and education are all too familiar with the employee who can only get training from his employer by continual badgering. The well-worn phrase 'you should have sent my boss on this course' shows the frustration of the junior employee whose knowledge and skills learnt on a college course are simply not implementable at work, however relevant. This problem is being determinedly attacked through competence based courses where performance at work provides the basis for assessment and an in-company mentor provides the connection between organizational needs and individual learning.

Furthermore many companies now understand that education and training must be available to the totality of employees if involvement and consistency of action in strategy implementation is to be achieved. This refers both to general training to improve the basic skills of management and also to technical training which not only prepares employees for changes but also renews and enhances their skills in performing familiar tasks. The latter is obviously best carried out in the context of continuous learning and improvement as described below.

Kinnie and Staughton (1991) point out the need for training when employee roles are subject to change. An instance they quote is when OPT as a methodology of production control was introduced in one factory along with changes in the payment system. No longer able to rely on the motivational effects of payment by results, supervisors had to be trained in communication and team building. More senior management also had to change their approach away from the crisis management of material flow control. The introduction of any new CAPM system without extensive training is likely to prove a disaster.

Payment systems, job evaluation and performance appraisal schemes must all be consistent with manufacturing strategy, in particular relating to quality control and in the context of the chosen process form. For instance, a jobbing form of production emphasizes the skills and ingenuity of individual craftspeople in a situation where meeting a particular customer's needs is paramount. Thus quality is related to customer satisfaction in a way not dissimilar to service operations and the ability to communicate and to solve problems is very important. By contrast a traditional form of production line job requires consistency and speed rather than ingenuity and payment by results may be one of only a few feasible motivational approaches. In this context the JIT approach of continual improvement makes motivational as well as productive sense, but payment by volume is problematic in the context of pull scheduling.

Drawing up detailed job descriptions may also be impossible where flexibility and multi-skilling are the norm. In such situations communication on the ends to be achieved at a given point in time may be more useful than detailed specifications of the means to be employed at all points in time.

Staffing issues include recruitment, redeployment, promotion and redundancy. This encompasses manpower planning at the organizational level and the allocation of an individual to a role or task at the tactical level. Flexibility is obviously important to the organization but one might consider its effects on the individual employee. For instance in one factory an extensive programme of multi-skilling was followed by a long period where production requirements meant that most workers simply carried out their previous roles. This led to frustration and cynicism directed at the competence of senior management who in turn were baffled by this response to what they considered was responsible modern management practice. The problem here may have been a lack of communication and openness on future strategy but this is by no means an easy problem to handle in practice.

Kinnie and Staughton also speculate on the classic approaches adopted by companies in dealing with human resource management issues. These are:

- The wait and see approach – care in avoiding unnecessary cost is traded against the possibility of being late in implementing new systems.
- The 'predict and pre-empt' approach – obviously praiseworthy if your predictions are reliable.
- The 'learn as you go' approach – of value if you learn and communicate quickly enough.

The disadvantages of the first of these are obvious though it was typical of five of the seven case studies quoted by the researchers. Even if a prudent attitude to expenditure is to be commended, waiting to see what happens is a feeble management strategy compared with the third alternative. In this latter case a culture of learning is encouraged along with a modesty in one's forecasting ability. These appear to be desirable characteristics in the current environment but such a strategy may be defeated by lead-times and the speed of change, that is having learnt what one should be doing can one perform in time?

One key to solving this problem is to remember that one's situation is not entirely unique. A company faced with implementing, say, a CAPM system is following in the footsteps of thousands of predecessors. Whilst the operation of CAPM in a given company will have idiosyncratic features, many of the human resource implications of such an innovation are well understood and much training and organizational change can be planned in advance. The optimum seems to be a prudent mixture of anticipation and learning, diffusion and sharing of the latter being widely promoted.

One of the major barriers to this, all too present in many companies, is the 'not invented here' syndrome. Some managers appear to be so intoxicated with a sense of their uniqueness and the need for heroic action that they are contemptuous of the experience and learning of others. This provides an interesting contrast with the Japanese approach, based originally on copying the best practice of others and then gradually improving on it, all in the context of a management style which insists on group consensus and action. In many companies, the application of even a simple techniques such as bench-marking (see Chapter 6) is valuable in promoting systematic learning from a wide range of sources.

HUMAN RESOURCE ISSUES IN SERVICE AND OFFICE OPERATIONS

Much of the above discussion relating to research in manufacturing industry carries over to service and office contexts. The principal difference, obvious from the very definition of service, is the human resource issues of staff having direct client contact. This is hardly a new issue in personnel management as, for instance, the training of sales staff is a well-explored area of work. However, operational staff are likely to have a different set of tasks and responsibilities when dealing with clients. The objective is not only to make a sale but also to provide aspects of service. For instance an assistant in a travel agency has a selling role but must also be competent in the actual clerical and computer-based tasks of booking travel.

The relationship between service providers and clients has been mentioned a number of times above, in particular in Chapter 5 in the context of service process choice and capacity management. Our concern here is with the interface between human resource and operational strategies. One key component of this relationship is the provision of a methodology for the analysis of operational situations into a series of tasks. This listing may then be used by personnel and training staff in recruitment, training and the design of staff welfare systems. Lovelock (1992), for example, includes several papers on this theme which is of particular importance in situations of high labour intensity and where flexibility is needed to match supply and demand.

There is much general management literature on the need for an appropriate service culture, in particular the 'excellence' series of books (including the original Peters and Waterman (1982)) emphasize this as a key feature of modern corporate life. It should also be remembered that the adoption of TQM in any organization carries with it an emphasis on internal as well as external client-provider relationships. Thus the skills of dealing with a 'client' (as well as being one) become essential for all organizational workers and the need for a service culture is ever present.

Air traffic control – an example of job design

A great deal of current research centres on the social organization of work in a context of information technology. An interesting example is provided in a report by Coops and Hobson (1992) on work carried out by researchers from Lancaster University on air traffic control (ATC) organization.

Air traffic control is a manual system aided by a great deal of technology. It is important, stressful and involves complex communication with a variety of outside agents in real-time decision situations. One principal researcher, John Hughes, comments:

> Control systems with reactive databases can only be effective when systems designers have access to guidance on the social aspects of work.

Such an operational context poses more extreme problems than the majority of factories and offices, but the same basic lessons apply. The human and machine parts of IT systems must be capable of working together to meet the objectives of the total system.

MOTIVATION AT WORK

We now turn to a brief consideration of some issues, common to all operational contexts, which demand special care and a strategic approach. In Figure 9.1 we compare two damaging ways in which poor performance is self-reinforcing. Just as low current profitability impairs an organization's ability to perform well financially in the future, it can also lead to a downward spiralling of motivation, morale and productivity in a workforce. Determined strategic action is needed to counter both of these effects.

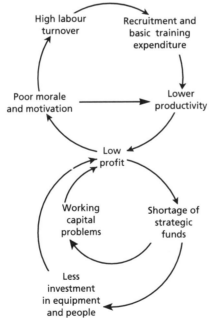

Figure 9.1
Dynamics of poor performance

The sources of individual and group motivation is a major preoccupation of organizational theorists and of managers. A straightforward summary of work in this complex area, and one which relates well to operations management, is given in Huczinski and Buchanan (1992). Motivation is related to five features of a work situation:

- Skill variety – where a job uses differing skills and abilities.
- Task identity – where a job is a whole and meaningful piece of work.
- Task significance – where the job affects others in an organization or affects clients.
- Autonomy – where there is freedom and independence in decision making and control.
- Feedback – where information is readily available on performance levels, including quality.

The first three of these together give what is referred to as 'experienced meaningfulness of work'. A particular job may require, say, skill variety more than task identity but some positive and coherent mixture of these three features is necessary for the job to be seen as meaningful.

Autonomy gives a job 'experienced responsibility for outcomes' and feedback gives 'knowledge of actual results'. It is then argued that high motivation, quality and satisfaction at work is the result of a job which is meaningful, responsible and for which actual performance is known.

The value of this framework is that a number of common approaches to job design may be contrasted in terms of these features. For instance the combining of tasks (job enlargement) addresses issues of skill variety and task identity but not necessarily the others. In contrast many jobs involving direct service provision score well on feedback, at least directly from the client. The extent to which the other features occur will depend on the context, for example nursing may be highly meaningful but lacking in autonomy in some situations. Teaching is a profession which traditionally has all the motivational factors but which may be organizationally and environmentally constrained, in particular by a reduction in autonomy.

This raises a particular problem with professional workers where a high score on all five motivational factors might be expected as a matter of right. Thus a particular work situation which falls below this ideal might be considered demotivating. In contrast workers accustomed to very routine tasks may feel threatened and uncertain if the job is changed without explanation, consultation and training. Motivation cannot therefore be separated from expectations and the history of work in a particular context.

The now classic device of job enrichment addresses all five motivational factors. More recently TQM, through its insistence on a pro-active approach to client relationships, can be seen to potentially score well motivationally though the issue of empowerment is related to the degree of autonomy of an individual.

This framework of motivation may also be applied to a small group. An example is a cell in a manufacturing unit. The cell as a unit may score well on all factors but at a given point of time individual members may lack, say, skill variety or autonomy. This may be handled by imaginative cell leadership in rotating tasks and fully communicating objectives, plans and performance levels to cell members.

The operational strategist therefore has a number of options available in job design for individuals and groups but changes must be strategic both in the sense of relating to corporate planning and also in their dynamics. Over a period of time changes to job structures must be coherent and positive to all concerned.

PROJECT MANAGEMENT AND ORGANIZATIONAL STRUCTURE

An issue which has taxed organizational theorists for some time is the link between organizational structure and operational process form. Are some forms of organization more suitable for a process industry rather than a batch producer? What is the best organizational form for either of these situations? We explore this issue in a particular context which has arisen on a number of occasions earlier in this book. The question we will ask is what is the most appropriate organizational structure to support project management activity.

In Figure 3.5 we showed how the technical side of project management, the setting of objectives and use of project management planning and control techniques, must not be divorced from considerations of organizational structure. We must in all cases know who is to be responsible for the completion of tasks within set parameters of quality, time and cost. This issue is very well explored in Meredith and Mantel (1989) and further light is cast onto it by the explorations into the car industry described in Womack et al (1990). The discussion below is based on these references and assumes a basic knowledge of organizational structure on the part of the reader.

The most obvious answer is to use an organizational structure based directly on project management teams formed specifically for particular projects. This has a large number of advantages but may be seen as wasteful in resources. It may also inhibit the diffusion of learning, particularly in technologically sophisticated situations, between experts who find themselves in different project teams. A project management structure may lead to personnel problems in terms of career structure and continuity of employment.

At the opposite extreme is the use of a traditional functional hierarchy where a project is given to the most appropriate functional department.

This department then has to manage the project and develop or buy in any skills it does not possess. A number of problems have been seen to arise in such a context, in particular a lack of coordination if extensive outside help is needed and a failure to fully identify with the client.

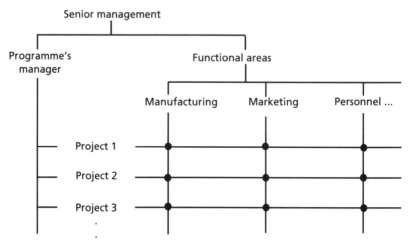

Figure 9.2
Matrix organizations

Thus a compromise seems to be necessary and the one chosen is likely to be a matrix form of organization. As illustrated in Figure 9.2 this involves a series of task orientated project teams being overlaid on a functional structure. However, the exact way in which this is to be done is the cause of much debate and concern. Larson and Gobeli (in Meredith and Mantel (1989)) postulate that three quite different matrix structures are in fact possible. The first is the functional matrix where a project manager is employed to coordinate the work of staff from a number of functional areas and subcontractors. Such an individual may have a vast budget but few direct subordinates. The project manager has to work through a number of functional managers to keep control of the project and the problems which may arise in such a context are graphically illustrated in Womack et al (1990) in the context of the GM-10 car design project.

The second form of matrix structure is the balanced matrix where the project manager has authority on an equal basis with functional heads and must manage the project jointly with them through a series of negotiated arrangements. This emphasizes the importance of communications in project management and appears an attractive arrangement provided the project manager is a skilful negotiator and can cope with high levels of stress. This form should work well in a mixed management context where ongoing non-project work can be managed by functional heads at the same time as a limited commitment to a small number of projects.

The third form is the project matrix where functional staff are seconded to a project team for limited periods of time. This appears to have many advantages from the point of view of the project itself, though functional managers may resent their loss of power. In a reported survey of experienced project staff this is the form thought to be the most effective. However, it may cause considerable resourcing and personnel scheduling problems for functional managers if key members of their staff are absent for some length of time.

Thus it appears that even within the limited context of project management, a variety of approaches are possible, each with their advantages and disadvantages. In a given context one of the above is likely to be most suitable. However, one should not separate issues of organizational design from a consideration of the skills needed by project staff, in particular the interpersonal skills of the project manager.

This issue is considered in depth in Boddy and Buchanan (1992). Based on empirical research in a number of contexts they suggest a two dimensional framework as follows. Firstly one must consider stakeholders in the project and thus be able to manage in the following four directions:

- Managing up: relating to senior managers.
- Managing across: relating to other departments and external organizations.
- Managing the team: full-time and part-time project staff.
- Managing the staff: ensuring the commitment of contributing and supporting individuals who are not actually team members.

Then we consider the actual skills of the project manager in influencing these groups:

- Communicating
- Negotiating
- Team-building
- Involving (encouraging a sense of ownership and commitment)

The result is another matrix where the principal diagonal is of particular importance (that is communication is crucial when managing up and so forth). We can easily see the importance of these results in the context of the varieties of project organizational structures.

THE ORGANIZATIONAL CHALLENGE OF CIM AND APS

Computer integrated manufacturing provides a range of acute challenges for operational management. Ebers and Lieb (1989) argue that CIM is an attempt at a technical solution to an organizational problem. CIM implementation is only likely to succeed if accompanied by appropriate organizational changes.

One problem with CIM implementation is that as automation progresses, a company searches for economic advantages through the reduction of organizational buffering. For instance many books recommend a reduction in stock holding as an initial step to free finance for investment in equipment. This reduction in organizational slack removes one of the measures used to cope with environmental uncertainty.

Another problem is the greater effect that data inaccuracies have on an integrated system. It is astonishing to see, in a traditional company, how little accurate data is kept beyond the minimum of engineering, financial and commercial information. Stock levels, costs, bills of materials, product routings are often inadequately documented. Indeed companies who attempt to implement CAPM systems from scratch must always allow a period of time and a considerable budget for the development of databases that one might have expected to be in existence already. In an integrated system, the effects of unreliable data can be considerable, not only in terms of immediate errors but in a loss of faith in data outputs and a development of parallel informal systems as *ad hoc* checks proliferate.

In this context, Campbell and Warner (1990) discuss the 'information technology paradox'. They argue that greater technical complexity leads to increases in organizational dependency and hence to greater difficulties in managing the organization as a whole. Yet one of the stated advantages of such systems is the potential for greater control of operations. They comment:

> With CIM in the full sense, however, the tension between the need for flexibility of organization and the need for integration of disparate operations, functions and databases, already critical with CADCAM and flexible manufacturing systems (FMS), may be such that no optimal or even operable form of management or work organization can be suggested.

A further point to explore in this context is how an organizational structure is 'designed'. We might expect a technical system to be designed by a group of experts who then train other individuals in its cost-effective operation. Though some post-implementational adjustments and learning may take place there will come a time when the design is effectively finished and operation is routine and well understood.

However, is this an appropriate metaphor for the design and implementation of a social system or even of a system such as CAPM or CIM? At every level of operation, such a system must be considered in relation to its effects on individuals and their roles. Is the 'human component' in such a system required merely to act out a part following a script or the system intended as a support for human decision making and action? The latter scenario has greater chance of coping with a varied and uncertain environment. It is consistent with commonly held views of the relationship between technology and professional and managerial staff. However, in this case the operation of the system is less predictable and the integrated nature of the system means that individual decisions taken in one part of the system may reverberate through the system as a whole.

It is, of course, a normal challenge for systems designers to anticipate and allow for such effects. However, as a massive and complex system grows and continues, through its human counterparts, to evolve and adapt, can we be sure of its stability and reliability? One suspects that the answer lies in the ability of those same human counterparts to develop and adapt appropriate control mechanisms.

This leads us to a consideration of what have recently been referred to as anthropocentric production systems (APS). Cooley (1987) argues that the split between designer and operator, evident in many operational situations, is potentially damaging in terms both of the economic health of the total system and the work satisfaction and effectiveness of the individual. This is evident in the operation both of stand-alone machining systems and in the context of CIM.

It should also be said that much APS orientated writing seeks to oppose an extremely mechanistic conception of manufacturing operations. Many APS recommendations are actually perfectly consistent with fairly standard management approaches to production work design (see the section on motivation above) and will seem natural to many working in the delivery of professional services. The benefit in the APS approach is that of an integrated approach to a number of aspects of production work and its implications for large, technologically sophisticated integrated manufacturing systems.

Charles and Roulstone (1991) survey developments in APS in the UK and in Europe. The basic premises are that technology is embedded in a social context of work and that human beings bring a distinct set of capabilities to socio-technical systems. They define an APS as one which:

- allows a unity of conception and execution
- is skill enhancing
- allows some user control over work processes and technology
- utilizes human competencies
- allows a healthy and socially interactive work environment

The first of the points made above is central to Cooley's thesis. It argues against a separation of mental and manual work in favour of the unity of thinking and doing which is so natural to most human activity but has been forced out of much industrial work. Perhaps the 'do as you are told and leave the thinking to me' mentality is still too ingrained in our work culture. It is also the target of much of Deming's writing. Indeed his concept of the skilled craftsperson as having 'profound knowledge' of their craft follows a similar path, though in the context of quality rather than technology management.

The idea that APS is skill enhancing and to some degree promotes autonomy is clearly in line with the literature on motivation at work. The final point in the above list, however, raises a crucial issue which may obscure the debate. Is the fundamental purpose of APS economic or social? Should organizations invest in such systems to make a profit or to preserve jobs and the dignity of their employees?

The assumption in this book is that operations strategy is principally driven by the need to ensure long-term competitiveness. Thus we are examining APS in terms of its economic advantage, though this may in turn be enhanced through policies which promote social welfare.

Another way to explore this is to imagine that a totally technocentric (or 'lights out') production system was being proposed as an economic form of manufacture in a given situation. We would analyse this by asking whether such a system could really be of long-term utility? It might produce short-term profits through economies of scale but is this all we require? Obviously some chemical process industries, for example, are of this form though even then the production unit is embedded within an organization and its use may depend to a considerable extent on human competence in maintaining it and optimizing its operating parameters.

The point is that there is no logical reason why a technocentric approach, based entirely on machinery or partly on routine human activity, should not work in some environments but the most consistent message we receive about the modern manufacturing situation is that it is quickly changing, requires a constant stream of new products and so forth. Such a high variety environment must be matched by high variety and responsive operational units in both manufacturing and service industries. The technocentric answer to this may be CIM but its organizational implementation will be difficult. If we envisage CIM as a support for an essentially human-centred production system (based on the APS definition given above) then interesting possibilities emerge.

Charles and Roulstone, discussing an EC funded FAST programme to which they contributed, contrast CIM with CHIM (computer and human integrated manufacturing). One key difference between the two is that while CIM is based on full technical integration, CHIM has integration based on a decentralized framework of decision makers. However, CIM does not appear from the evidence to be the only development in production organization. The following are alternative responses:

- Automated variable mass production – further automation to reduce bottlenecks, increase variety and ensure conformance quality (USA).
- Diversified quality production – using highly skilled labour to achieve economies of scope (Germany).

- Flexible mass production – using team working and JIT in a repetitive manufacturing environment to ensure high quality and innovativeness (Japan).
- Flexible specialization – small batch production through a collaborative network of small firms using advanced technology and skilled and flexible labour (Italy).

Thus CIM, the APS approach and the variety of forms listed above need organizational and human innovativeness as much as its technological counterpart. In total they represent human and technological opportunities for the operational strategist coping with the variety and uncertainty inherent in a modern competitive environment.

ETHICS IN OPERATIONS MANAGEMENT

It has often been stated that one of the most important contributions made by senior management to an organization is the dominant working culture of the organization. Senior management set standards of behaviour both by example and through reinforcing or deterring certain types of behaviour. Thus a major strategic input to a company is in terms of ethical standards.

Business ethics is a major area of research and popular writing in business. Much of the concentration is currently on corporate responsibility but implicit within operational strategies are moral considerations regarding what is and is not acceptable behaviour.

An obvious example of this is in the health care industry where ethical dilemmas may face nursing, medical and managerial staff at any time. Much has been written on ethics in medical research but resource allocation in hospitals may have similar impact on the well-being of patients.

A systematic and detailed treatment of ethics in business is contained in Donaldson (1989) which sets out the historical and philosophical basis for the analysis of moral issues in the context of organizations, including the Trade Unions. Donaldson ends with a set of procedures for improvement, the first of which is 'matching values to strategies'. Though Donaldson is not directly concerned with operational management, we have here an indication of the importance of ethics at the grass roots level. Another is contained in a later suggestion:

> More open procedures and less secrecy in decision making could be developed within firms ... Safety, low morale and stress, and equitable pay and opportunities are specific issues at the level of the firm and industry.

An interesting possibility for operationalizing the consideration of ethical issues is contained in Atkinson (1989) which links ethics with soft systems methodology. This in turn leads us to Seedhouse (1988) which, though set in the context of health care, includes a practical device, the 'ethical grid', to be used as a framework for analysing particular ethical problems.

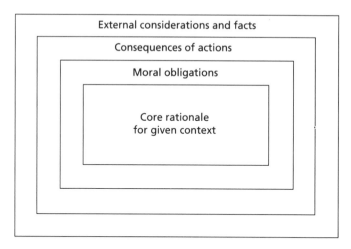

Figure 9.3
The ethical grid

The Seedhouse grid has four levels which lead us through a set of necessary considerations for analysing a given case (see Figure 9.3). The first layer consists of external considerations, including the law, codes of practice, the facts of a case and the wishes of other parties. Also included at this level are criteria such as efficiency, effectiveness and the need to assess risk. The contents of the first layer will be familiar to most managers but should not be seen as the totality of ethical considerations.

The second layer of the grid relates to the consequences of possible actions for individuals and groups including society in general. One might think of this as a form of decision theory but with moral as well as material pay-offs ('goods' in both the moral and the economic senses of the word) for a wide range of stakeholders.

The third layer will sound more esoteric to most managers but is in fact based on well-known principles. It relates to the deontological considerations associated with our actions. Donaldson defines deontology as 'The doctrine that ethics is grounded in notions of duty; that some acts are morally obligatory regardless of consequences in terms of practice'. Thus we might feel that telling the truth, keeping promises and not doing harm to others are overriding considerations.

This, however, is the point where the use of the ethical grid is likely to prove valuable in a particular case. It may well be that by this stage problems and inconsistencies have shown up. For instance, the perfectly legal action we wish to take to improve productivity will result in our making three workers redundant and we specifically promised three months ago that this would not happen.

The fourth layer is what Seedhouse calls the 'core rationale' for a given context and in his study of ethics in health care he includes respect for the autonomy of the individual and equality of treatment. These might carry over into, say, an educational context but in a business context the core rationale might differ. The important point, however, is that it should reflect the key values of an organization.

The ethical grid, seen perhaps in the context of soft systems methodology, is a vehicle for uncovering issues and debating them. In particular its use by groups of individuals can help in reconciling differences of approach to major moral issues in management. One point that is evident from even a cursory examination of general management is that managers are often encouraged to base their actions on expected consequences, within some general framework of rules, while 'the workers' are required to follow more detailed rules and instructions. Both reflect a limited set of ethical considerations and ignore the clashes which may occur with common rules of behaviour and perceived key values.

CONCLUSIONS

As management in general, and operations management in particular, is largely about people, most of this book has related to human resource issues either directly or obliquely. In this chapter we have explored several specific issues thought to be worthy of special mention. A number of further issues are briefly explored in Harrison (1990) in the specific context of the management of advanced manufacturing technology. These include:

- The social environment which provides a context for operational activity and which obviously varies around the world.
- Training and management development, with a particular emphasis on the concept of the learning organization.
- Human resource barriers to technological change and reasons for failure in technological innovation.
- Safety at work and employee welfare.
- Trade unions and industrial relations.

These are, of course, very broad areas of concern which affect management strategies in general but their relevance for operations strategy should not be forgotten in the midst of the wide range of concerns dealt with above.

BIBLIOGRAPHY

Abernathy, W. J. and Wayne, K. (1974) 'Limits of the Learning Curve', *Harvard Business Review*, Sept.– Oct, 47–57

Ackoff, R. L. and Emery, F. E. (1972) *On Purposeful Systems*, Tavistock, London

ACME (1990) *Report of the CAPM Supply Industry Conference*, March

Andreasen, M. M. and Hein, L. (1987) *Integrated Product Development*, IFS Publications, Bedford

Amara, R. and Lipinski, A. J. (1983) *Business Planning for an Uncertain Future*, Pergamon, Oxford

Andreou, S. A. (1991) 'Capital resource allocation for strategic quality management', *International Journal of Technology Management*, Special Issues on Manufacturing Strategy, Vol. 6, Nos 3/4, 415-426

Ansoff, I. and McDonnell, E. (1990) *Implanting Strategic Management* (2ed), Prentice Hall, New York

Atkinson, C. J. (1989) 'Ethics: a lost dimension in soft systems practice', *Journal of Applied Systems Analysis*, vol. 16, 43-53

Bank, J. (1992) *The Essence of Total Quality Management*, Prentice Hall, New York

Beer, S. (1981) *Brain of the Firm* (2ed), Wiley, Chichester

Beer, S. (1985) *Diagnosing the System for Organizations*, Wiley, Chichester

Bell, R. and Gaafar, O. M. (1990) 'Small Firm Growth and the Ambition Dilemma', in Carrie, A. and Simpson, I. (eds) *Advances in Manufacturing Technology V*, Strathclyde University, 28 – 32

Belussi, F. (1989) 'Benetton: a case-study of corporate strategy for innovation in traditional sectors', in *Technology Strategy and the Firm: Management and Public Policy* (ed. M. Dodgson)

Bennett, D., Lewis, C. and Oakley, M. (1988) *Operations Management*, Philip Allan, London

Bennett, D. J. and Forrester, P. L. (1990) *The DRAMA Methodology for Analysing Strategy and its links with Production System Design*, Proceedings of the 5th International Conference of the Operations Management (UK), MCB Press, Bradford

Berliner, C. and Brimson, J. A. (1988) *Cost Management for Today's Advanced Manufacturing*, Harvard Business School Press, Boston

Berry, G. and Carter, M. (1992) *Assessing Crime Prevention Initiatives: The First Steps*, Home Office Crime Prevention Unit, Paper No. 31

Bodily, S. E. (1985) *Modern Decision Making*, McGraw Hill, New York

Boddy, D. and Buchanan, D. (1992) *Take the Lead*, Prentice Hall, New York

Bowman, C. (1990) *The Essence of Strategic Management*, Prentice Hall, New York

Bowman, C. and Verity, J. (1991) *Surfacing Managerial Patterns of Competitive Strategy*, Research Review, Cranfield School of Management, Summer

BPICS (1990) *Industrial Computing Sourcebook: 1990/1*, Emap, London

Browne, J., Harhen, J. and Shivnan, J. (1988) *Production Management Systems*, Addison Wesley, Wokingham

Buxey, G. (1991) 'The Nexus between CAD-CAM and Quality', *International Journal of Operations and Production Management*, Vol. 11, No. 10, 19–32

Campbell, A. and Warner, M. (1990) 'Managing Advanced Manufacturing Technology', in Warner, M., Wobbe, W. and Brodner, P. (eds) *New Technology and Manufacturing Management,* Wiley, Chichester

Charles, T. and Roulstone, A. (1991) *Prospects and Conditions for Human Centred Production Systems in British Manufacturing,* TORU Occasional Paper No 2, Staffordshire Polytechnic

Checkland, P. (1981) *Systems Thinking, Systems Practice,* Wiley, Chichester

Checkland, P. and Scholes, J. (1990) *Soft Systems Methodology in Action,* Wiley, Chichester

Clark, J., McLoughlin, I., Rose, H. and King, R. (1988) *The Process of Technological Change: New Technology and Social Choice in the Workplace,* Cambridge University Press, Cambridge

Cooley, M. (1987) *Architect or Bee? The Human Price of Technology,* Hogarth Press, London

Cullen, J. and Hollingum, J. (1987) *Implementing Total Quality,* IFS (Publications)/Springer-Verlag, Berlin

Dale, B. G. and Plunkett, J. J. (eds) (1990) *Managing Quality,* Philip Allan, New York

Deming, W. E. (1986) *Out of the Crisis,* Cambridge University Press

Dilworth, J. B. (1992) *Operations Management,* McGraw-Hill, New York

Donaldson, J. (1989) *Key Issues in Business Ethics,* Academic Press, London

DTI (1989) *Manufacturing into the Late 1990s,* HMSO, London

Dwyer, J. (1990) *Mis-aligned integration,* Manufacturing Systems, June, 25-29

Ebers, M. and Lieb, M. (1989) 'Computer integrated manufacturing as a two-edged sword', *International Journal of Operations and Production Management,* 9, 2, 69-92

Eilon, S. (1976) *Applied Productivity Analysis for Industry,* Pergamon, Oxford

Ferdowes, K., Miller, J. G., Nakane, J. and Vollmann, T. E. (1989) 'Evolving global manufacturing strategies: projections into the 1990s' in Sheth, J. and Eshghi, G. (1989) *Global Operations Perspectives,* South-Western, Cincinnati

Flood, R. L. and Jackson, M. C. (1991) *Creative Problem Solving,* Wiley, Chichester

Garvin, D. A. (1988) *Managing Quality,* Free Press, New York

Garvin, D. A. (1992) *Operations Strategy: Text and Cases,* Prentice Hall, New York

Giffi, C. A., Seal, G. M. and Roth, A. V. (1990) *Operating Principles for the 1990s: Assessment of the Elements Comprising World Class Manufacturing,* Proceedings of the 5th International Conference of the Operations Management (UK), MCB Press, Bradford

Goldhar, J. D., Jelinek, M. and Schlie, T. W. (1991) 'Flexibility and competitive advantage - manufacturing becomes a service business', *International Journal of Technology Management,* Special Issue on Manufacturing Strategy, Vol. 6, Nos 3/4, 243-259

Goldratt, E. M. (1985) 'Devising a coherent production, finance and marketing strategy using OPT rules', *BPICS Control,* April/May

Goldratt, E. M. and Cox, J. (1986) *The Goal,* North River Press, New York

Goldratt, E. M. and Fox, R. E. (1986) *The Race,* North River Press, New York

Harrison, M. (1990) *Advanced Manufacturing Technology Management,* Pitman Publishing, London

Hayes, R. H. and Clark, K. B. (1986) 'Why some factories are more productive than others, *Harvard Business Review,* Sept.– Oct, 66–73

Hayes, R. H. and Wheelwright, S. C. (1984) *Restoring our Competitive Edge: Competing through Manufacturing,* Wiley, Chichester

Hayes, R. H., Wheelwright, S. C. and Clark, K. B. (1988) *Dynamic Manufacturing,* Free Press, New York

Henry, J. and Walker, D. (eds) (1991) *Managing Innovation,* Sage Publications, London

Hill, T. (1985) *Manufacturing Strategy*, Macmillan, London

Hill, T. (1991) *Production/Operations Management: Text and Cases*, Prentice Hall, New York

Hill, T. and Chambers, S. (1991) 'Flexibility – A Manufacturing Conundrum', *International Journal of Operations and Production Management*, Vol. 11, No 2, 5-13

Hollier, R. H., Boaden, R. J. and New, S. J. (1992) *International Operations; Crossing Borders in Manufacturing and Service*, North-Holland, Amsterdam

Hollins, G. and Hollins, B. (1991) *Total Design; Managing the design process in the service sector*, Pitman Publishing, London

Huczynski, A. and Buchanan, D. (1991) *Organizational Behaviour* (2ed), Prentice Hall, New York

Jackson, S. (1990) *Benchmarking: Its Development and Application in Royal Mail*, Unpublished MBA Dissertation, Staffordshire Polytechnic

Johnson, G. and Scholes, K. (1989) *Exploring Corporate Strategy; Text and Cases*, Prentice Hall, New York

Johnson, H. T. and Kaplan, R. S. (1987) *Relevance Lost*, Harvard Business School Press, Boston

Johnston, R., Chambers, S., Harland, C., Harrison A., and Slack, N. (1993) *Cases in Operations Management*, Pitman Publishing, London

Jolley, A. and Patrick, A. (1990) 'The Office Factory', *Management Today*, July, Jones, P. (ed) *(1989)* Management in Service Industries, Pitman, London

Kanji, G. K. (1990) 'Total quality management: the second industrial revolution', *Total Quality Management*, Vol. 1, No 1, 3-12

Kaplan, R. S. and Atkinson, A. A. (1989) *Advanced Management Accounting* (2ed), Prentice Hall, New York

Kerr, R. (1991) *Knowledge-Based Manufacturing Systems*, Addison Wesley, Sidney

Kinnie, N. J. and Staughton, R. V. W. (1991) 'Implementing Manufacturing Strategy: The Human Resource Management Contribution, *International Journal of Operations and Production Management*, Vol. 11, No 9, 24-40

Klein, J. A. (1989) 'The Human Costs of Manufacturing Reform', *Harvard Business Review*, March-April

Krajewski, L. J. and Ritzman, L. P. (1990) *Operations Management; Strategy and Analysis (2ed)*, Addison Wesley

Lei, D. and Goldhar, J. D. (1991) Computer-integrated Manufacturing (CIM): Redefining the Manufacturing Firm into a Global Service Business, *International Journal of Operations and Production Management*, Vol. 11, No 10, 5-18

Little, D. and Johnson, S. B. (1990) *Survey of UK Manufacturing Control Practice: A brief report*, BPICS Control, Vol. 16, No 3, pp.31-33

Lockyer, K. and Gordon, J. (1991) *Critical Path Analysis (5ed)*, Pitman Publishing, London

Lovelock, C. H. (1988) *Managing Services; Marketing, Operations and Human Resources*, Prentice Hall, New York

Lovelock, C. H. (1992) *Managing Services; Marketing, Operations and Human Resources (2ed)*, Prentice Hall, New York

Lubben, R. T. (1988) *Just-in-Time Manufacturing*, McGraw-Hill, New York

Lumby S. (1988) *Investment Appraisal and Financing Decisions* (3ed), VNR International, Wokingham

McLoughlin, I. and Clark, J. (1988) *Technological Change at Work*, Open University Press, Milton Keynes

McNamee, P. B. (1985) *Tools and Techniques for Strategic Management*, Pergamon, Oxford

Makridakis, S. and Wheelwright, S. C. (1989) *Forecasting Methods for Management* (5ed), Wiley, Chichester

Marsh, P., Barwise, P., Thomas, K. and Wensley, R. (1988) 'Managing strategic investment decisions', in *Competitiveness and the Management Process* (ed. Pettigrew, A. M.), Blackwell, Oxford

Maull, R., Bennett, J. and Hughes, D. (1992) 'MAESTRO: Management Evaluation of Strategic Options', in *International Operations*, ed. Hollier, R. H., Boaden, R. J. and New, S. J., Elsevier, Amsterdam

Maull, R. and Hughes, D. (1990) *Stratagem*, a Systems Methodology for Matching Manufacturing Strategy to Business Requirements, Proceedings of the 5th International Conference of the Operations Management (UK), MCB Press, Bradford

Maull, R., Hughes, D., Childe, S., Weston, N., Tranfield, D. and Smith, S. (1990) 'A Methodology for the Design and Implementation of Resilient CAPM Systems', *International Journal of Production and Operations Management*, Vol. 10, No 9, pp.27-36

Mercer, D. (ed) (1992) *Managing the External Environment*, Sage Publications, London

Meredith, J. R. and Mantel, S. J. (1989) *Project Management; a managerial approach* (2ed), Wiley, Chichester

Mill, R. C. (1989) 'Productivity in service organisations', in Jones (ed) *Management in Service Industries*, Pitman Publishing, London

Moores, B. (1991) 'Lessons from some of the USA's most respected service providers', *Total Quality Management*, Vol. 2, No 3, 269-277

Morgan, G. (1986) *Images of Organization*, Sage Publications, London

Murdick, R. G., Render, B. and Russell, R. S. (1990) *Service Operations Management*, Allyn and Bacon, Boston

Newell, S. and Clark, P. (1990) *Technological Innovation and Organizational Learning*, Proceedings of the Sixth International Conference on Production Research, University of Strathclyde

Oakland, J. S. (1989) *Total Quality Management*, Heinemann, Oxford

Parasuraman, A., Zeithaml, V. A. and Berry, L. L. (1985) 'A Conceptual Model of Service Quality and its Implications for Future Research', *Journal of Marketing*, Fall, 41-50

Pfeffer, N. and Coote, A. (1991) *Is Quality Good for You?*, Institute for Public Policy Research, Social Policy Paper No. 5

Phadke, M. S. (1989) *Quality Engineering Using Robust Design*, Prentice Hall, New York

Platts, K. W. and Gregory, M. J. (1990) *A Manufacturing Audit Approach to Strategy Formulation*, Proceedings of the 5th International Conference of the Operations Management (UK), MCB Press, Bradford

Porter, M. E. (1985) *Competitive Advantage*, Free Press, New York

Peters, T. (1987) *Thriving on Chaos*, Macmillan, London

Peters, T. and Waterman, R. (1982) *In Search of Excellence*, Harper and Row, London

Reading, B. (1992) *Japan: The Coming Collapse*, Weidenfeld and Nicholson, London

Rhodes, E. and Wield (ed) (1985) *Implementing New Technologies*, Blackwell, Oxford

Rose, H. (1990) *Opening the Black Box: The Relationship between Technology and Work*, TORU Seminar Paper, Staffordshire Polytechnic, Oct.

Rosenhead, J. (ed) (1989) *Rational Analysis for a Problematic World*, Wiley, Chichester

Rowe, A. J., Dickel, K. E., Mason, R. O. and Snyder, N. H. (1989) *Strategic Management, A Methodological Approach* (3ed), Addison-Wesley, Wokingham

Samson, D. (1991) *Manufacturing and Operations Strategy,* Prentice Hall, New York

Sarson, R. (1992) 'Multimedia medic support', *Guardian,* 30 July

Schlosser, M. (1989) *Corporate Finance, a model-building approach,* Prentice Hall, New York

Schroeder, R. G. (1989) *Operations Management* (3ed), McGraw-Hill, New York

Schonberger, R. J. (1982) *Japanese Manufacturing Techniques,* Free Press, New York

Schonberger, R. J. (1986) *World Class Manufacturing,* Free Press, New York

Schumacher, P. C. (1988) *The Planner's Dilemma: Centralised Control versus Individual Motivation and Freedom,* Proceedings of the 23rd European Conference on Production and Inventory Control, BPICS, Birmingham

Seedhouse, D. (1988) *Ethics: The Heart of Health Care,* Wiley, Chichester

Silver, E. A. and Peterson, R. (1985) *Decision Systems for Inventory Management and Production Planning,* Wiley, Chichester

Silvestro, R., Fitzgerald, L., Johnston, R. and Voss, C. (1992) 'Towards a Classification of Service Processes', *International Journal of Service Industry Management,* Vol. 3, No 3, 62-75

Slack, N. (1987) 'Flexibility and the Manufacturing Function-Ten Empirical Observations', *in Proceedings of the Operations Management Association (UK) Conference* (ed. Rhodes, D.), Nottingham

Slack, N. (1991) *Strategic Flexibility,* Proceedings of the 6th Conference of the Operations Management Association (UK), MCB Press, Bradford

Small, B. (1990) *Manufacturing Strategy: Bridging the Gap,* Proceedings of the 5th International Conference of the Operations Management Association (UK), MCB Press, Bradford

Stacey, R. D. (1991) *The Chaos Frontier; Creative strategic control for business,* Butterworth-Heinemann, Oxford

Stevens, G. C. (1989) *MRPII - The Second Time Around,* Proceedings of the BPICS Annual Conference, Birmingham

Taguchi, G., Elsayed, E. A. and Hsiang, T. (1989) *Quality Engineering in Production Systems,* McGraw-Hill, New York

Thomson, R. (1992) 'Case of the vanishing banks', *Independent on Sunday,* 9 Aug.

Toksvig, N. (1992) 'Going down the tubes', *Guardian,* 3 Jan

Twiss, B. (1992) *Managing Technological Innovation,* Pitman Publishing, London

Ure, A. (1835) *The Philosophy of Manufactures,* Knight, London (reprinted F Cass (1967))

Vollmann, T. E., Berry, W. L. and Whybark, D. C. (1992) *Manufacturing Planning and Control Systems,* Irwin, Homewood

Vonderembse, M. A. and White, G. P. (1991) *Operations Management,* West, St. Paul

Voss, C. A. (1986) *Implementing Manufacturing Technology - A Manufactuirng Strategy Perspective,* Proceedings of the UK Operations Management Association Conference, University of Warwick

Voss, C. A. (ed) (1987) *Just-in-Time Manufacture,* IFS Publications, Bedford

Voss, C. A. (1989) 'The Managerial Challenges of Integrated Manufacturing', *International Journal of Production and Operations Management,* Vol. 9, No 5, pp.33-38

Voss, C. A., Armistead, C., Johnston, B. and Morris, B. (1985) *Operations Management in Service Industries and the Public Sector,* Wiley, Chichester

Ward, J., Griffiths, P. and Whitmore, P. (1990) *Strategic Planning for Information Systems,* Wiley, Chichester

Waterlow, J. G. and Clouder Richards, F. J. (1988) *Report of the CAPM Workshop and Tutorial* (Sept.), ACME, Swindon

Waterlow, J. G. and Monniot, J. P. (1986) *A Study of the State of the Art in Computer-Aided Production Management*, ACME, Swindon

Wilson, B. (1984) *Systems: Concepts, Methodologies and Applications*, Wiley, Chichester

Wolstenholme, E. F. (1990) *System Enquiry; A System Dynamics Approach*, Wiley, Chichester

Womack, J. P., Jones, D. T. and Roos, D. (1990) *The Machine that Changed the World*, Rawson Associates, New York

Wood, G. R. and Munshi, K. F. (1991) 'Hoshin Kanri: a systematic approach to breakthrough improvement', *Total Quality Management*, Vol. 2, No 3, 213-226

Zairi, M. (1991) *The Management of Advanced Manufacturing Technology: A Study of User-Supplier Networks*, Unpublished PhD Thesis, Staffordshire Polytechnic

Zuboff, S. (1988) *In the Age of the Smart Machine*, Heinemann, Oxford

INDEX